Kristofer Dorosz

Malcolm Lowry's Infernal Paradise

Uppsala 1976

Distributor:
Almqvist & Wiksell International
Stockholm

Doctoral dissertation at the University of Uppsala 1976

© Kristofer Dorosz

ISBN 91—554—0459—6

Printed in Sweden by
Borgströms Tryckeri AB, Motala

Phototypesetting by
TEXTgruppen i Uppsala AB

I have two selves and one lives free in hell,
The other down a well in Paradise.

Malcolm Lowry, "Conversations with Goethe"

Table of contents

Acknowledgements

I should like to express my gratitude to Professor M. C. Bradbrook, University of Cambridge, who was the first to encourage my initial interest in Malcolm Lowry, and who kindly agreed to discuss my work when this study was well under way; to my adviser, Dr. Sven-Johan Spånberg, whose pragmatic and sober approach to literature has often saved me from the entanglements of much unnecessary speculation; to Professor Gunnar Sorelius, who has carefully read the manuscript at every major stage of my work-in-progress and contributed valuable suggestions.

I should also like to thank Dr. Louis Jacobs, London, whose expert advice on the Jewish Cabbala has proved invaluable in my assessment of the "Cabbalistic layer" of *Under the Volcano*; Mr. Harold Osborne, the Editor of *The British Journal of Aesthetics,* who kindly found the time to discuss with me Ingarden's concept of "metaphysical qualities". His illuminating comments encouraged me in my attempts to apply Ingarden's theories to literary research. My thanks are also due to Mr. Mark Troy, whose intimate knowledge of James Joyce has helped me to perceive many similarities as well as differences between Joyce and Lowry; to Mr. Michael Srigley for valuable and interesting comments on some esoteric themes in *Under the Volcano* and for the stylistic improvements; to Mr. Hermann Wüscher for useful editorial directions and suggestions.

Introduction

"Malcolm Lowry is at this time recognized as one of the greatest novelists of the twentieth century", writes Professor M. C. Bradbrook in *Malcolm Lowry: His Art and Early Life—A Study in Transformation,* published in 1974.[1] Indeed, a lot has changed since *Under the Volcano* was censured in 1945 by Jonathan Cape's reader for its initial tedium and excessive length, its weakness in character drawing, "eccentric word-spinning and too much stream-of-consciousness stuff".[2] To the publishers' strictures Lowry reacted by writing an involved thirty-one page critical analysis of *Under the Volcano*, in which he admirably explained and defended the novel's design. The defence fulfilled its task and the book was unconditionally accepted. Acclaimed as a masterpiece immediately after its publication, and subsequently neglected (it has been ignored by a number of histories and surveys of twentieth century English literature), the novel has now attracted considerable critical attention. Yet despite its established reputation and despite the wealth of insight provided by the growing Lowry criticism, *Under the Volcano* seems to remain elusive.

The elusiveness is no doubt due to the obscurity of much of the novel's symbolism and to the extraordinary richness of its meanings: never final and definitive, but always changing and surprising with every fresh look at the text. Its enormous evocative powers and the multiplicity of its various levels seldom allow our interpretations to crystallize in well-defined shapes. In other words, the resources of the novel are well-nigh infinite and critics rarely fail to point that out. To David Markson, author of a study on the book's symbolism, *Under the Volcano* is a preeminently Joycean work, "in the *Finnegans Wake* sense of all-embracing mythic evocation".[3] To Professor Bradbrook it is an "open myth" which, like oral literature, "can work at all sorts of levels, and in different combinations of emphasis for different people."[4] No wonder it eludes classification,

---

[1] *Malcolm Lowry: His Art and Early Life* (Cambridge: Cambridge University Press, 1974), p. 1.

[2] *Selected Letters of Malcolm Lowry,* ed. Harvey Breit and Margerie Bonner Lowry (London: Jonathan Cape, 1967), p. 60. Hereafter cited as *Letters.*

[3] David Markson, "Myth in *Under the Volcano*", *Prairie Schooner,* 37 (1963/64), 340.

[4] Bradbrook, pp. 55, 12.

analysis, or synthesizing formulae. Lowry was himself very well aware of the manifoldness and the polysemous character of his work. In the preface to the French edition of the novel, he admits his intention of expressing as much as six things at a time,[5] and in the letter to Cape he suggests a number of possible approaches to *Under the Volcano*:

The novel can be read simply as a story which you can skip if you want. It can be read as a story you will get more out of if you don't skip. It can be regarded as a kind of symphony, or in another way as a kind of opera—or even a horse opera. It is hot music, a poem, a song, a tragedy, a comedy, a farce, and so forth. It is superficial, profound, entertaining and boring, according to taste. It is a prophecy, a political warning, a cryptogram, a preposterous movie, and a writing on the wall. It can even be regarded as a sort of machine: it works too, believe me, as I have found out. In case you think I mean it to be everything but a novel I better say that after all it is intended to be, and, though I say so myself, a deeply serious one too. But it is also I claim a work of art somewhat different from the one you suspected it was, and more successfull too, even though according to its own lights. (*Letters*, p. 66)

Indeed, judged by the standards of realistic fiction, *Under the Volcano* must appear a failure.[6] Deficient in adequate character drawing, it does not depict "man in society". There is almost no "story", no external action that would lend coherence to the "eccentric word-spinning" saturated with exuberant imagery. The book seems misshapen and overwritten. But the essential features of Lowry's writing are never embedded in the traditional art of the novel. "If there is no external action", writes Lowry's biographer and critic, Professor Douglas Day, "there is almost a surfeit of movement internally; and there is enough tension within the mind of the protagonist to render any other conflict superfluous."[7] Hence the absence of full-blooded characters. However desirable in most novels, they seem inconsistent with Lowry's fundamentally poetic conception of *Under the Volcano* (cf. *Letters*, p. 59). By the same token they are not essential for the purposes of an Eliot or a Joyce.[8] *Ars poetica,* as we know, does not depend for its success on either plot or characters.

The art of poetry relies primarily on the manipulation of linguistic resources, capable of rendering such complex and "volatile" meanings as remain beyond the reach of factual down-to-earth prose. Free from the order of our empirical existence, poetry employs myth, metaphor, symbol, or image, and enters the

[5] Malcolm Lowry, "Preface to a Novel", *Canadian Literature,* No. 9 (Summer 1961), p. 23.

[6] Cf. George Woodcock, "Malcolm Lowry's *Under the Volcano*", *Modern Fiction Studies,* 4, No. 2 (Summer 1958), 153.

[7] Douglas Day, Preface to Malcolm Lowry, *Dark as the Grave Wherein My Friend is Laid* (Harmondsworth: Penguin Books, 1972), p. 8.

[8] See Harry Levin, *James Joyce: A Critical Introduction* (London: Faber, 1968), p. 116.

sphere of the wonderful and the improbable. Often its characteristic mode of expression consists in implication and suggestion rather than statement. Especially where ambiguity and evocation prevail, factual statement recedes into insignificance. When it has no story to tell, poetry has no use for facts and their sequences. In that it is more like contemplation than action. Without being ruled by the sweep and dynamics of events, it can hold the reader's attention by single metaphors, images, or words. While in novelistic prose the smallest unit of aesthetic perception is usually the event, in poetry it is the individual word. "Good poetry", says David Daiches, "is the result of the adequate counterpointing of the different resources of words (meaning, association, rhythm, music, order and so forth) in establishing a total complex of significant expression."[9]

Considered by poetic standards, *Under the Volcano* must indeed appear a considerable achievement. Its "significant expression" evidently relies on the word rather than event. The reader is invited not so much to follow the story as to contemplate the extraordinary verbal display composed of layers upon layers of meaning. Lowry, however, never went as far as Joyce, who in *Finnegans Wake* made individual words carry whole constellations of semantic charges.[10] Instead, he counterpointed themes, images, and metaphors turning them into the fundamental units of his art. Yet his brilliant polyphony, unsupported by the solid framework of a plot, seems to lose itself in stream of consciousness and drunken phantasmagorias. To recover it, it is necessary to approach *Under the Volcano* the way most poetry is approached. "Poems", Lowry reminds his publisher, "often have to be read several times before their full meaning will reveal itself, explode in the mind" (*Letters*, p. 59).

The same requirement, imposed by the characteristic stasis of poetry, has to be met by readers of Joyce's *Ulysses*, where "all the factual background—so conveniently summarized for the reader in an ordinary novel—must be reconstructed from fragments, sometimes hundreds of pages apart, scattered through the book. As a result, the reader is forced to read *Ulysses* in exactly the same manner as he reads poetry—continually fitting fragments together and

---

[9] David Daiches, *A Study of Literature* (New York: W. W. Norton & Company Inc., 1964), p. 139. My brief discussion on the nature of poetry has been also based on the following works: Owen Barfield, *Poetic Diction: A Study in Meaning* (Middletown, Connecticut: Wesleyan University Press, 1973); Susanne K. Langer, *Feeling and Form: A Theory of Art* (New York: Scribner, 1953), Ch. 13, "Poesis"; Winifred Nowottny, *The Language Poets Use* (London: The Athlone Press, 1965); Krishna Rayan, *Suggestion and Statement in Poetry* (London: The Athlone Press, 1972).

[10] Cf. Daiches, p. 44.

keeping allusions in mind until, by reflexive reference, he can link them to their complements."[11]

Exactly the same can be said of Lowry's work. But what applies to the factual background of the novel is no less true of its every other level, down to the ultimate poetic significance. We cannot grasp *Under the Volcano* all at once, and our understanding of it grows with each successive reading. Time and again the reader must probe the apparently amorphous mass of details until it reveals an immensely intricate network of relationships: a scaffolding, or a multitude of scaffoldings, on which larger thematic patterns may be fashioned. Nor is this all. The labour of poetic reconstruction is further stimulated by the novel's wheel-like structure which leads the reader on an endless circular course through the protagonist's life. "The book was so designed", Lowry informs Cape, "counterdesigned and interwelded that it could be read an indefinite number of times and still not have yielded all its meanings or its drama or its poetry" (*Letters*, p. 88). Obviously no ordered 'reading', no linear argument can do justice to all this profusion of meanings. If we compare Lowry's novel to a vastly complicated score of polyphonic music, we shall see that the critic's task lies not so much in interpretation but in devising a sort of instrument on which the "symphony" of the *Volcano* could be played.

To complicate matters further, *Under the Volcano* is *par excellence* a symbolic novel. Like the French symbolists, Lowry used the poetic resources of language not only to evoke and suggest rather than state,[12] but also to present "a reality on one level of reference by a corresponding reality on another".[13] Thus the ruined garden, for example, one of the recurrent motifs in the novel, does not merely signify a plot of land in a state of confusion, abandoned and covered with weeds. Symbolically, it reflects the protagonist's ruined life, neglected love and destroyed marriage, or the earth in danger of destruction by the forces of political oppression. As a mythical symbol, both Christian and Cabbalistic, it refers to the lost paradise and the abuse of mystical powers and occult knowledge. The garden is one of the more comprehensive symbolic images in the novel, comprising all the five levels of meaning distinguished by Douglas Day in his analysis of *Under the Volcano*: the chthonic, the human, the political, the magical, and the religious.[14] But "life is a forest of symbols", as Lowry

---

[11] Joseph Frank, "Spatial Form in Modern Literature", *Sewanee Review,* 53 (1945), 234. This quotation was first applied to *Under the Volcano* by Victor Doyen in *English Studies,* 50, No. 1 (February 1969), p. 65.

[12] Cf. Edmund Wilson, *Axel's Castle* (New York: Scribner, 1959), pp. 20–21.

[13] Ananda K. Coomaraswamy, article on "Symbolism" in *Dictionary of World Literary Terms* (London: Allen & Unwin, 1970), p. 322.

[14] See Douglas Day, *Malcolm Lowry: A Biography* (London: Oxford Univ. Press, 1974), pp. 326–350. Hereafter cited as *Biography*.

liked to repeat after Baudelaire,[15] and any detail, however insignificant, may reveal unsuspected depths of meaning. The hero's dark glasses, which on reflection turn out to symbolize his fear of light, truth and salvation, are a case in point. Likewise, the apparently casual references to Atlantis implicate us in the theme of destruction by fire and water, a symbolic reflection—as we shall see—of the tragedy depicted by the whole novel.

But how to find one's way in this forest of symbols where the often unmarked paths and misleading signposts seem to mock our sense of orientation? How to approach the variety of mythical and literary allusions which, in order to evoke and symbolize, are severed from the cohesion of our non-poetic everyday experience? How to come to terms with motifs from Christianity, Greek, Aztec, Buddhist, and Hindu mythology; from the occult sciences such as the Cabbala, alchemy, astrology, the Tarot; from the sacred literature of the Old and New Testaments, The Cabbalistic *Zohar*, the Hindu *Mahabharata*, or the *Rig Veda*; and, finally, from the works of Marlowe, Dante, Shakespeare, Goethe, Blake, Boehme, Pascal, and many others?[16]

Certainly we cannot afford an immediate response to all these messages assembled from systems of ideas accessible to us mostly through scholarship. Together they have never formed any living, cultural or religious, tradition; nor have they been ordered within an organic whole until the creation of *Under the Volcano*. Their guiding principle therefore lies in the novel itself and has to be discovered there. Otherwise Lowry's symbols might appear simply as "a heap of broken images", to borrow T. S. Eliot's phrase. Uninformed by a common faith and cultural tradition, dependent for their elucidation on learning and research, they might often be found to mean practically everything and nothing. Indeed, the science of comparative religion has often demonstrated that, above the common archetypal substratum, mythical symbols display a variety of meanings determined by particular mythologial and religious contexts.[17] Therefore most images, whose context in *Under the Volcano* suggests a nonliteral symbolic and mythical significance, are exposed to what Karl Jaspers calls "the random interpretability of symbols". And so, until we decide to what

[15] See *Letters*, p. 78, and *Biography*, p. 273.

[16] Without any claim to completeness we might also mention Baudelaire, George Berkeley, Rupert Brooke, John Bunyan, Thomas Burnet, Cervantes, John Clare, Cocteau, Coleridge, De Quincey, Dickens, John Donne, I. Donnelly, Dostoevsky, La Fontaine, Thomas Gray, A.E. Housman, Edward Lear, Frey Luis de León, Eliphas Lévi, Jack London, Andrew Marvell, S. L. MacGregor Mathers, Melville, Poe, W.H. Prescott, Racine, Sir Walter Raleigh, Henryk Sienkiewicz, Sophocles, Oswald Spengler, Swedenborg, Swinburne, Tolstoy, Virgil, Wordsworth.

[17] See Mircea Eliade, "Methodological Remarks on the Study of Religious Symbolism", in *The History of Religions, Essays in Methodology*, ed. by M. Eliade and Joseph M. Kitagawa (Chicago and London: The Univ. of Chicago Press, 1959), pp. 93—94, 99—100, 106—107.

particular symbolism they belong, our interpretation cannot become conclusive.[18]

Needless to say, Lowry's verbal exuberance as well as the whirl of ambiguities characteristic of his work make such decisions sometimes very difficult. The interpreter is often stranded in his research into the Cabbala or Swedenborgianism, for example, trying to fit the relevant bits and pieces into the appropriate context. Is it not a poor work of art, he might ask himself, which renders immediate response so excessively difficult? Is the game of research worth the candle of final elucidation? Difficulty of access to a work's meaning, however, does not have to detract from its aesthetic excellence. This applies above all to works of literature written in languages we do not happen to know. As regards *Under the Volcano*, we have to assume that all the arcane sciences, all the myths and literary allusions of which it is composed, are analogous to foreign languages inaccessible to most speakers of English. We may regret the situation on cultural, but not necessarily on aesthetic, grounds. If so, we shall ascribe the obscurity, the lack of cohesion, or the fragmentariness not so much to the shortcomings of the writer but to the breakdown of a culture. Because European civilization—less and less permeated by a universal faith and by the canons of a common literary tradition—is increasingly incapable of reanimating whatever "broken images" it still cherishes, the twentieth-century writer has often had to rely on the power of his own personal vision and the resources of other cultures. "He has had to be, in a sense, his own priest, his own guide, his own Virgil. He has been condemned by the cultural circumstances of his time to draw from within himself everything that forms and orders his art ... he has had to plunge deep in his search for the principles by which the anarchy of experience might be controlled and given a shape and a significance."[19]

In the case of *Under the Volcano*, however, the shape and the significance have not escaped a measure of anarchy. Most readers have found the novel not only enormously complex but also obscurantist.[20] An essentially romantic piece of fiction, remote from the atmosphere of a well-tempered classicism, it tends, as I have been trying to point out, to escape our grasp and understanding. Through all-embracing poetic evocation it can work at all sorts of levels, its wheel-like structure creates perpetually open meanings, and its mani-

[18] See Karl Jaspers, *Philosophy* (Chicago and London: Univ. of Chicago Press, 1969), III, pp. 126–27.

[19] Nathan A. Scott, Jr., "The Broken Center: A Definition of the Crisis of Values in Modern Literature", in *Symbolism in Religion and Literature*, ed. Rollo May (New York: G. Braziller, 1960), p. 185.

[20] See *Biography*, p. 321.

fold symbolism, rooted in a variety of cultural and religious traditions, can make it both inaccessible and unduly ambiguous. Not surprisingly Lowry critics have on the whole concerned themselves with various aspects of the novel, without attempting what Douglas Day terms a *"Gestalt* approach".[21]

However unsatisfactory from a *Gestalt* point of view, most critical contributions have undoubtedly increased our understanding of *Under the Volcano.* The life-and-work studies have put the novel in perspective and elucidated it through Lowry's other works and through biographical details. The source studies—notably by Kilgallin and Costa—have brought to light the book's literary kinships as well as the materials that have gone into its making. Articles concerned with the peculiar form of the novel have made us aware that Lowry's work, through its characteristic "spatial form" (Doyen) and "stasis" (Wright), "is intended to evoke something of the aesthetic response of poetry, music or even the visual arts".[22] And the one-aspect studies—to give some examples—have examined *Under the Volcano* in terms of myth (Markson), myth and ritual encounter (Albaum), the Cabbala (Epstein), jazz (Epstein), the cinema (Tiessen), the phenomenological consciousness (Corrigan), sea metaphor (Wild), or the immediate (human) level (Edmonds).[23] Finally we have to mention Professor Day's biography of Malcolm Lowry which contains a short *"Gestalt* reading" of the novel.

Without questioning the merits of Day's excellent analysis to which I gratefully acknowledge my debt, it might be pointed out that his *"Gestalt* reading" lacks a well-defined centre or ordering principle. His five levels, which comprehend the whole of the novel, do not seem to contain any mainspring other than a moral cause said to be advanced by *Under the Volcano* in its entirety. To say that the novel advances a moral cause on five levels simultaneously is, of course, basically correct but it is still far from getting to the heart of the matter. More perhaps we cannot expect from a short essay incorporated into a biography of Lowry.

The present dissertation is an attempt to look more closely into this moral cause or problem, and trace its thematic implications in *Under the Volcano.* The task is both difficult and full of hazards because the fundamental moral issue is embedded in Lowry's complex mythical polyphony, unsupported, as I

---

[21] See ibid., pp. 321—22.

[22] Terence Wright, "*Under the Volcano:* the Static Art of Malcolm Lowry", *Ariel*, No. 4 (October 1970), p. 67.

[23] For the works of critics mentioned above see bibliography. Cf. also D. Day's survey of Lowry criticism, *Biography,* pp. 321—22.

have already pointed out, by the solid framework of a plot. To come to terms with the moral problem of the book, therefore, we shall have to search for some order in the confusion of mythical and literary evocations. This will expose us to the dangers of a reductive interpretation, but to leave *Under the Volcano* working at "all sorts of levels" is to miss its specific essence or *Gestalt*. In this study we shall approach the novel as a whole, and in chapter 4 below try to discover the guiding principle of its mythical layer. This principle, in as much as it creates a pattern underlying the protagonist's moral problem and radiating throughout the whole of *Under the Volcano,* will reveal the peculiar essence of the novel. As we shall see, this fundamental pattern springs from the motif of black magic and permeates the book as the *Gestalt* quality of "infernal paradise" .

Nevertheless, our search for the *Gestalt* quality of "infernal paradise" will not enable us to disentangle all the complexities of Lowry's work or fill out all the obscure areas. The discovery of the underlying pattern of *Under the Volcano* may reveal its essential quality but it cannot remove its essential flaw: the overabundance of suggestive detail which, while creating many potential rather than actual meanings, sometimes tends to dissolve the imaginative experience of the novel. For the sake of our investigation, however, we shall try to make the best of Lowry's potential meanings, suspending our judgement until the Conclusion.

Now in order to indicate in a preliminary way the meaning of the quality of "infernal paradise" we shall have to anticipate our discussion of the novel's esoteric layer and take a short look at the theme of black magic. *Under the Volcano* is, as most critics agree, based, at least to a certain extent, on the Jewish esoteric wisdom, the Cabbala. At the same time it contains, if only by poetic implication, a host of other esoteric and mythical ideas and images. Of these the most important— and in my view more important than the Cabbala—is the theme of black magic and the black magician. Black magic is evoked by allusions to Faustus, Prometheus, the destruction of Atlantis, which in esoteric tradition is said to have perished through necromantic practices, and to the Tower of Babel, built, according to a Cabbalistic legend, by means of magical sciences and for the purpose of man's self-deification. But the magical substance, so to speak, conjured up by many mythical allusions of which I have given just a few examples, is constantly reflected by the more tangible reality of the novel, that is, by the protagonist's drunkenness.

Although drunkenness is the main theme of Lowry's book, "the drunkenness of Geoffrey Firmin", as a critic puts it, "is the correlative of the drunkenness of the world as seen by both Dostoevsky and Hesse, a world reeling down the corridors of disaster filled with the sins of both commission and, particularly, omission, a world which had apparently condemned itself to impotence in the dark night presided over by palpable evil".[24] More specifically, the alcoholic addiction depicted in *Under the Volcano,* because it creates a confusion of heaven and hell, is the correlative of the quality of "infernal paradise".

Consul Geoffrey Firmin is no ordinary drunkard who in alcohol seeks merriment or forgetfulness. On the contrary, in drinking the Consul finds mystical enlightenment and fulfilment of his spiritual aspirations. He appears as a mystic in search of the lost paradise and eternity. He drinks as if he "were taking an eternal sacrament" (p. 40)[25], often regarding mescal, his favourite drink, as the nectar of immortality. At the same time, he is suffering the "tortures of the damned" (p. 85), on the magico-mystical plane manifested by sheer demonic horrors, and on the human, by profound estrangement and an almost total inability to love. Obviously there is something amiss with his mysticism. It seems that he is trying to reach divinity by way of hell, without being fully aware of it. Overwhelmed by despair and surrounded by darkness, he fondly imagines that he has reached a state of bliss. Darkness appears to him as light, and the true light, of which he is mortally afraid, as darkness. One of the cantinas for which his whole being yearns is significantly called "El Infierno". Just as significantly perhaps a "lamp of hope" is hanging over its door; a lamp of hope, of course, since alcohol provided by the cantinas appears as the way to God and eternity.

In Cabbalistic terms Geoffrey is probably still ascending the Tree of Life (one of the central images of the Cabbala) but the Tree must have been turned upside down by demonic powers.[26] And in as much as he is a Faustus, the Consul—as Lowry indicates in the letter to Cape—has sold his soul to the devil (see *Letters*, p. 70). In return the devil provides him with his own brand of *Imitatio Dei:* a mysticism which involves an almost total confusion of heaven and hell. To be sure, *Demon est deus inversus,* just as the black magician is an inversion of the saint. According to the nineteenth-century authority on magic, the Cabbala, and things occult, Éliphas Lévi (whose *Transcendental Magic* is mentioned in *Under the Volcano*), black magic forever "apes the Magic of Light, but takes it, as it were, backwards".[27] Hence the Consul's search for celestial joys in the inferno and his constant confusion of good and evil bespeak a diabolic mysticism as practised by a would-be saint or contemplative.

Perhaps Geoffrey's demonic magic, buried in countless evocations, sym-

---

[24] Daniel B. Dodson, *Malcolm Lowry* (New York and London: Columbia Univ. Press, 1970), p. 46.

[25] Malcolm Lowry, *Under the Volcano* (London: Jonathan Cape, 1967), p. 209. Henceforward all page references to this edition will be given in the text in parentheses.

[26] Cf. *Biography*, p. 324.

[27] Eliphas Lévi, *The History of Magic* (London: Rider, 1969), p. 204.

bolized by his drunkenness and never stated as fact, would be better left alone, were it not for its overall effect upon the whole novel. Since it truly radiates throughout *Under the Volcano,* it gives the novel a characteristic stamp and becomes a central metaphor, capable of ordering the significance of the book. As a demonic inversion it has permeated each of the five levels distinguished by Day:

> The chthonic imagery [for example] is, clearly, archetypally demonic in nature: that is, it employs the traditional affirmative apocalyptic images of the Mount of Perfection, the fertile valley, the cleansing stream or fountain, and the blossoming garden, but employs them in an inverted, ironic form. What had indicated fruition, now indicates sterility; what had represented cleansing, now represents corruption, and what had symbolized the soul's striving upward toward salvation, now symbolizes the descent into damnation. It is of a world turned upside down that Lowry writes.[28]

Indeed, as we shall see in the eight chapters of this dissertation, the magical inversion has spread itself onto the eight fundamental themes of Lowry's novel. Like the Cabbalistic Tree turned upside down, the eight themes represent man's spiritual aspirations brought down by the powers of evil. We see ascent turned into downfall, light into darkness, immortality into perdition, a search for eternity and paradise terminated in hell, love and charity giving way to lovelessness and indifference, life transformed into death, salvation appearing as damnation, and freedom as captivity.

But the demonic inversion in *Under the Volcano* involves much more than a transformation of one thing into its opposite. It is an attitude, a state of mind, or an atmosphere which envelops events, motifs, fragments of dialogue, sometimes even single phrases and words. Not confined to images, symbols, ideas, themes, or metaphors, it is something which permeates *Under the Volcano* through and through. It cannot be enclosed by any of the objects in the world depicted by the novel nor by any of the common categories of literary criticism. It appears therefore that demonic inversion has in *Under the Volcano* assumed the role of a quality, a *Gestalt* or essential quality, peculiar to the novel as a work of art. Hence the proper subject of this study is not the protagonist's black magic but its thematic and aesthetic consequence, the quality of "infernal paradise".

Gestalt qualities which permeate the whole of a work of art and determine at the same time its aesthetic status have been investigated (even though incompletely) and described under the name of "metaphysical qualities" by the Polish aesthetician and philosopher Roman Ingarden.[29] Here we are not concerned with the theoretical aspects of the metaphysical qualities. Their brief

---

[28] *Biography,* pp. 329–30.
[29] See R. Ingarden, *O dziele literackim* (Warszawa: PWN, 1960), §§ 47–50.

presentation is included in the appendix. Two things, however, are to be noted now.

First, according to Ingarden, metaphysical qualities possess aesthetic value. It follows therefore that their existence in a work of art implies the work's aesthetic excellence. In the case of *Under the Volcano* it means that, because the book displays metaphysical qualities, it is aesthetically valuable. To carry full conviction, however, such a statement would have to be further substantiated. But to attempt a technical description of the aesthetic qualities inherent in Lowry's novel would take us too far afield. Here I would simply like to suggest that the subject of this dissertation, "Malcolm Lowry's Infernal Paradise", is a quality which has to do not only with the human condition but also with beauty. As much emerges from a general application of Ingarden's theories. Consequently, the present study explores *Under the Volcano* not exclusively from a thematic but also, indirectly, from an aesthetic point of view.

Secondly, it should be emphasized that metaphysical qualities do not form part of all the different objects depicted by the novelist or poet. Nor do they manifest themselves when we merely name them. They hover, as it were, above and around single objects in the novelist's world, but more often around whole complexes of objects, situations, events, or processes. They can be seen and contemplated but not rationally defined. This is one of the reasons why it is very difficult to describe or define metaphysical qualities contained in a particular work of art.[30]

Nevertheless, it is certain that literary criticism could help metaphysical qualities come in sight. The critic would first have to perceive them in his aesthetic experience of a work of art and then somehow point them out. I say "somehow", because we could imagine a number of ways in which they might be brought to the reader's attention. Certainly one way of doing it is to discover in a given work patterns of meaning governed by the metaphysical quality in question. Then a description of these patterns would bring into awareness the metaphysical quality attendant upon them. This is a modest task which does not involve elaborate and technically complex analyses of aesthetic phenomena. For the purposes of this study I have accepted this task and therefore refrained from any detailed application of Ingarden's theories. Instead, I have drawn upon them in order to gain some theoretical clarity, some point of departure which determines the subject as well as the general direction of research.[31] It is true that the prevailing pragmatic tradition of Anglo-American

---

[30] The foregoing discussion has been based on Ingarden's treatment of metaphysical qualities, see note 29 above.

[31] My application of Ingarden's theories may also be regarded as an exercise in critical theory: an exploration of one of the many "open fields" of literary research suggested by Ingarden's

literary criticism has often ignored theoretical considerations.[32] I believe, however, that criticism, although its proper subject is literature, cannot afford to be cut off from a theoretical awareness. As the British aesthetician Harold Osborne writes:

To be coherent with itself criticism must be controlled within a framework of ideas supplied by aesthetics; otherwise it will remain precarious, chaotic and damaging. If by accident it were successful, there would exist no criteria by which its success could be discriminated from failure. And though there be no consciously articulated body of theoretical principles to guide and direct research, some principles are nevertheless presupposed in every act of analysis; if the theoretical ground has not been formulated and rendered pure from inconsistencies and irrelevances, practical research will incorporate all the inconsistencies and irrelevances of undisciplined popular thought. Criticism cannot be without aesthetics; if it has no sound aesthetic ground, it must work with a bad aesthetics and therefore work badly.[33]

Taking thus a clue from aesthetics, we shall in the following pages be concerned with the metaphysical quality characteristic of *Under the Volcano*. It is a quality most conspicuously reflected in the novel's main moral problem which is evoked by the theme of black magic and represented by the protagonist's drunkenness. I have decided to call this quality "infernal paradise" although in point of fact this name refers to an object. But according to Ingarden, metaphysical qualities are organically connected with (aesthetically concretized) objects or situations, and "infernal paradise" conveniently epitomizes the kind of situation in which our quality comes into fullest view. While the term is thus, to a certain extent, arbitrary, I assume that its full meaning will emerge when many of its elements have been examined and described. So far I have tried to approximate the meaning of "infernal paradise" through the preliminary discussion of black magic and demonic inversion.

"The gods exist, they are the devil" (p. 209), the Consul is told by a randomly singled-out quotation, which succintly characterizes the mental and physical world he inhabits. We shall now examine this world by selecting out of its complexity different themes, strands, and motifs, and organizing them with-

work in aesthetics. Although he was primarily a philosopher and aesthetician concerned with ontology and cognition of art, he always hoped that literary critics would take up his clues and apply them in their literary research.

[32] See R. Wellek, *Concepts of Criticism* (New Haven and London: Yale Univ. Press, 1963), p. 264; Cleanth Brooks, "Implications of an Organic Theory of Poetry", in M. H. Abrams, *Literature and Belief* (New York: Columbia Univ. Press, 1958), p. 53; Malcolm Bradbury, "Introduction: The State of Criticism Today", in *Contemporary Criticism,* ed. M. Bradbury and D. Palmer (London: Edward Arnold, 1970), pp. 27–29.

[33] Harold Osborne, *Aesthetics and Criticism* (London: Routledge, 1955), p. 28.

in some more inclusive and basic patterns. In this way I hope to bring out the quality of "infernal paradise" and show how it permeates the eight fundamental themes of *Under the Volcano*. The first of these, "Ascent", prepares the ground for the moral issue of the novel. Through the mountain-volcano symbolism and its negative counterpart of the fall, it shows man in the context of his highest aspirations and their failure. "Light", the second of the themes, reveals the demonic inversion in the dialectics of light and darkness. "Draught of Immortality" brings us close to the central issues in the protagonist's predicament. We see how Geoffrey's spiritual and physical thirst cannot be quenched by alcohol, notwithstanding its mystical faculties. These indeed turn out to be deceptive and, instead of mystical illumination and eternity, the Consul finds destruction and death. The fourth theme, "Eternity", contains the essence of his mystical-metaphysical strivings. Through a variety of mostly mythical evocations it shows him as a former mystic and an earnest seeker for God and eternity, now turned into black magician and bound for hell. "Love" brings into view a world contaminated by estrangement and indifference, devoid of charity and genuine personal relations, while "Life" presents the exuberance of vital forces turned into disintegration and death. "Salvation" discloses the spuriousness of human efforts towards rebirth and redemption. So great is the spuriousness that genuine salvation appears as damnation and vice versa. "Freedom", finally, gives us a picture of the Consul's abuse of freedom and its transformation into spiritual imprisonment. And since the abuse of freedom implies its initial existence, the theme reveals the protagonist as essentially and fundamentally free, responsible for his actions and the tragedy depicted by the whole novel.

The eight themes examined in the eight chapters of this dissertation have been selected with a view to the quality of "infernal paradise". Hence they do not claim to exhaust the richness of Lowry's imaginative universe contained in *Under the Volcano*. Because this universe appears to be in a state of continual creation, other themes, perhaps equally fundamental, could be discovered in the novel. Nor do the eight themes cover every phenomenon that properly belongs to them. To do this would require a study at least twice the size of the present one. No completeness is therefore claimed for the themes whose components have been chosen in a representative, rather than systematic, fashion. Other elements and in a different arrangement could possibly do just as well. I hope, nevertheless, that the significance of the eight themes lies in their governing principle, the quality of "infernal paradise" which I take to be the characteristic *quidditas* of Lowry's novel.

Finally a word on the scope of this thesis. I have confined myself exclusively to *Under the Volcano* not only because this difficult complex, and immensely rich symbolic novel deserves to be studied in its own right, but because I believe that the primary task of literary criticism consists in a descriptive analysis of the individual literary work. And because its meaning is, in my view, first of all determined by the internal relationships of its various elements, I have avoided relying on Lowry's biography and other material external to the novel itself.[34]

The present dissertation is thus an attempt to examine one work of literary art in order to discover its *Gestalt* quality. It explores eight fundamental themes in Lowry's *Under the Volcano*; themes which reveal the metaphysical quality of "infernal paradise". This quality, rooted in the poetic evocation of black magic and reflected in the protagonist's moral problem, bespeaks a world turned upside down by demonic forces. If, by investigating a number of different themes and strands of the novel, this study succeeds in bringing this quality into the awareness of the reader, its aim will have been realized.

[34] It is true that in my analysis of *Under the Volcano* I have to a considerable extent drawn upon Lowry's letter to Cape. But whatever its biographical interest, I have taken the letter for what it primarily is: a piece of very perceptive criticism of the novel rather than a fragment of biography.

Chapter 1
Ascent

"Whoever unceasingly strives upward ... him can we save", states the novel's third epigraph taken from Goethe's *Faust* and strikes the note of ascent and salvation. However faintly sounded at the beginning of *Under the Volcano,* the note establishes a connection between these two archetypal themes, which are also connected in much religious and mythological symbolism.[1] Thus when the theme of ascent makes its first appearance, it has already acquired religious overtones through its relation to salvation. As we shall see in this chapter, these overtones are woven into the theme mainly through the protagonist's mystical strivings. Geoffrey Firmin—we are often obliquely told—has been a mystic, a magician, a religious seeker engaged in a search for transcendental reality. Before his present ruin and disintegration, "he had striven upwards, as at the beginning with Yvonne". Had he succeeded, there would have been "an infinite widening, an infinite evolving and extension of boundaries, in which the spirit was an entity, perfect and whole" (p. 361). Yet perfection and wholeness, as *Under the Volcano* persistently shows, are very far from the Consul. In actual fact the novel presents his fall into damnation, a fall which, given his enormous spiritual aspirations, becomes an inverted ascent.

The other protagonists are likewise shown within the context of their highest—though more earthbound—aspirations: Hugh, with his somewhat naive left-wing faith, Laruelle, hoping to change the world through his films, and Yvonne, trying to save Geoffrey. "For man, every man [...] must ceaselessly struggle upward", affirms Hugh as he muses about conscience and the political vicissitudes of Mexico (p. 108).[2] The Goethean epigraph, thus restated and transposed, acquires a broad moral and political significance. Characteristically enough, Lowry unfolds the strivings of his characters not only through the plot but through manifold images of ascent. In the case of Hugh and the Consul, the most tangible image is that of climbing mountains.

[1] See J. E. Cirlot, *A Dictionary of Symbols* (New York: Philosophical Library, 1962), pp. 19—20 ("Ascension"); and Mircea Eliade, *Patterns in Comparative Religion* (London and Sydney: Sheed & Ward, 1958), pp. 102—108.

[2] In order to avoid confusion between Malcolm Lowry's three dots and my own ellipses the latter will be put in square brackets.

They both want to climb the volcano, and both are shown to aspire at more than merely physical heights. But whereas Hugh, even though motivated by a desire to improve the world, often indulges in bravado, Geoffrey's ascent has unmistakable metaphysical implications. In a phantasmagoric vision at the very beginning of Chapter Five, the Consul imagines a pilgrimage to the holy mountain Himavat (also mentioned by T. S. Eliot in *The Waste Land*). From the Hindu book of *Mahabharata* he quotes a passage describing a mystical ascent to the top of the Himalayas:[3]

And by degrees they reached the briny sea. Then, with souls well disciplined they reached the northern region, and beheld, with heaven-aspiring hearts, the mighty mountain Himavat. (p. 125)

The mountain motif in *Under the Volcano* is thus reinforced with religious connotations. As in many mythological traditions, this image indicates the point where heaven and earth meet and evokes the sacred mountain or the mountain of salvation.[4] But the Consul's ascent to salvation appears unsuccessful. His never completed pilgrimage to the top of the mountain Himavat foreshadows his visionary attempt to climb Popocatepetl at the end of the book. A moment before his death the Himalayas merge in his vision with the volcano and Geoffrey reaches its peak, convinced that "this greatest ascent of all had been successfully [. . .] completed" (p. 375). Yet the illusion is soon broken and the mountain of salvation turns into the violently erupting volcano. In this fashion Lowry lets mountain and volcano merge, creating a new symbolic entity, richer in connotations and better able to sustain the inverted ascent and the quality of "infernal paradise".

While the Himavat, as well as the mountains, which form part of the imagery contained in the visions of a perfect union of Geoffrey and Yvonne, suggest serenity, happiness, and ultimate fulfilment, the volcano brings the turmoil of destruction and death. "*Ignivome* mountains", says the Consul with apparent irrelevance when speaking about the submergence of Atlantis (p. 148). Yet everyone acquainted with the legend of Atlantis knows—and the Consul is said to be writing a book on Atlantis—that the continent perished as a result of volcanic eruptions. All this is set forth in great detail by Ignatius Donnelly,[5] an influential authority on Atlantis of almost a century ago, who is mentioned by the Consul (see p. 86). Thus we see how the Atlantis motif, though properly belonging to the theme of destruction and catastrophe, is here interwoven with *Ascent*.

[3] Cf. Monier Williams, *Indian Wisdom* (London: Wm. H. Allen & Co., 1875), p. 412.
[4] Cf. Cirlot, pp. 208—11, and M. Eliade, *The Sacred and the Profane* (New York: Harcourt, 1959), pp. 38—39.
[5] Ignatius Donnelly, *Atlantis* (New York: Rudolf Steiner Publications, 1971), On Lowry's use of Donnelly see A. Kilgallin, *Lowry* (Erin, Ontario: Press Porcepic, 1973), p. 136.

Popocatepetl, however, does not need the support of the Atlantis theme, which is only indirectly implied, to reveal its destructive character. An awareness of its evil nature accompanies both Geoffrey and Hugh; only for Yvonne are the volcanoes simply a spectacle of stunning beauty. The Consul acknowledges the beauty; he even once thinks of Popocatepetl and another volcano called Ixtaccihuatl in terms of "that image of the perfect marriage" (p. 93), but more often he finds himself in a mood which invests the volcanoes with lifelessness and despair. He feels

his desolation go out to those heights where even now at midmorning the howling snow would whip the face, and the ground beneath the feet was dead lava, a soulless petrified residue of extinct plasm in which even the wildest and loneliest trees could never take root [. . .] (p. 144)

This description, one might say, is only a prelude: a mere spectacle of inert death on the verge of non-being. Later in the book, Popocatepetl becomes an active force of destruction. The volcano is identified with the *Máquina Infernal*, one of the images of the Consul's hell, and described in its destructive aspects. At the end of the novel it erupts, even though only in Geoffrey's dying vision. Because of its metaphoric associations, the explosion becomes identified with the Consul's death, war, holocaust, and the annihilation of the world:

now there was this noise of foisting lava in his ears, horribly, it was in eruption, yet no, it wasn't the volcano, the world itself was bursting, bursting into black spouts of villages catapulted into space, with himself falling through it all, through the inconceivable pandemonium of a million tanks, through the blazing of ten million burning bodies [. . .] (p. 375)

In *Under the Volcano* the imaginative impact of the whole mountain motif takes its force not only from the different aspects of volcanoes and mountains but from the juxtaposition suggested by the title of the novel.

Popocatepetl towered through the window, its immense flanks partly hidden by rolling thunderheads; its peak blocking the sky, it appeared almost right overhead, the barranca, the Farolito, directly beneath it. Under the Volcano! It was not for nothing the ancients had placed Tartarus under Mt. Aetna [. . .] (p. 339)

It is not for nothing Lowry places the abyss of perdition under the mountain of salvation. The abyss, represented most conspicuously by the fearful ravine, the barranca, is moreover shown to be eternal and ubiquitous; more tangible and substantial than the Consul's visions of a mystical pilgrimage towards higher reality, Yvonne's "blue mountains with snow and blue cold rough water" (p. 277) in her dream of a new life with Geoffrey, and Hugh's irresistible urge for climbing. "One was [. . .] always stumbling upon the damned thing, this immense intricate donga" (p. 130), remarks the Consul to himself while contem-

25

plating a tequila-supported descent into this "general Tartarus and gigantic jakes" (p. 131). A year later, towards the end of the sequence of events presented by the story, but at the beginning of the book, Jacques Laurelle makes essentially the same observation: "Wherever you turned the abyss was waiting for you round the corner. Dormitory for vultures and city Moloch!" (p. 15). The ubiquity of the barranca overcasts the salvific overtones of the mountain motif which are also undermined by the sinister cantina Farolito. Situated right above the ravine but under the volcano, the cantina is more than once compared to, and actually identified with, hell. This place where the Consul is finally killed appears to be in a sense the real goal of his strivings.

In *Under the Volcano* human strivings are represented not only by the mountain. Another, less concretely physical but more symbolic, image of man's aspirations used by Lowry is the tower. Its most widely known symbol in Western culture is the Biblical Tower of Babel which is alluded to a number of times in the novel. It is mentioned for the first time quite early in the book. In Chapter One Laruelle recalls the Consul insisting that the ruined pyramid in Cholula (a Mexican town with ancient Aztec ruins) was the original Tower of Babel (see p. 11). The reader may wonder what makes the Consul confuse the Hebrew story of the ancient Middle East with Aztec ruins in Mexico: is it the mere sight of the collapsed pyramid accompanied by a drunken fantasy, or does it have some deeper and significant reasons which are not immediately apparent? It seems that in this case Lowry's novel allows for some interpretative speculation.

If we assume that the cultural-geographic transfer that Geoffrey makes does possess a rational significance other than his "babel of thoughts" in the immediate context, we might take it for granted that it supports itself on some specialized body of knowledge. If we follow up this clue, we shall discover that the already mentioned Ignatius Donnelly relates the story of the Cholula pyramid, finding it to be an almost exact parallel of the Tower of Babel. Moreover, "both legends were", according to the American scholar, "probably derived from Atlantis, and referred to some gigantic structure of great height ..."[6] Were this an isolated allusion to the lost continent and Donnelly, we might dismiss the reference as scarcely relevant, but in view of the clearly audible Atlantis theme it certainly merits attention. The same chapter offers yet another allusion to Atlantis, where the "hidden meaning" is hinted at in much the same way:

it was one of those occasions when the Consul had drunk himself sober [Laruelle continues his recollection, looking now into the barranca]—he had spoken to him about

[6] Donnelly, p. 203.

the spirit of the abyss, the god of storm, "huracán," that "testified so suggestively to intercourse between opposite sides of the Atlantic." Whatever he had meant. (p. 16)

Neither Laruelle nor the reader can immediately fathom what the Consul has in mind. But a look into Donnelly considerably clarifies the situation. *Hurakan*, the name of a Mexican deity, and its European counterparts like English hurricane or Spanish huracán, are said to reflect the destruction of Atlantis as it was retained in human consciousness on the two opposite shores of the Atlantic. "While the ships from Atlantis carried terrified passengers to tell the story of the dreadful catastrophe to the people of the Mediterranean shores", relates Donnelly, "other ships, flying from the tempest, bore similar awful tidings to the civilized races around the Gulf of Mexico."[7] Lowry also follows Donnelly in calling huracán "the spirit of the abyss", in a context where, a few sentences before, "abyss" has been applied to the barranca. Thus we may imagine the destructive spirit *Hurakan* residing in the infernal barranca, a symbol of "finality indeed, and cleavage" (p. 15).

Donnelly further informs us that *Hurakan* was an agent of destruction and deluge,[8] and, finally, that "the pyramid of Cholula was erected 'as a means of escape from a second flood, should another occur' ".[9] This, in turn, ties in very well with Laruelle's towers and his fears of flood and cataclysm:

It was still raining, out of season, over Mexico, the dark waters rising outside to engulf his own zacuali in the Calle Nicaragua, his useless tower against the coming of the second flood. Night of the Culmination of the Pleiades! (p. 29)

Now the last sentence of the above quotation is apparently so incongruous with what both precedes and follows it as to become an almost blank space. The space fills with significance only after a work on Mexican mythology has been consulted, where the culmination of the Pleiades is given to signify the end of the world.[10]

It might be objected that the unfolding of all these allusions—though they certainly merit attention—is, strictly speaking, outside the text of Lowry's novel and should not be taken into account in its interpretation. Unless allusions, some scholars would maintain, work within the text through their suggestive power, they are not worth pursuing and, indeed, fall into the category of false intentionalism.[11] But while this objection is theoretically sound, it does not seem

[7] Ibid., p. 103.

[8] See ibid., pp. 102–103.

[9] Ibid., p. 203.

[10] See Lewis Spence, *The Myths of Mexico and Peru* (London: George G. Harrap, 1913), p. 41. That Lowry used Spence's work has been pointed out by Perle Epstein in *The Private Labyrinth of Malcolm Lowry* (New York: Rinehart, 1969), p. 190.

[11] See W. K. Wimsatt and M. C. Beardsley, "The Intentional Fallacy", in W. K. Wimsatt, *The Verbal Icon* (London: Methuen, 1970), pp. 14–18.

to bear upon the three cases so far considered. Here the allusions, because their meanings cannot be satisfactorily accounted for by the context, "attract" the outside information which not only might but has to be fitted into the text. In effect, Lowry's motif of the tower accumulates a variety of meanings of which destruction or collapse is the dominant note. Destruction is represented by the Biblical Tower of Babel, the Mexican Cholula, Atlantis, and, more indirectly, the barranca. The associations with the flood introduce the element of cosmic punishment inflicted on the sins of humanity. The Tower of Babel, the Cholula pyramid and the towers of Laruelle's house suggest man's self-aggrandizement attempted, as we shall see in chapter 4 below, by means of black magic.

Man's self-aggrandizement, his aspiration to reach ever higher, indicates the aspect of ascent in an image otherwise dominated by qualities rooted in the idea of downfall. That the tower is symbolic of ascent we learn also through Laruelle's recollection of the Chartres Cathedral. Its "twin spires [. . .] slowly rising into the sunlight" (p. 12) suggest the European Middle Ages during which towers symbolized a link between earth and heaven.[12] Yet the tower as a symbol of aspiration is, as we have seen, essentially flawed and it is the flaws which make for its total effect. In the first place, we are affected by the Biblical significance of the Babel myth which Lowry substantiates by weaving it skilfully into the Consul's alcoholic predicament:

In how many glasses, how many bottles had he hidden himself, since then alone? Suddenly he saw them, the bottles [. . .] the glasses, a babel of glasses—towering [. . .] built to the sky, then falling, the glasses toppling and crashing, falling downhill [. . .] the bottles breaking [. . .] smashing [. . .] or bursting into smithereens . . . (p. 292)

In a different and more tragic key, the theme of Babel recurs in the Farolito, where the only voice capable of rising above an infernal confusion of tongues is that of the pimp who has been instrumental in pushing the Consul towards the catastrophe.

The medieval towers do not remain untouched by Lowry's irony. Jacques Laruelle's rapture over the French cathedral appears to be stained by some unfulfilled moral obligations and guilt. This is implied by setting together the fascination of Chartres with the spell cast fifteen years later by his love for Yvonne, as well as by the consequent juxtaposition of guilt feelings accompanying the two enchantments. The first is not broken by "the fact that he was scandalously in debt" (p. 12), and the second by "any remorse for the Consul's plight" (p. 13) whom Laurelle betrays by having an affair with his wife. In other words, the delights of artistic and erotic magic prove much stronger than moral considerations. "An artist with a murderer's hands", the

---

[12] See Cirlot, pp. 326–327 ("Tower").

French film producer comments on the poster of *The Hands of Orlac,* and significantly adds: "or was it, by some uncomfortable stretch of imagination, M. Laruelle himself?" (p. 25).

The towers of Laruelle's house, the cataclysmic context of which has already been pointed out, are also expressive of a basic dualism: one is unadorned except for its crenellations, the other boasts two angels but the angels are set opposite "two nameless objects like marzipan cannonballs" (p. 194). The towers are compared to the s.s. *Samaritan*—the Consul's disguised warship whose actions defy and mock its name—and to the police watchtowers commanding the landscape of *Under the Volcano.* These appear throughout the novel, and their presence is as oppressive as that of the barranca. While "the eternal mirador [Spanish: watchtower] of Parián state" (p. 63) recalls "the [Chartres] cathedral eternally sailing against the clouds" (p. 12), it actually suggests an excessive interference of the police and, on a more general plane, man's enslavement by dark forces. "The world was always within the binoculars of the police" (p. 106) states Hugh, and we may take this to represent the actual nature of the tower image in *Under the Volcano.* Clearly, the infernal has prevailed here over the paradisal.

The same may be said of the recurrent and manifold images of soaring.

Birds were sailing up there, ascending higher and higher. Infernal bird of Prometheus!
They were vultures, that on earth so jealously contend with one another, defiling themselves with blood and filth, but who were yet capable of rising, like this, above the storms, to heights shared only by the condor, above the summit of the Andes— (p. 317)

This is the only place in the book where vultures acquire any dignity; otherwise they are an unmistakable sign of death and horror. And even when "more graceful than eagles", they hover "like burnt papers floating from a fire" (p. 93) and thereby point to the floating ashes of the Consul's letter. The letter, expressing the essence of Geoffrey's despair and an acknowledgement of the absolute necessity of love, could have led to his salvation had it ever been posted. A year after his death, when Laruelle accidentally discovers it and on a sudden impulse sets it on fire, it is only "a burning castle, collapsed [. . .] a dead husk [. . .] faintly crepitant . . ." (p. 42).

There are two cases in *Under the Volcano* of birds actually soaring, and what is significant, soaring as a result of being released. Hugh's sea-gull—"pure scavenger of the empyrean" with "angelic wings" (p. 151)—and Yvonne's eagle—"a little world of fierce despairs and dreams" in a cage, now flying off into "the deep dark blue pure sky above" (p. 320)—suggest a dramatic uplifting heavenwards. But, just as the tower image, they are tinged by their specific context. Hugh's setting free of the bird has the character of an empty gesture, an overdramatization of the wish to be and do good. Yvonne's action is far more difficult to understand because, even though it asks to be read symbolically, Lowry seems to withold clues to its significance.

All the same, we might venture to suggest that the act of freeing the eagle is an "objective correlative" of Yvonne's nervous apprehension; her feeling of constant emotional pressure created by the demands of the situation and the failures to achieve a reunion with Geoffrey. The eagle may also point to her awareness of the imprisoned potential for good in both the Consul and herself (cf. Yvonne's letters to him). At the same time Yvonne's release of the bird is too desperate, too reminiscent of Hugh's gesture not to share in the quality of the somewhat spurious enthusiasm displayed by the young man.

The image of soaring is also modified by the frequent appearance of the cigarettes *Alas* where both the Spanish (wings) and the English meaning of the name is indicated. The word becomes an intensely dramatic counterpoint when, shortly before his death, the Consul is reading Yvonne's letters which— just as his own unsent confession—could have led to his salvation, had he had the physical and moral power to read them before. Yvonne writes passionately and with love. She regrets having been childless but desires children now, at once. She speaks of "life filling and stirring" her, of happiness and peace. At this moment Geoffrey pauses, fumbling for a cigarette: "Alas; the tragic word droned round the room like a bullet that had passed through him" (p. 346). On the resumption of reading, the letter has changed tone and message: "You are walking on the edge of an abyss where I may not follow" (p. 346).

Alas appears to be, in turn, connected with the airplane image—if we agree that soaring implies flying, and that the planes mentioned in *Under the Volcano* can be treated metaphorically. "Everyone comes flying to see me these days" (p. 60), remarks the Consul, and we may associate this coincidence with the fact that both Yvonne and Hugh, who have chosen to travel by air, are trying in their own ways to save Geoffrey. However, Hugh's journey has been possible only thanks to a fascist acquaintance of his, and Yvonne's plane is ominously called a "winged emissary of Lucifer" (p. 44). The other planes—though their role is not altogether obvious—seem to be terrifying portents of some undefined evil.

Before we pass on to the final stage of the inverted ascent, we might consider the question of Yvonne's journey to the stars at the end of Chapter Eleven. The difficulty seems to lie not so much in determining the fact of her death on the basis of the text alone, but in coming to terms with what happens, regardless of whether Yvonne is actually dying or simply losing consciousness. Lowry's own comparison of Yvonne to Goethe's Gretchen seems somewhat strained (cf. *Letters*, p. 84). As Douglas Day tells us, Lowry

did leave in the final version of the novel the ecstatic and lyrical conclusion to Chapter Eleven, in which Yvonne feels herself being "gathered upwards and borne towards the stars," and told Cape that he was thinking of Yvonne's death as being like that of Margarete in *Faust*, Part I, in which she is translated to heaven as Faust is sent to hell; but since the passage had existed from the time when, in the early drafts of the novel, Yvonne's ecstasy was caused by sexual intercourse with Hugh, Lowry's Faustian allusion strikes one as after-the-fact, a happy accident.[13]

Whatever the origin of the passage in question, the most significant textual indication we can resort to is the persistent revolving of almost all the heavenly bodies described or mentioned in Chapter Eleven which finally gathers Yvonne up towards the Pleiades. She seems thus to be left for ever travelling on a gigantic cosmic wheel, in much the same way as the Consul on the Máquina Infernal. But is it legitimate to compare Geoffrey's infernal journey with Yvonne's heavenly? We may answer in the affirmative, if we realize that the wheel images in *Under the Volcano* suggest senselessness and infinite unfulfilment. For even though "the diamonded brightness" of the stars contemplated by Yvonne should "gleam an instant on the soul, touching all within that in memory was sweet or noble or courageous or proud" (p. 322), their incessant circling movement appears as a spectacle of cosmic purposelessness:

And the earth itself still turning on its axis and revolving around that sun, the sun revolving around the luminous wheel of this galaxy, the countless unmeasured jewelled wheels of countless unmeasured galaxies, turning, turning, majestically, into infinity, into eternity, through all of which all life ran on—all this, long after she herself was dead, men would still be reading in the night sky, and as the earth turned through those distant seasons [. . .] would they not, too, still be asking the hopeless eternal question: to what end? (p. 322)

Let us now proceed to the ascent turned full circle, that is to say, to what the Consul calls "his downward flight" (p. 362). Certainly the choice of phrase is not accidental. Lowry lets its ambivalence develop in a remarkably intricate way since Geoffrey becomes fully aware of his "downward flight" only in the Farolito, the goal of his escape from life, where now, despite the very palpable danger, his powerful urge to run away is curiously arrested: "The Consul produced his blue package of cigarettes with the wings on them: Alas! He raised his head again; no, he was where he was, there was nowhere to fly to" (p. 362). Nowhere, save the barranca: the erupting volcano and the exploding universe into which the dying Consul will imagine himself falling.

The way Geoffrey dies is foreshadowed, or echoed—depending on whether we see the first chapter as the beginning of the book or as the conclusion of the story—by Laruelle's significant misreading of Marlowe: "Then will I headlong fly into the earth . . ."[14] The lapsus, through which "run" has become "fly", so

---

[13] *Biography*, p. 340.

[14] Cf. Christopher Marlowe, *Doctor Faustus* (London: Methuen, 1962), xix, 155. Henceforward cited as *Faustus*.

powerfully affects Laruelle that he stares for a while "at the words that seemed to have the power of carrying his own mind downward into a gulf" (p. 34). His mistake and the reaction it elicits establish a parallel between Doctor Faustus and the Consul which is a little later reinforced by another randomly selected passage from Marlowe's tragedy. This time it is the moral of the play spoken by the chorus, but Lowry lets it break at words significant for his own purpose: "Faustus is gone: regard his hellish fall—" (p. 34). Prompted by this sudden break, the reader may pause to reflect on Marlowe's words and take them to be actually a prologue; an invitation to witness the drama that is about to unfold. What follows is indeed an account of the different forms of the hero's fall and in the middle of the novel comes a direct confirmation of its hellish nature. Geoffrey looks at a horrifying prohibitionist poster which, he will realize a moment later, only too adequately reflects his own situation.

Down, headlong into hades, selfish and florid-faced, into a tumult of fire-spangled fiends, Medusae, and belching monstrosities [. . .] shrieking among falling bottles and emblems of broken hopes, plunged the drunkards; up, up, flying palely, selflessly into the light toward heaven, soaring sublimely in pairs [. . .] shot the sober. (p. 199)

Presently, the name of Parián is mentioned which is soon associated in the Consul's mind with the infernal cantina Farolito. Geoffrey takes another look at the poster and suddenly wakes to the shocking yet curiously tranquillizing certainty of his own being in hell. From now on his downward movement becomes both more deliberate and more pronounced. The next chapter (Chapter Eight) begins with "Downhill . . ." and this opening is substantiated by the direction of the erratic bus journey on the one level and by the tragically ironic transposition of the story of the Good Samaritan on the other.

Later, in a conversation with Yvonne, the Consul goes so far as to admit his downfall, but the high hopes evoked by the moment of truthfulness prove to be very short-lived. The conversation is interrupted by Geoffrey drinking the habanero, and immediately afterwards a powerful image of illusion presents itself: a consoling and soothing sight of water turns out to be a broken roof of a greenhouse, full of weeds and shot through with the sunlight (p. 279).

Another instance of the Consul acknowledging his downfall proves equally frustrating. In a prayer, he admits having sunk low and asks, among other things, for a recovery of his purity, and for happiness with Yvonne. But on one condition: "if it's only out of this terrible world. Destroy the world!" (p. 289). This wish to opt out of the world becomes a fact at the end of the chapter when Geoffrey, breaking with Yvonne and Hugh, consciously and deliberately chooses hell. Henceforward we shall encounter him only in the Farolito where the Consul more acutely than ever realizes the extent of his ruin. But just as in the previous instances, the mere awareness is not of much avail. The cantina, through Geoffrey's actions and inaction, becomes, as it were, an infernal spring-board from which he plunges into the barranca.

Nevertheless, the hero's fall is in *Under the Volcano* set off against various hints of salvation. If we witness inverted ascent, we also get glimpses into man's ultimate aspirations before they have been turned upside down. In one of her letters, Yvonne reminds Geoffrey of his immense spiritual potentialities:

"Your are one born to walk in the light. Plunging your head out of the white sky you flounder in an alien element. You think you are lost, but it is not so, for the spirits of light will help you and bear you up in spite of yourself and beyond all opposition you may offer." (pp. 364—65)

In other words, the ascension into the light is affirmed as the essential part of the Consul's existence and his calling which he constantly chooses to resist. Because of this choice which, musically speaking, constitutes the key of *Under the Volcano,* the theme of "striving upwards" has turned into its opposite and yielded only inverted images: spiritual heights and the mystical mountain Himavat have merged with the volcano which, defined by what is under it, stands for individual and global destruction. Soaring to heaven has been, as we have observed, first transformed into the Tower of Babel and the police watchtowers; secondly arrested by the immobile wings (alas); and then imprisoned in infinite senseless rotation. Finally, flight has become escape, "downward flight", and ultimate fall.

Chapter 2
Light

The theme of *Ascent* examined in the previous chapter contains, as we have seen, a number of mythical overtones. The same is true to a greater or lesser extent of most of Lowry's imagery in *Under the Volcano*. Although in the case of *Light* we can speak perhaps more legitimately in terms of mythical parallels rather than overtones, it seems obvious that the imagery of this theme is embedded in the general light symbolism in which "the numinous is essentially the luminous".[1] Not surprisingly therefore the Consul's mystical aspirations are, as we saw at the end of the previous chapter, conceived as an ascent into the light. In this chapter we shall trace the interplay of light and darkness as it manifests itself in the Consul's cantinas, in his relationship with Yvonne, and in her dreams and fears. We shall also see how Geoffrey's inability to face the light leads him to the Dantean dark forest which in *Under the Volcano* signifies not so much a test for the hero's soul as darkness, death, and destruction.

The light symbolism employed by Lowry is general enough to evoke a great many echoes from different mythological traditions. Of these the most appropriate for gaining an insight into the Consul's plight is probably the Cabbala, the poetic substance of the novel. One short description, or an image, of the Cabbala given by Lowry in the letter to Cape discloses the fusion of *Ascent* and *Light:*

The Cabbala is used for poetical purposes because it represents man's spiritual aspirations. The Tree of Life, which is its emblem, is a kind of complicated ladder with Kether, or Light, at the top and extremely unpleasant abyss some way above the middle. The Consul's spiritual domain is probably the Qliphoth, the world of shells and demons, represented by the Tree of Life upside down . . . (*Letters*, p. 69)

In this schematic exposition of the Cabbala, Light, because it is situated at the top of the Tree of Life, represents the goal of human aspirations. This cor-

---

[1] Edwyn Bevan, *Symbolism and Belief* (Boston: Beacon Press, 1957), p. 130. "In all great religions of antiquity", writes Bevan, "the chief gods are characterized by their connexion with light. In Egypt [for example] this led to the chief god being identified with the sun—the Ra or Re of Heliopolis" (pp. 129—30). Likewise the Old and New Testaments provide many examples of light being associated with God (e.g. Ps. 43:3., Isa. 49:6., John 1:9., I John 1:5.).

responds to the "ascension into the light" touched upon in the previous chapter and encourages us therefore to imagine the Consul as a Cabbalist ascending the Tree of Life into the Light of Kether. But in fact Geoffrey is doing nothing of the kind. Because he is in the "domain of shells and demons",[2] represented by the Tree of Life *upside down,* he must be making a descent into darkness, even though he is often unaware of the true nature of his predicament. Only in an utterly hopeless situation does he really take notice of his infernal whereabouts. When the fascist pseudo-policemen begin their "investigation" of his case and when the urge to escape finally leaves him, the Consul recalls the prohibitionist poster and identifies himself with those who are falling into hell, visualizing at the same time the others, "more noble, the higher they ascended into the light" (p. 361). Also in the unsent letter to Yvonne he tries to clarify his real position on the Cabbalistic Tree. Far from approaching its top, where Yvonne might perhaps picture him, he is in the Qliphoth: the world of evil and demonic forces.

But apart from such dramatic moments of insight, the Consul appears to be oblivious of the total reversal of values within his mystical frame of reference. In so far as he is a Cabbalist, he is likely to think that he is still ascending the Tree of Life into the Light at its top. Thus he finds himself in an "infernal paradise", or in a situation where the quality of "infernal paradise" appears with particular clarity. The infernal cantina which represents the goal of his downward path is to him a source of light and bliss. It is called the *Farolito*, which in Spanish means "a little beacon". Accordingly, the Consul does not fail to point out that it is the Lighthouse although, he adds, it is "the lighthouse that invites the storm" (p. 200). Yet neither this qualification nor the atmosphere of sorrow and evil with which the cantina is permeated diminish his longing for its heavenly peace and light:

He saw the dawn again [. . .] in the violet-shaded light, a slow bomb bursting over the Sierra Madre—*Sonnenaufgang!*—the oxen harnessed to their carts with wooden disc wheels patiently waiting outside for the drivers, in the sharp cool pure air of heaven. (p. 200)

If to long for heaven is to hope, it is natural that Geoffrey should be impatiently waiting for the glowing "lamp of hope" of a cantina. Nevertheless, the cantina is revealingly called *El Infierno* (see p. 350) and the Consul realizes that all his cantinas are more or less infernal. Yet he allows this insight into his consciousness only half-heartedly, merely with a part of his mind. Sometimes a word, a phrase, or a peculiar mood gives away his otherwise blissfully ecstatic

---

[2] This is the "sinister demonic world of evil which forms the dark side of everything living and threatens it from within". G. Scholem, *Major Trends in Jewish Mysticism* (New York: Schocken Books, 1961), p. 239.

cantina fantasies and prayers: "Outside the cantina El Puerto del Sol in Independencia the *doomed* [italics mine] men would be already crowding into the warmth of the sun, waiting for the shutters to roll up with a crash of trumpets" (p. 70).

On another occasion the Consul's recognition of the fact that all his love of life is imprisoned and turned to poison in the cantinas comes through what he imagines to be Yvonne's reproachful thoughts (p. 65). And because Yvonne often appears to him not as a voice of conscience but as a hostile force, Geoffrey avoids confrontation with the truth. Feeling that his wife is entirely incapable of appreciating the sunlight and the beauty of the cantinas, the Consul persists in seeing light precisely where he is surrounded by darkness:

Ah none but he knew how beautiful it all was, the sunlight, sunlight, sunlight flooding the bar of El Puerto del Sol, flooding the watercress and oranges, or falling in a single golden line as if in the act of conceiving a God [. . .] (p. 90)

But to Yvonne the cantinas are simply a world of darkness which sharply contrasts with the light she is bringing in together with her dreams of saving Geoffrey. Still conscious of the sunlight behind her (p. 46), "the seven o'clock morning sunlight" (p. 44) of the town square, she reluctantly enters the dark bar where the Consul is sitting. At the sight of him, however, "the terrific onslaught of sunlight" (p. 45) experienced during the flight to Quauhnahuac leaves her. Geoffrey's reaction to meeting her for the first time after their long separation seems only to confirm what Yvonne calls "the darkness of the sundering" (p. 50). "Oh Geoffrey, why do you do it", she cries silently in her exasperation over—as she feels it—the Consul's ultimate denial of her. "Must you go on and on forever into that stupid darkness, seeking it, even now, where I cannot reach you", she asks, and in the same imaginary conversation herself provides Geoffrey's answer in terms of the cantina: "you misunderstand me if you think it is altogether darkness I see [. . .] but if you look at the sunlight there, ah, then perhaps you'll get the answer [...] what beauty can compare to that of a cantina in the early morning?" (p. 50). While "the darkness of the severance" between Yvonne and Geoffrey persists throughout *Under the Volcano*, the light and the beauty that the Consul is seeking alone in the cantinas acquire a dark and sinister aspect. On the other hand, a similar atmosphere of beauty and sunlight in Yvonne's dreams seems to be aimed at dissolving the darkness of lovelessness and isolation, since it bespeaks happiness, renewal, and reunion:

How happy they seemed in one another; lovers they were, or on their honeymoon. Their future would stretch out before them pure and untrammelled as a blue and peaceful lake, and thinking of this Yvonne's heart felt suddenly light as that of a boy on his summer holidays, who rises in the morning and disappears into the sun. (p. 269)

36

Yvonne is often presented as if she had some mysterious but natural connection with the sun; almost as if the sun were her native element. "An ocean creature so drenched and coppered by the sun" (p. 54), she feels "part of the sun" (p. 254), and appears "entirely clothed in sunlight" to Hugh (p. 95). The Consul is also sensitive to Yvonne's radiant aspect and even remarks on her having had plenty of sun (p. 71). But when she suggests getting out into the sun, he shuns the idea by being first carefully noncommittal and later frankly hostile to the suggestion, which in the course of their conversation comes to stand for a radically new beginning of their life together. For Yvonne, despite her lack of faith and her failings, does introduce at least a possibility of salvation into Geoffrey's downward hopeless flight. Unfortunately, the Consul is so deeply involved with his own damnation that he dreads such a possibility. To part with his own misery, which he has come to love (cf. p. 14), and to accept Yvonne's dreams of sunshine would be too painful, too unbearable:

The Consul looked at the sun. But he had lost the sun: it was not his sun. Like the truth, it was well-nigh impossible to face; he did not want to go anywhere near it, least of all, sit in its light, facing it. (p. 205)

Outside his dark cantinas Geoffrey recoils from the light. The thought of a sunflower growing outside his bedroom window causes him real terror: "[It] stares. Fiercely. All day. Like God!" (p. 179).

Presumably the same kind of fear accounts for the Consul's dark glasses which are mentioned too persistently to signal merely the appearance of the main character. They often seem to indicate one of the many barriers Geoffrey has placed between himself and the reality he cannot and does not want to confront. "For everyone that doeth evil hateth the light, neither cometh to the light, lest his deeds should be reproved", the Gospel of John (3:20) seems to provide a comment on the Consul's condition. Indeed, without the sunglasses on, the world presents a tormenting vision invested with images of guilt, agony, darkness:

it was as though bits of his eyelids had broken off and were flittering and jittering before him, turning into nervous shapes and shadows, jumping to the guilty chattering in his mind [. . .] a picture of his soul as a town appeared once more before him [. . .] a town ravaged and stricken in the black path of his excess, and shutting his burning eyes he had thought of the beautiful functioning of the system in those who were truly alive [. . .] Christ, how it heightened the torture [. . .] to be aware of all this [. . .] the light now on, now off, now on too glaringly, now too dimly [. . .] then at last to know the whole town plunged into darkness [. . .] (pp. 144—45)

This rather extraordinary image is foreshadowed by the metaphor of an abandoned town which the Consul has earlier applied to his own predicament (p. 74), and evoked by Dr. Vigil's comments on the sickness of the soul. Vigil compares the nerves to what he calls "an eclectic systemë" and in his significantly

37

faulty English adds: "After much tequila the eclectic systemë is perhaps un poco descompuesto [. . .] as sometimes in the cine: claro?" (p. 144). The doctor's diagnosis recalls the complaint of the cinema manager: "I am very sorry the function must be suspended. But the wires have decomposed. Chingado. Every blessed week something goes wrong with the lights" (p. 25).

In this way the image of failing lights establishes a link between the Consul's soul and the cinema which is characterized not only through the defects in the electric system but, mainly, through *Las Manos de Orlac,* the film it is constantly showing. And since the hands of Orlac are a murderer's hands, the Consul's soul is thematically implicated with the murder of the Indian at the hands of the same Mexican fascists who are later to shoot the Consul. The Indian's death, set in the context of the ironically paraphrased story of the Good Samaritan, indicates the spiritual impotence of the world totally incapable of active compassion. It is also connected with the themes of disintegration, death, and disaster which at the end of the book are gathered into a conflagration of the whole world (p. 375). Thus Lowry's counterpointing leads to a very paradoxical relationship between light and darkness since the rays of the sun, unmediated by the sunglasses, reveal a reality plunged into dark shadows of spiritual and physical death, a reality associated with the image of the dark cinema and *Las Manos de Orlac.* The Consul may be striving towards light but actually he lives in a world where to face light is to face darkness.

The paradox does not become as apparent in the case of the other protagonists who, lacking assumptions of a mystical search, do not have to follow the Consul in pretending that the darkness they experience in their lives has anything to do with spritual illumination. Yvonne, as we have seen, is not willing to accept Geoffrey's account of his cantinas in terms of sunlight and beauty. Feeling rejected and unable to reach him, she becomes acutely aware of "this stupid darkness [. . .] the darkness of the sundering, of the severance" (p. 50). However, this realization comes to her when she notices "a curious familiar glare in his eyes that always frightened her, a glare turned inward now like one of those somberly brilliant cluster-lamps down the hatches of the *Pennsylvania* on the work of unloading, only this was a work of spoliation" (p. 49). In other words, darkness is again revealed through light, though the contrast between the two elements is less conspicuous than before. Unlike the Consul, Yvonne experiences darkness in a much more direct way.

When she wanders all alone among the lights of New York City, suffering from a profound sense of unfulfilment brought about by the divorce from her first husband and a decisive setback in her artistic career, she feels engulfed by a darkness not only of personal tragedy but of universal despair:

She'd stood once more [. . .] on that freezing night in Times Square [. . .] watching the illuminated news aloft travelling around the Times Building, news of disaster, of suicide,

38

of banks failing, of approaching war, of nothing at all, which, as she gazed upward with the crowd, broke off abruptly, snapped off into darkness, into the end of the world, she had felt, when there was no more news. Or was it—Golgotha? A bereaved and dispossessed orphan, a failure [...] Yvonne had felt far more desolate than a streetwalker; walking [...] through the numb brilliant jittering city [...] that awful darkness had persisted in her mind, blackening still further her false wealthy loneliness, her guilty divorced dead helplessness. The electric arrows thrust at her heart—yet they were cheating: she knew, increasingly frightened by it, that darkness to be still there, in them, of them. [...] Men muttered by in whose faces all hope seemed to have died. [...] And everywhere, that darkness, the darkness of a world without meaning, a world without aim [...] (pp. 265—66)

Yvonne's experience foreshadows (within the sequence of time covered by the novel) the vision of a final breakdown which comes upon the aimless, sunless world: "people stumbling through debris littering dark streets, hurrying thousands seeking shelter in bomb-torn darkness [...] Darkness, disaster!" (p. 153). This image—mediated to Hugh by "the pulse of the world beating in that latticed throat" (p. 154) of the radio he is listening to in Geoffrey's garden—is in turn anticipated (within the sequence of the novel's structure) in Chapter One by the confusion which breaks out at the onset of an unexpected storm. In Lowry's own interpretation "in the cinema and the bar, people are taking refuge from the storm as in the world they are creeping into bomb shelters, and the lights have gone out, as they have gone out in the world" (*Letters,* p. 69).

But the darkness of the world is never unrelated to the lights that have gone out in the individual human soul. Indeed, the Consul, in his capacity of a mystic who has abused his powers and turned black magician,[3] may be held responsible for playing havoc with the world. Not necessarily through any direct action but because of an occult connection between the soul and the universe. For the magician or mystic the split of reality into inward and outward, into spirit and matter, is not too radical. Aware of the unity underlying the cosmos, knowing that every man is a microcosm, he will perceive the most far-reaching consequences of his thought or feeling.[4] And so, Geoffrey's drunken fantasies in the bathroom become charged with the forces of the universe:

Who would have ever believed that some obscure man, sitting at the center of the world in a bathroom, say, thinking solitary miserable thoughts, was authoring their doom, that, even while he was thinking, it was as if behind the scences certain strings were pulled and whole continents burst into flame, and calamity moved nearer—just as now, at this moment perhaps, with a sudden jolt and grind, calamity had moved nearer, and, without the Consul's knowing it, outside the sky had darkened. (p. 146)

---

[3] For a discussion of the Consul as a magician and Cabbalist see chapter 4 below.

[4] See Cirlot, *A Dictionary of Symbols,* pp. 187—190 ("Man"), and Rudolf Steiner, *Occult Science: An Outline* (London: Rudolf Steiner Press, 1969), pp. 294—95. Cf. also Perle Epstein, *The Private Labyrinth of Malcolm Lowry,* pp. 115—16.

What the Consul does know, however, is that his inner sky has darkened. Just before he embarks upon this phantasmagoria of doom, he becomes aware of insanity coming near: "the approaching storm, the darkness that will come galloping out of nowhere across the fields of the mind" (p. 145). Insanity, however, is only one aspect of the Consul's spiritual state, evoked here by Dr. Vigil's insistence on the sickness of the soul and his professed interest in the insane (p. 145). At other times, Geoffrey's mind is shrouded by darkness that is unmistakably infernal:

... Night: and once again, the nightly grapple with death, the room shaking with daemonic orchestras, the snatches of fearful sleep, the voices outside the window, my name being continually repeated with scorn by imaginary parties arriving, the dark's spinets. (p. 35, cf. also p. 342)

This vision of nightly terrors forms the beginning of the unsent letter to Yvonne, in which the Consul discloses the essential fact of his life, namely, that he is a wanderer in hell (p. 36). Like Dante, he feels lost in a dark forest, only the forest has merged with a cantina: "The Terminal Cantina El Bosque [Spanish: forest, woods], however, seemed so dark that even with his glasses off he had to stop dead ... Mi ritrovai per una bosca oscura—or selva?" (p. 225).[5] Unlike the Italian poet, the Consul deliberately chooses hell as his destination, and after a quarrel with Yvonne and Hugh runs "toward the forest, which was growing darker and darker" (p. 314).

The theme of the Dantean dark forest can be felt throughout *Under the Volcano*. It makes its first appearance on the first page of the book in the name Hotel Casino de la Selva,[6] where Dr. Vigil and Laruelle are having a drink after a game of tennis (p. 3). It is audible in another reference to Casino de la Selva (p. 10), can be heard when Cantina El Bosque is mentioned in passing (p. 30), and returns somewhat more clearly at the beginning of Chapter Two in Yvonne's attempt to establish the meaning of Quauhnahuac. According to one version it means "near the wood" (p. 44). Then the mysterious forest meets us—even though only by implication—in the very first words of Chapter Six. "—Nel mezzo del bloody cammin di nostra vita mi ritrovai in..." (p. 150), says or thinks Hugh to himself, establishing thus the key-note to the account of his life that is about to follow. Later, on entering the cantina El Bosque, the

---

[5] The whole tercet runs as follows: Nel mezzo del cammin di nostra vita / mi ritrovai per una selva oscura / che la diritta via era smarrita. (In the middle of the journey of our life / I found myself in a dark wood, / Having lost the straight path. (T. S. Eliot's translation from his essay on Dante in *Selected Essays,* London: Faber, 1934, p. 241).

[6] "*Note:* the book opens in the Casino de la Selva. Selva means wood and this strikes the opening cord of the *Inferno*—remember, the book was planned and still is a kind of Inferno..." (Lowry: *Letters,* p. 67). It might seem that Lowry's claim is still at this point unwarranted by the text, but the development of the theme will bear it out.

Consul will supply the missing words and complete the Dantean line with "per una bosca/selva oscura". The lines, taken from the tercet which opens *The Divine Comedy,* stand at the beginning of the *Inferno* part. Accordingly hell merges, in the symbolic foreshortening of Lowry's novel with the dark forest: a place where human beings get lost. The Consul's way to perdition leads through this dark forest where he bends his steps in a hurry after having made the fateful decision in favour of hell. And it is precisely the same forest into which Yvonne and Hugh will follow the Consul, searching for him in all the cantinas along the way. They never succeed, however, themselves lost in the dark woods where the reader finally loses sight of them. As Douglas Day points out,

they do a truly sorry job of looking for him—getting drunk themselves, setting caged eagles free, buying guitars: acting, in short, more like a pair of tourists than people hurrying to save a man's life. And so the Consul dies, and Yvonne dies, and Hugh is left stumbling about in the dark forest in the midst of a wild thunderstorm.[7]

While Yvonne still continues the search, the Consul is reading her letters in the Farolito. The letters, which he has not had the courage to read ever before, at last bring him to an insight into "the darkness of the severance":

Restless and haunted nights follow in bitter routine: the sun shines without brightness, and the moon rises without light. My heart has the taste of ashes, and my throat is tight and weary with weeping. What is a lost soul? It is one that has turned from its true path and is groping in the darkness of remembered ways—" (p. 346)

The Dantean motif, hardly perceptible at the beginning of *Under the Volcano,* has now associated itself not only with a loss of way but with heartbreak, misery, fruitless ruin, death and perdition. Yvonne does not forget that they were in "a dark wood", amidst a multitude of bizarre images which invade her consciousness shortly before it is extinguished (p. 335). The Consul is also accompanied by the forest theme down to the very end. At the moment of his death, which symbolizes also an ultimate collapse and catastrophe, he becomes aware of falling not only into the volcano or into "the blazing of ten million burning bodies" (p. 375); his agonal stream of consciousness breaks off at "falling, into a forest, falling—" (p. 375).

Yet the forest where Yvonne is trampled by the panic-stricken horse, and outside of which the Consul is shot, is not absolutely dark. A violent storm is raging in nature and the darkness is constantly rent by flashes of lightning: the theme of lights twitching in the dark is seeking here its tragic culmination:

Again trying to rise she heard herself scream as the animal turned towards her and upon her. The sky was a sheet of white flame against which the trees and the poised rearing horse were an instant pinioned—(p. 335)

[7] *Biography*, p. 340.

Geoffrey's ultimate loss of bearings is also illuminated by the tempestuous sky:

The Chief of Rostrums pushed the Consul back out of the light, took two steps forward and fired. Lightning flashed like an inchworm going down the sky and the Consul, reeling, saw above him for a moment the shape of Popocatepetl, plumed with emerald snow and drenched with brilliance. (p. 373)

The black storm clouds, which symbolize darkness of catastrophe covering the world, have been gathering throughout the Day of the Dead on which the action of *Under the Volcano* takes place. But the actual outbreak is witnessed by the reader at the end and beginning of the book.[8] In Chapter One (which is both the prologue and the epilogue of the novel) the storm is associated with Laruelle's passion for Yvonne: "Dark swift horses surging up the sky. A black storm breaking out of its season! That was what love was like [. . .] love which came too late!" (p. 10). From his thoughts we sense that love has not brought happiness or fulfilment, and from the knowledge of the whole book we gain an insight into the destruction which the affair has wrought in the lives of all the protagonists.[9] Later in the chapter the storm heralds the war by making people run for shelter, and then becomes a torrential rain which threatens the Frenchman's towers with the second flood, signifying thus the end of the world. Finally, when the "prologue-epilogue" in its conclusion indicates a return to the proper action of the novel, darkness, lights, and storm fall together into one image: "Over the town, in the dark tempestuous night, backwards revolved the luminous wheel" (p. 42). This carries us into the story itself at the end of which another storm will make its fateful appearance and reveal a victory of darkness over light.

In this context the Consul's description of the infernal cantina Farolito as "the lighthouse that invites the storm" becomes pregnant with meaning. It will be recalled, however, that the cantina is to him also a source of light and bliss. Geoffrey's longing for it is likened to that of "the mariner who, sighting the faint *beacon* [italics mine] of Start Point after a long voyage, knows that soon

---

[8] "This chapter [the last one] is the easterly tower, Chapter I being the westerly, at each end of my churrigueresque Mexican cathedral, and all the gargoyles of the latter are repeated with interest in this." (Lowry, *Letters*, p. 85).

[9] Yet all the essential themes are anticipated in the first chapter. It is hardly possible to feel how effective these anticipations are before going through the rest of *Under the Volcano*. The reader who is just beginning the novel will probably miss a great deal in the introductory chapter, which will become progressively clearer and more meaningful with each consecutive reading. It may be remarked in passing that the experience of listening to music is somewhat similar in that respect: sometimes, say, the fifth hearing reveals the scattered passages, anticipating some more central themes we have so far enjoyed without suspecting them of having any antecedents in the earlier part of a composition.

he will embrace his wife" (p. 201). Light is thus related to love, to the Consul's longing for Yvonne. And yet Geoffrey presently realizes that his wife and the Farolito are poles apart, and that he cannot be faithful to them both. Once again a dim awareness of being in the dark pit awakens in him and the Consul tries to lift his soul towards the light:

Christ, oh pharos of the world, how, and with what blind faith, could one find one's way back, fight one's way back, now, through the tumultuous horrors of five thousand shattering awakenings, each more frightful than the last, from a place where even love could not penetrate, and save in the thickest flames there was no courage? On the wall the drunks eternally plunged. (p. 201)

Let us observe that the invocation to the pharos of the world is immediately followed by a summoning of "blind faith", as if the light did not illuminate but blind. Indeed, as we have seen in this chapter, the Consul evades the light which merely illuminates the infernal horrors which he cannot bring himself to face. To escape them, therefore, he needs to become blind. Yet the blind faith does not seem to bring liberation. As though in answer to Geoffrey's question comes the picture of the drunks' eternal punishment.

The lighthouse image is also present in one of Yvonne's visions of a new life. Inspired by Geoffrey's confession of love and his apparent willingness to begin all over again, Yvonne dreams of their new tiny house on the beach which appears to her as "a haven and a beacon" (p. 279). But the vision ends with a dissonance. Yvonne realizes that she has built on too slender foundations, and the peaceful picture of their new home fades in her mind into "a figure of a woman having hysterics, jerking like a puppet and banging her fists upon the ground" (p. 279).

Neither the lighthouse nor light is ever unequivocal. The light that the Consul seeks is not only spurious; it is in reality darkness itself, the infernal darkness of his cantinas. Geoffrey persists in this fundamental confusion because he cannot face the real light. The sun that Yvonne tries to bring into his misery is too painful for him since it discloses only darkness. He takes refuge in the cantinas, pretending that the darkness of the sundering with which they are permeated is the light of heaven. At the same time he becomes aware—even though very dimly—that his favourite Farolito which promises the greatest celestial joys is in fact a lighthouse that invites the storm, while another cantina merges with the Dantean dark forest in which the human soul becomes lost. Geoffrey realizes also that his own soul is plunged into the darkness which cannot be redeemed by the twitching failing lights. Indeed, it is his very soul which is in a mysterious way responsible for the calamity of the world. Just as the soul moves towards insanity so the world moves towards destruction; just as the soul is plunged into the night so the world is shrouded with darkness. A storm breaks out—in the soul, in nature, in the whole world—and the darkness is shaken by flashes of lightning: "heliographs" (pp. 323—24) which reveal the death of Yvonne, the Consul, and a universal catastrophe.

There is no doubt that Geoffrey has failed in his search for the light. Confusing light with darkness, he has become like those who, according to Swedenborg, are in "corporeal love":

[They] see nothing in the light of heaven; to them the light of heaven is thick darkness; but the light of hell, which is like light from burning coals, is to them as clear light. Moreover, in the light of heaven their interior side is so darkened that they become insane; consequently, they shun that light and hide themselves in dens and caverns, more or less at a depth in accordance with the falsities with them derived from their evils.[10]

Why is this so? It seems that light has turned into its opposite because the Consul has sought not light itself but mere promise of brightness, as Lowry indicates in one of his mythical evocations. In a scene much reminiscent of the Tantalus myth Geoffrey desperately yet unsuccessfully tries to quench his thirst. Neither the falling rain nor the stream, nor the cool marshes, nor the lake are of any avail. The Consul is lying face downwards and drinking from a lake but his thirst remains unslaked:

Perhaps because he was drinking, not water, but lightness, and promise of lightness—how could he be drinking promise of lightness? Perhaps because he was drinking, not water, but certainty of brightness—how could he be drinking certainty of brightness? Certainty of brightness, promise of lightness, of light, light, light, and again, of light, light, light, light, light! (p. 125)

Just as striving upwards has ultimately proved to be a downward flight, so the light has turned into darkness since its appearance has been mistaken for its reality.

---

[10] Emanuel Swedenborg, *Heaven and Its Wonders and Hell* (London: The Swedenborg Society, 1966), p. 362. Lowry has not only read Swedenborg (see P. Epstein, pp. 13, 220), but mentions him in the first chapter of *Under the Volcano* (p. 37) and in *Dark as the Grave wherein my Friend is Laid* (Harmondsworth: Penguin, 1972), pp. 146, 222.

Chapter 3
Draught of Immortality

The metaphor of drinking mere promise of brightness, set in the context of mountain Himavat, suggests the Consul's mystical ascension towards the light as well as its inversion. Spiritual illumination, if sought through drink provided by the sinister cantinas, results in growing darkness and increasing thirst. So much is apparent to Yvonne, even though she does not share Geoffrey's esoteric quest. She is nonetheless exposed to its effects on the plane of her relations with him. The "darkness of the sundering" signifies the divorce they have gone through and expresses the Consul's denial of Yvonne for the sake of the light and beauty of the cantinas. The divorce is also symbolized by Oaxaca, a town "where the Consul had gone when she left, as if into the heart of the sundering, of the severance" (p. 49). Reminded of Oaxaca by Geoffrey, Yvonne becomes painfully conscious of its significance. "The word was like a breaking heart, a sudden peal of stifled bells in a gale, the last syllables of one dying of thirst in the desert" (p. 48). Thus Yvonne's image of Oaxaca associates thirst with the divorce, with the "darkness of the sundering" and, indirectly, with the Consul's denial of her caused by his love for the cantinas.

As we shall see in this chapter, *Under the Volcano* is permeated with a sense of thirst reminiscent of the tortures of Tantalus. Tantalus, as we remember, was deprived in the infernal regions of fruit and water which, seemingly accessible, perpetually receded from his reach. In Lowry's novel this mythical motif is suggested by thirst and drought being set off against the exuberant Mexican nature, fertile and overflowing with water. The antithesis between deprivation and abundance reflects the dilemma created by the Consul's thirst. Surrounded by the "fecund fountains of the new life" (p. 371) which remain closed to him, he tries to quench his thirst by alcohol, his mystical "draught of immortality", but in vain. Whatever its alleged mystical and holy powers, the alcoholic aqua vitae destroys the new life, leading the Consul to hell rather than heaven. His drunkenness involves him in a vicious circle analogous to a continual, ever more profound, exile from paradise. Mythologically speaking, Geoffrey has been cut off from the legendary source of life situated in the Garden of Eden. He has lost eternal life which he is trying to regain by means of his alcoholic "draught of immortality". Yet the more he drinks the further he is from the fountain of life, and the deeper his exile from the Garden. The fiery water of alcohol only increases his thirst, and his drunkenness—"a magnetic field where everything is driven toward its inescapable link with everything else"[1]—creates a waste land, visited by death and destruction.

Thirst, a classical symbol of human desire, manifests a want of life-giving substance, whether in a physical or spiritual sense. "My soul thirsteth for God, for the living God" (Ps. 42:2), says the Psalmist, "in a dry and thirsty land, where no water is" (Ps. 63:1). Both the human soul and the earth suffer from the drought and its death-bringing consequences. The theme of dying by thirst has in the twentieth century found a classic expression in T.S. Eliot's *The Waste Land,* which depicts the sterlility of a culture devoid of a living spiritual faith. And it has been noticed that *Under the Volcano* is likewise a description of a waste land.[2] Moreover, it is a waste land dramatized by the Tantalus myth, since the aridity and thirst are set amidst an abundance of water and drink.

The grass that Yvonne notices on the way to Geoffrey's house is not sufficiently green: it testifies to a dry spell "though the gutters on either side of the road were brimful of rushing mountain water" (p. 58). In the Consul's garden plants are perishing of thirst but the thirst is said to be unnecessary (p. 65). Indeed, there is plenty of water for the small swimming pool which is not overflowing only because the hose by which it is connected with the hydrant is leaky. Also the natural exuberance of the garden in its jungle-like state suggests not so much the plague of drought as neglect and the ensuing ruin. After all, the neighbouring garden, incessantly sprinkled by water, seems immaculate. The greenness of its lawn, the loveliness of its English-like turf arouse the Consul's nostalgia, reminding him of his exile from home and, symbolically, from paradise (see chapters 5 and 6 below). Natural semi-paradisal plenitude is also manifested in the Mexican landscape. The way from Tomalin to Parián, for example, is marked by the exuberance of water and nature, as Yvonne, estranged from Geoffrey, is trying to find him in the "rich cantina country" (p. 285). Two trees embracing one another strike her as an image of love drawing its sustenance from water:

The intertwined roots of the two tree lovers flowed over the ground towards the stream, ecstatically seeking it, though they didn't really need it; the roots might as well have stayed where they were, for all around them nature was out-doing itself in extravagant fructification. (p. 320)

[1] Alfred Kazin, *Bright Book of Life: American Novelists and Story Tellers* (Boston and Toronto: Little, Brown & Co., 1971), p. 19.

[2] See "A Prose Waste Land", unsigned essay in *The Times Literary Supplement* (May 11, 1962), and Anthony R. Kilgallin, "Eliot, Joyce and Lowry", *Canadian Author and Bookman,* 40 (1965), pp. 3—6.

At the same time *Under the Volcano* is permeated with a sense of dryness signalled by references to the dry spell, images of desert, the omnipresent dust and, of course, thirst. The combination of thirsty walls of houses and dust (p. 280), for example, makes one almost reach for a drink. But the particles of sand and earth point not only to the dry land; "dust, dust, dust—it filtered in through the windows, a soft invasion of dissolution, filling the vehicle" (p. 250). Twice is dust mentioned in connection with Cholula (pp. 11, 205), among whose ancient ruins, at least according to the Consul, lie the remnants of the original Tower of Babel. And so in terms of Lowry's juxtapositions, destruction and ruin are intertwined with the theme of thirst.

"Might a soul bathe there and be clean or slake its drought?",[3] asks the Consul of his swimming pool (p. 73), but the water seems to answer only with a ticking as of a clock. The question is twice more repeated in the book but neither the memory of the fountain in the court of the Trinity College in Cambridge (pp. 79—80) nor Laruelle's collection of books provide deliverance from the drought, which through Marvell's words has acquired a metaphorical meaning. And yet the very same man who has brought the memory of Cambridge and, wearing the striped college tie, in a way represents the Trinity fountain, offers the Consul a drink. Not of living water, however, but of Irish whisky. The Consul gratefully takes a long draught of the acqua vitae and his thirst is for some time quenched. If the scene with the Englishman only hints at the ambiguity of thirst and points to the transformation of water into alcohol, Geoffrey's image of the "desert of perdition" illustrates it more fully:

The day before him stretched out like an illimitable rolling wonderful desert in which one was going, though in a delightful way, to be lost: lost, but not so completely he would be unable to find the few necessary water-holes, or the scattered tequila oases where witty legionnaires of damnation [. . .] would wave him on, replenished, into that glorious Parián wilderness where man never went thirsty [. . .] (p. 139)

The Parián desert, almost synonymous, as we shall see, with the cantina Farolito and with death, is the Consul's "promised land", offering him not only heavenly light but also the bliss of drinking without limits. "He that believeth on me shall never thirst" (John 6:35, 4:14, 7:37); in his quasi-religious zeal the Consul could well have applied Christ's words to his paradisal cantina which alone is able to bring relief. All the swimming pools, all the lakes, and all the fountains have no such power. As we learn on the very first page of the novel, Quauhnahuac has four hundred swimming pools "filled with the water that ceaselessly pours down from the mountains", but the refreshing cool they so evidently offer seems beyond the Consul's reach. Saturated with alcohol and

---

[3] Cf. Andrew Marvell, "Clorinda and Damon", in *The Poems and Letters of Andrew Marvell* (Oxford: The Clarendon Press, 1927), vol. 1, p. 18.

having begun to drink the calamity-bringing mescal, he will find the sight of a natural waterfall in Tomalín "less cooling than grotesquely suggestive of some agonized ultimate sweat" (pp. 284—85). Neither is his own swimming pool of much use for it merges with the ticking of a mysterious clock, a clock signifying conscience, remorse, a call for decision, an awareness of waiting fearfully for the right moment that may never come. "The water still trickling into the pool—God, how deadeningly slowly—filled the silence between them" (p. 75). Lacking forgiveness, Geoffrey is unable to open himself to Yvonne and establish anew the kind of communication they have experienced before her betrayal and the divorce. The silence continues and he addresses the swimming pool with the Shakespearean words: "Thou art the grave where buried love doth live" (p. 143).[4] The love of Yvonne and Geoffrey has died and its death—as if to increase the tortures of Tantalus endured by the Consul—is set against extraordinary abundance of water. The grave is in the pool but the pool seems to offer the life-giving substance: "Fresh mountain water trickled into the pool, which was almost overflowing, from the cracked broken hose whose length was a series of small spouting fountains" (p. 143).

That water has that life-giving property also on the human plane is suggested by the characteristic imagery that appears in Yvonne's dream of love and happiness. Not only does the future of a happy pair of lovers seem to her like "a blue and peaceful lake" (p. 269) but she actually sees one, elated by the prospect of a new beginning with Geoffrey: a "little silver lake glittering cool, fresh, and inviting before them" (p. 279). However, all this turns out to be no more than the sight of fruit and water for the suffering Tantalus, since the alluring lake is just a broken roof of a greenhouse. The Consul, who is quick to dispel Yvonne's illusion, tells the story of "somebody dying of thirst in the Tasmanian desert [who] had a similar experience. The distant prospect of Cradle Mountain had consoled him a while, and then he saw this water . . . Unfortunately it turned out to be sunlight blazing on myriads of broken bottles" (p. 279). It seems that the mountain motif once more joins here with the theme of water in order that striving upward and regeneration by water might be all the more mercilessly negated by the underlying alcoholic reality. Despite the abundance of water, both the inner and the outer landscape of *Under the Volcano* are, as we can see, permeated by thirst.

The alcoholic reality has created a waste land in which fountains, wells and springs (ancient symbols of the source from which all the life forces perennially flow)[5] seem to have lost their regenerative powers. A "deep, cool well with its

---

[4] Cf. Sonnet 31.

[5] See J. E. Cirlot, *A Dictionary of Symbols*, pp. 107—108 ("Fountain"), p. 350 ("Well"); M. Eliade, *Patterns in Comparative Religion*, pp. 199—202.

guardian figure" appears in Yvonne's vision of a new life with Geoffrey (p. 271) and dimly reminds us of the well by which they met in the gardens of Granada (p. 292), when the "eternal hopes" (p. 87) of their marriage made striving upward still possible. But Yvonne's dream of the future explodes the moment she is knocked down by the horse; all its beautiful ingredients, together with the guardian figure on the well, catch fire, and, burning, pass before her mind (p. 336). A similar note of unfulfilled dreams is struck when the Consul considers the different paths leading from the town of Tomalín to Parián and the Farolito. The paths, one of which follows the stream, suggest that Tomalín probably held "some irrigational importance. Then [...] schemes, cleavable and lustrous, evolved for a spa, were abandoned sulphurously". To-day, the paths lead to what the Consul calls the "rich cantina country" (p. 285). Here a connection between water and alcohol, or regeneration and destruction, emerges again: hopes and promises inspired by the life forces come to nought while their place is taken over by alcoholic reality.

The Consul's thirst for water is genuine enough but it is invariably transformed into a craving for alcohol. So powerful is the craving that reality itself sometimes seems to comply with it. In "the huge dark well" of a hotel dining room in Oaxaca, where Geoffrey has descended in search of a drink, a carafe of water turns out to be a bottle of wine. Certainly this is what Geoffrey must have wished for, although he has been well aware of the fatal character of his thirst:

—the thirst that was not thirst, but itself heartbreak, and lust, was death, death, and death again and death the waiting in the cold hotel dining room, half whispering to himself, waiting, since El Infierno, that other Farolito, did not open till four in the morning [. . .] waiting for the Infierno whose one lamp of hope would soon be glowing beyond the dark open sewers. (p. 350)

The Consul's thirst, manifested in his alcoholic addiction, condemns him to look for light, hope, and salvation nowhere else but in the cantina Infierno. Yet shortly before his death it dawns on him that the alcoholic inferno is not the only source of hope. Suddenly he attacks his fascist persecutors, accusing them for the first time of the evil of which they have made themselves guilty. This change of mood appears to have been caused by a fragmentary radio message which the Consul—imagining it to be some kind of an order—hears just before he begins to offer resistance. The message speaks, Renaissance-like fashion, of the inconceivably marvellous creations of man which make hap-piness, perfection, and freedom possible. It concludes with a statement of man's unrealized potentialities: "Without parallel the crystalline and fecund fountains of the new life which"—nevertheless—"remains closed to the thirsty lips of the people who follow in their griping and bestial tasks" (p. 371). The fountains of the new life do not fulfil their promise. They may have inspired the

Consul to oppose evil but they are powerless to stop the course of events. Geoffrey is killed by the fascist thugs and the world, which now more than ever seems controlled by the dark forces, goes towards catastrophe symbolized by the eruption of the volcano at the end of the novel.

Also on the mythical plane the fountains of the new life do not fulfil their promise. Indeed, the waters of the baptismal font in the church where Indian dignitaries were for the first time baptized in the New World have not proved fruitful. As god-fathers served Hernan Cortez and his men who, within the novel, represent the injustice of the conquest and social exploitation; and the Indians were senators of the republic of Tlaxcala which throughout *Under the Volcano* symbolizes betrayal. This ironic juxtaposition voids the regenerative powers of water and the fountain, of which the baptismal font is a widely known symbol.[6] Needless to say, the effects of sacred waters are also destroyed by the fiery water of alcohol. When the trip to Cascada Sagrada (sacred waterfall) is proposed, mescal, the most mystical of Geoffrey's drinks, creates a magic of rainbows but it also strikes a discord: a "succession of plaintive discords", suggesting deception, illusion, misguided search, and unrealized goals (p. 286).

All the negative transformations of the images representing regeneration by water are, mythologically speaking, analogous to the fall of man which, as we know, involved a loss of immortality. Exiled from Eden, man was cut off from the legendary source of the four rivers of the terrestrial paradise which, situated at the foot of the Tree of Life itself, is said to be "the *fons juventutis* whose waters can be equated with the 'draught of immortality'—*amrita* in Hindu mythology."[7] Similarly, the ever-thirsty Consul seems to be hopelessly cut off from the source of life.

The analogy between the waste land depicted by Lowry and man's exile from paradise gains additional force in view of the Consul's claims to immortality and eternity (which we shall more fully explore in the following chapter) and the generally mythical "aura" of *Under the Volcano*. So far we have seen Geoffrey's fall into darkness: a paradoxical result of his aspirations to mystical heights and struggling towards the light. Now we are going to consider his efforts to attain immortality and mystical illumination by way of drinking.

---

[6] See Alan W. Watts, *Myth and Ritual in Christianity* (Boston: Beacon Press, 1968), pp. 177—79.

[7] Cirlot, p. 107; cf. also Henrich Zimmer, *The King and the Corpse* (Princeton: Princeton Univ. Press, 1971), p. 37; Eliphas Lévi, *Transcendental Magic* (London: Rider, 1923), p. 10.

50

Although drinking involves, as we shall see, death, disaster, and actual limitations of consciousness, it remains the Consul's "royal" way to God. In the personal letter to Cape Lowry may talk in terms of his own "booze" (*Letters*, p. 64) but in the novel he provides his hero's alcoholic experiences with religious connotations. The Consul may drink for the prosaic purpose of steadying his hand but he also drinks "as if [he] were taking an eternal sacrament" (p. 40). Even if not all the intoxicants possess that numinous quality, mescal, the most powerful of them all, the awesome Mexican drink most prized, respected, and feared by the Consul, is in his consciousness identified with "soma, Amrita, the nectar of immortality, praised in one whole book of the Rig Veda" (p. 307).[8] Without mescal, Geoffrey is convinced, eternity is forgotten (p. 287).

In the Rig Veda soma is often pictured as a source or stream but also as a paradisal plant and a wondrous drink assuring life, fruitfulness, and regeneration.[9] It corresponds to the Greek ambrosia, "the liquor of life, the drink and fare of eternity, which the gods enjoy in their abode: they are sustained by it in their immortality and bestow it on the heroes of their choice".[10] As we know, Tantalus was chosen by the gods to be a guest at their banquets of ambrosia until "he betrayed Zeus's secrets and stole the divine food to share among his mortal friends".[11] For his presumption, which extended to serving the Olympians the body of his son in a stew, he was cast into Tartarus where, like the Consul, he suffers tortures of hunger and thirst amidst an abundance of food and drink. In the next chapter we shall discuss the Consul's betrayal of divine mysteries and his identification with Prometheus, another thief of heavenly riches. Meanwhile we may note that the stolen goods in question are drink and fire, components of "fiery water", Geoffrey's aqua vitae of which daily and in different forms he partakes.

Thirsty as Tantalus yet drinking—tequila, beer, whisky, or mescal—he imagines that he is engaged in fighting a great battle "for the survival of the human consciousness" (p. 217). For drink, as Laruelle has to admit in a conver-

---

[8] "The Consul here of course has the whole thing wonderfully and drunkenly mixed up: mescal in Mexico is a hell of a drink but it is still a drink you can get at any cantina, more readily I dare say than Scotch these days at the dear old Horseshoe. But mescal is also a drug, taken in the form of buttons, and the transcending of its effects is one of the well-known ordeals that occultists have to go through. It would appear that the Consul has fuddledly come to confuse the two, and he is perhaps not far wrong" (Lowry, *Letters*, p. 71). Mescal, Professor Day explains, "is often erroneously supposed to possess some of the hallucinatory qualities of mescaline, the drug derived from peyote; and Lowry seems to have subscribed to this error." *Biography*, p. 227.

[9] See Eliade, *Patterns in Comparative Religion*, pp. 281–82.

[10] Zimmer, *The King and the Corpse*, p. 37.

[11] Robert Graves, *The Greek Myths* (Harmondsworth: Penguin, 1960), II, p. 25.

sation with the Consul, enhances "clear seeing" and effects a release of some mystical substance (pp. 217—18).[12] According to William James whom Lowry invokes both in his letter to Çape (*Letters,* p. 71) and in *Dark as the Grave wherein my Friend is Laid:*[13]

The sway of alcohol over mankind is unquestionably due to its power to stimulate the mystical faculties in human nature, usually crushed to earth by the cold facts and dry criticism of the sober hour... It brings its votary from the chill periphery of things to the radiant core. It makes him for the moment one with truth ... The drunken consciousness is one bit of the mystic consciousness, and our total opinion of it must find its place in our opinion of that larger whole.[14]

Clearly, the Consul's drinking reaches far beyond the ordinary.[15] From the recesses of his soul it releases visions of mystical pilgrimage (pp. 125—26) or "the seeker and his goal" (p. 286); it offers bliss and enlightenment. Like mystics or magicians the Consul and Dr. Vigil are called "major adepts in the Great Brotherhood of Alcohol" (p. 139). And even if we are not always sure whether drink does indeed heighten Geoffrey's "metaphysical consciousness", it is certainly not oblivion he seeks in it but enhanced awareness.[16] Alcohol puts him in touch with his situation (p. 345), makes him apparently sober, awake, and "able to cope with anything that might come his way" (p. 284). Without a drink he cannot look Yvonne in the face (p. 196); and without a drink he does not know whether the belated postcard he has got from her is a good omen or not (p. 197). Also, forgetfulness is supposedly counteracted by drink since it has the power to bring back suppressed memories (p. 308). In a

[12] It might be objected that, since it is Laruelle who makes the connection between drinking and mystical consciousness, it does not necessarily throw light on the Consul. Yet at the end of their conversation Geoffrey's own thoughts assume Laruelle's voice, so that a certain identification between the two is effected (p. 219).

[13] "Fundamentally the truth, or part of the truth, about his own drinking was to be found in William James. 'It heightened the metaphysical consciousness in man,' he said. Whatever that was, he vaguely suspected such an effect now, and wanted it prolonged and intensified." (Lowry, *Dark as the Grave wherein my Friend is Laid,* p. 46).

[14] William James, *The Varieties of Religious Experience* (London: Collins, 1960), p. 373. Douglas Day reports that William James's *Varieties* was Lowry's bedside reading (*Biography,* pp. 294, 335). From this and from Lowry's own references to the American psychologist it would appear that James was certainly "on his mind". The author's consciousness does not, of course, prove the existence of Jamesian ideas within *Under the Volcano* but strengthens the case for using them as an illustration of what is suggested in terms of the novel itself.

[15] It is interesting to note that for Lowry himself, "intellectually at least, alcoholism was not necessarily only a weakness, or disease: it could also be a source of spiritual strength, even of mystical insights—a positive force, one of which any man might be proud." *Biography,* p. 25.

[16] See Stephen Spender's Introduction to *Under the Volcano,* p. xvii (edition used in this dissertation).

word, alcohol becomes, in the Consul's view, a consciousness-expanding agent, having little to do with drunkenness of which he strongly disapproves (pp. 220, 293). No wonder then the Consul feels deeply insulted by Yvonne's promptings to get sober so that he might be able to cope with her plans for a new life together:

And what right had Yvonne to assume it, assume either that he was not sober now, or that, far worse, in a day or two he *would* be sober? And even if he were not sober now, by what fabulous stages, comparable indeed only to the paths and spheres of the Holy Cabbala itself, had he reached *this* stage again, touched briefly once before this morning, this stage at which alone he could, as she put it, "cope," this precarious precious stage, so arduous to maintain, of being drunk in which alone he was sober! (pp. 84—85).

For the most part, however, this alcoholic sobriety is an illusion, making the Consul less rather than more capable of coping with his problems. Or else it may become an awareness of suffering and damnation, just like the light which reveals no more than darkness. When mescal does bring Geoffrey in touch with his situation, it only too often manifests the "abject confirmation of his own lostness, of his own fruitless selfish ruin" (p.345). Truth is revealed, but it is a tragic, fatal truth, limited, moreover, by what the Consul calls "the dreadful tyranny of the self" (p. 289). Thus his awareness does not extend beyond his own misery and his feeling of guilt towards Yvonne. It is bound by the silence of his love: it seems on the one side created or evoked by that silence, on the other unable to break through it (p. 345).[17]

In this way, consciousness is correlated with personal isolation which, according to Stephen Spender, is the price the Consul has to pay for being fully aware.[18] We might suppose with Yvonne that Geoffrey finds some kind of companionship in drink (p. 365) but he knows better than that: pulls at the bottle are just "burning draughts in loneliness" (p. 360). Moreover, mescal has a curious power of shutting off the call of human voices. It may be indispensable in reminding the Consul of eternity, but at the same time it makes him lose touch with "the clear sweet voices of the young Mexicans outside: the voice of Yvonne too, dear, intolerable" (p. 287). In the Farolito, at the beginning of the final stage of his life, Geoffrey deliberately shuts out all awareness of Yvonne. After two swift mescals, her pleading voice as well as the reproachful voices wailing "Borraaaacho!" abruptly cease. There is a hint of conscience in these

---

[17] This is suggested by the fact that the Consul discovers his "lostness", as it were, between two "silences" encountered in Yvonne's letters. He stops at the "silence that frightens me", with the help of mescal becomes for the moment overwhelmed by a sense of guilt and devastation he has wrought in his own life, and resumes reading at the very same words (p. 345).

[18] See Spender, p. xvii.

voices, for they seem both to reprove the Consul and summon him to put a stop to his "fruitless selfish ruin". They send their plea over the roar of the falls, "above the noise of the maelstrom" (p. 288), as if trying in the last moment to warn against "the rising waters of possible catastrophe" (p. 63). But the roar of water muffles Geoffrey's conscience (p. 293). Accompanied in the Farolito by the sound of "rushing water", he cuts himself off not only from Yvonne but from a recognition of his own guilt; a recognition represented by the voices which mingle with the accusations he has flung at his own misery (p. 337).

Yet mescal—it may be objected—has also been said to bring the Consul in touch with his guilt and misery. In terms of human relationships, however, the alcoholic consciousness is tantamount to a renunciation of awareness. Mescal does awaken the Consul to his predicament but long after the pleading and reproachful voices of Yvonne and others have been left behind: when estrangement is almost complete. True, Geoffrey is at that moment reading Yvonne's letters, but the insight they provide into his misery is both preceded and followed by Yvonne's cry over the silence between them.[19] Besides, his sense of guilt and suffering verges on a certainty of damnation. What use is conscience to him if, born of isolation, it proves entirely impotent? The subsequent events confirm Hugh's statement that "conscience had been given man to regret [the past] only in so far as that might change the future" (p. 108). In the Farolito the Consul accepts the prostitute's offer, even though he knows perfectly well that the "adventure" involves "the final stupid unprophylactic rejection" (p. 348), and destroys whatever chances there still are for a reunion with Yvonne, for a new life and salvation. But knowledge that is completely divorced from action is powerless to change anything:

Some reckless murderous power was drawing him on, forcing him, while he yet remained passionately aware of the all too possible consequences and somehow as innocently unconscious, to do without precaution or conscience what he would never be able to undo or gainsay [...] (p. 348)

Conscience thus becomes incompatible with consciousness, the alcoholic "clear seeing" which, as we can see, can just as well turn into "innocent unconsciousness". If alcohol, as William James would have us believe, makes its votary "for the moment one with truth", this truth is in the Consul's case strangely limited. "Everything seems perfectly clear, because indeed it is perfectly clear, in terms of the toe-nail", mockingly comments Laruelle. That is why Geoffrey's "battle for the survival of the human consciousness" leaves out of account "the things [...] on which the balance of any human situation depends" (p. 217). And yet whatever has been excluded from his feeling of omniscience—as if in accordance with Freud's law of repression—will return.

[19] Cf. footnote 17 above.

"I'll say it returns," the Consul said, listening at this point. "There are other minor deliriums too, *meteora,* which you can pick out of the air before your eyes, like gnats. And this is what people seem to think is the end . . . But d. t.'s are only the beginning, the music round the portal of the Qliphoth, the overture, conducted by the God of Flies . . . Why do people see rats? These are the sort of questions that ought to concern the world, Jacques. Consider the word remorse. Remord. Mordeo, mordere. La Mordida! Agenbite too . . . And why rongeur? Why all this biting, all those rodents, in the etymology?" (pp. 218—19)

The Consul comes here quite close to admitting the ambivalence of the alcoholic consciousness: the space between one drink and another fills with remorse, and bliss turns into "the tortures of the damned" (p. 85). Besides, drinking can become just a draught of absolute coldness, of boiling ice: as if "there were a bar of red hot iron across one's chest, but cold in its effect, for the conscience that rages underneath anew and is bursting one's heart burns so fiercely with the fires of hell a bar of red hot iron is as a mere chill to it" (p. 350).[20] These tortures, increasing towards the novel's dénouement, culminate in the Consul's death at the hands of the fascist police. Their victory is, in some measure, a result of Geoffrey's passive consciousness, in particular of his inability to draw conclusions from what he knows about the Unión Militar, his moral impotence in the face of evil. When in the end he becomes convinced of their villainy and decides to act, it is far too late. He finds himself in a situation where, as Lowry points out, "power ends conscience" (p. 369, cf. also p. 94), and is crushed by brute force. Paradoxically, conscience is subdued not only under the impact of power but also through powerlessness born of an excess of consciousness.

The paradox touches here on the Faustus theme, bringing it, as it were, to its modern twentieth-century conclusion. The quest for knowledge which leads Marlowe's hero to magic as power, thus giving rise to what Harry Levin calls "science without conscience",[21] seems to have diametrically opposed consequences in modern times. As we shall see in the following chapter, the quest for knowledge also makes the Consul occupy himself with magic, but magic apparently devoid of the Renaissance appetite for worldly power, conceived rather in a modern intellectualist spirit as pure cognition of divine mysteries. No longer concerned with the subjection of forces and elements, this magic turns away from the world and, in forcing the doors of perception open, it becomes con-

---

[20] Cf. A.E. Waite, *The Secret Doctrine in Israel: A Study of the Zohar and Its Connections* (London: Rider, 1913). Waite gives the following description of tortures in hell: "The chastisement is by fire and ice, but an elucidation in another place explains that the waters which fall from above are cold as ice, while the fire which comes up from below is water which burns" (p. 180).

[21] See Harry Levin, *Christopher Marlowe: The Overreacher* (London: Faber, 1961), chapter V.

sciousness without conscience, a floating awareness powerless to act. But, as the Consul will have occasion to discover, the world, action, and power neglected for the sake of the mystico-alcoholic consciousness do not merely disappear and dissolve. The unintegrated and subdued opposite of his transcendental magic will inevitably show its face and return as the pure evil of fascism, the evil that will destroy him together with the world.[22]

Mescal "would be the end even though a *damned* [italics mine] good end perhaps", one of the familiars informs Geoffrey (pp. 69—70), who himself admits as much in the conversation with Laruelle (p. 216). No doubt the heavenly bliss of drinking has its dark infernal side. We have already observed the ambiguity of the thirst which, in a mysterious way, seems capable not only of repelling water and attracting alcohol but of replacing one with the other. The transformation certainly has an infernal air about it when the thirst is conceived of as death, and when the Consul is impatiently waiting for El Infierno to open, but it can also appear as a sign of divine grace. Geoffrey is almost convinced that the carafe of water miraculously turned into a bottle of French wine from Salina Cruz must have been sent by Jesus who has been following him after all. Indeed, how otherwise could water suddenly become wine? The Consul drinks the wine, his thirst assuaged by "the blessed ichor" trickling down his throat (p. 350). In a sense he partakes of the divine blood, for ichor is no less than a fluid flowing in the veins of the gods. Yet at the same time the ambiguity of the word suggests an inversion of the heavenly, created by the kind of infernal irony which turns a holy mass into a black one: ichor designates also a watery discharge from wounds and ulcers. And however blissful the drink might have appeared, it casts the Consul into "a cold shivering shell of palpitating loneliness" (p. 350) and causes him unspeakable suffering, from which he so passionately wants to escape to the cantina El Infierno. Such is the logic of drink, even of the more innocent tequila, the effects of which already indicate that Geoffrey's happiness is far from being pure. "Bliss. Jesus. Sanctuary ... Horror" (p. 127) is a characteristic reaction to his draught of immortality. Not for nothing then is the bottle of Anís labelled with "a florid demon [brandishing] a pitchfork" (p. 4); not for nothing is the Consul's mystical vision of pilgrimage immediately followed by "an inconceivable anguish of horripilating hangover" (p. 126).

The Consul himself is not unaware of the toll extracted by alcoholic beatitude. He complains of his "chronic, controlled, all-possessing and in-

---

[22] Cf. Zimmer, pp. 48—49, for an interesting mythological exposition of the theme of unintegrated evil: "For every lack of integration in the human sphere simply asks for the appearance, somewhere in space and time, of the missing opposite. And the personification, the embodiment, of that predestined antagonist will inevitably show its face."

escapable delirium tremens" (p. 138), compares iced mescal to agony (p. 129), or despairs over his lost identity: his essential self buried in one of an infinitude of broken bottles, broken like fragments of a Tower of Babel falling to the ground:

Bottles of Oporto, tinto, blanco, bottles of Pernod, Oxygénée, absinthe, bottles smashing, bottles cast aside, falling with a thud on the ground in parks, under benches, beds, cinema seats, hidden in drawers at Consulates, bottles of Calvados dropped and broken, or bursting into smithereens, tossed into garbage heaps, flung into the sea, the Mediterranean, the Caspian, the Carribean, bottles floating in the ocean, dead Scotchmen on the Atlantic highlands [. . .] bottles, bottles, and glasses, glasses, glasses, of bitter, of Dubonnet, of Falstaff, Rye, Johnny Walker, Vieux Whisky blanc Canadien, the apéritifs, the digestifs, the demis, the dobles, the noch ein Herr Obers, the et glas Araks, the tusen taks, the bottles, the bottles, the beautiful bottles of tequila, and the gourds, gourds, gourds, the millions of gourds of beautiful mescal [. . .] How indeed could he hope to find himself, to begin again when, somewhere, perhaps, in one of those lost or broken bottles, in one of those glasses, lay, forever, the solitary clue to his identity? How could he go back and look now, scrabble among the broken glass, under the eternal bars, under the oceans? (pp. 292—93)

Neither do the cantinas offer an unmixed blessing even though they may be capable of radiating a "healing love" (p. 200). The fancy and pleasing names of some of them—Farolito, El Puerto del Sol (the Gates of the Sun), El Amor de los Amores (the Love of Loves), Todos Contentos y Yo También (Everybody Happy Including Me)—indicate the light of the sun, love, happiness. But the heavenly joys so passionately sought for by the Consul are within the cantinas interfused with hopelessness and disaster which show through the longing for his alcoholic oases. The impression is thus created that Geoffrey in a way welcomes his damnation, as long as it implies an eternal sojourn in his cantinas. Like Doctor Faustus, he confounds hell with Elysium[23], and like Doctor Faustus he finds it difficult to recognize the power of heaven:

Not even the gates of heaven, opening wide to receive me, could fill me with such celestial complicated and hopeless joy as the iron screen that rolls up with a crash, as the unpadlocked jostling jalousies which admit those whose souls tremble with the drinks they carry unsteadily to their lips. All mystery, all hope, all disappointment, yes, all disaster, is here, beyond those swinging doors. (p. 50)

Indeed, El Amor de los Amores happens to be a fascist joint, Todos Contentos y Yo También provides shelter for the pelado, the man who has shamelessly robbed the dying Indian, and the Farolito is situated not only right under the volcano but it faces the reputed Unión Militar headquarters.[24] The juxtaposi-

[23] See *Faustus*, iii, 62; cf. also Levin, ibid., p. 154.

[24] In Chapter Six the Consul identifies Unión Militar with the Sinarquistas (an ultrareactionary, semifascist movement organized in Mexico about 1937) and indicates their connection with the Military Police (p. 183).

tion of the cantina and the headquarters of the fascist police is neither accidental nor exceptional, for whenever the Farolito is mentioned in *Under the Volcano* it almost invariably appears together with Parián (a fictitious Mexican state) which in most cases stands for the fascist centre. Farolito and Parián are also linked by a somewhat intricate reference to *Kubla Khan*. Looking into the bottomless barranca the Consul finds the beginning of Coleridge's poem strangely appropriate: "In Parián did Kubla Khan . . ." (p. 338). Whether or not the unfinished line is to suggest that the Farolito is a "pleasure-dome" and the fearful ravine corresponds to "that deep romantic chasm", *Kubla Khan* is also suggested to the Consul by "the enormous drop on one side of the cantina into the barranca" (p. 200). And so both the Farolito and Parián are associated with the abyss of the barranca. Like this gigantic sewer, they represent death, catastrophe, and perdition. Parián is the very centre of the dark evil forces; Farolito is either hell itself or at least a portal of damnation: an infernal custom-house where the Consul is almost completely divested of his divine image before his body will be received by the barranca. More on the theme of perdition will be said later, especially in chapter 7. Here we are mainly concerned with the "other side" of drinking: with pointing out that the Farolito is not only a cantina of bliss but also a "Café Chagrin" (p. 201), not merely a paradise but "a paradise of despair" (p. 338), "un infierno" in Dr. Vigil's words (p. 147). And Parián, even though, as Lowry points out, innocently suggestive of old marble and the gale-swept Cyclades (p. 130),[25] is, because of its connections with fascism and antisemitism, with the Mexican sinarquistas and the Nazis, representative of disaster which strikes individual human beings as well as whole societies and civilization; it signifies dissolution of conscience, loss of human dignity, oppression, violence, murder, extermination of life. Evidently, Geoffrey's draught of immortality does not lead him to paradise.

Dr. Vigil is also apprehensive of the relation between drinking and catastrophe. When the Consul describes to him his fateful vision of the sinking Atlantis, Vigil only nods gloomily: "Sí, that is tequila. Hombre, un poco de cerveza, un poco de vino, but never no more tequila. Never no more mescal" (p. 148). Here an important suggestion emerges: drinking is associated with the end of the world represented by the destruction of Atlantis. Atlantis, as we know, is supposed to have perished by fire and water, that is to say, by volcanic explosions and flood:[26]

[25] Parian is an adjective pertaining to the island of Paros (one of the Cyclades) noted for its white marble.

[26] See Donnelly, *Atlantis,* pp. 11, 44, part II "The Deluge"; see also Spence, *The Occult Sciences in Atlantis* (London: Rider, 1943), p. 93.

The lightning of Zeus, which consumed the Titans, ignited a world conflagration, *ekpy-rôsis*, and it would have burned up everything had not Ocean-Atlas implored Zeus to extinguish the fire with a flood. This union of water with fire in the destruction of the first world is repeated in the immemorially ancient, common dream of humanity, from the Sais hieroglyphics and Babylonian cuneiforms to the ancient Mexican codices.[27]

As if responding to the call of the ancient archetype, the Consul brings about disaster by means of the fiery water of alcohol.[28]

Water as a destructive element has already been mentioned in connection with Laruelle's towers which are not able to withstand the approaching flood. Nor is the Consul's conscience, as we have noticed, able to resist "the rising waters of possible catastrophe" (p. 63). And mescal, when it gets out of his control, produces "a hangover like a great dark ocean swell finally rolled up against a foundering steamer" (p. 293). Drink literally submerges and over-whelms the Consul. Its sheer amount and variety, as we have seen, take the shape of a Tower of Babel which, crashing, buries the clue to his identity. The fiery water can submerge the Consul simply in "impending unconsciousness" (p. 293) but it also drowns him in isolation, physical and spiritual impotence, meaningless suffering or despair, and finally plunges him into the infernal bar-ranca. Drink is, in fact, at the root of all evil and tragedy that Lowry depicts in *Under the Volcano,* and it is the principal cause of the hero's downfall.

It goes without saying that in a life devoted almost entirely to drinking there is no room for tending the garden. The point would be rather trifling were it not for the fact that within the terms of the novel the Consul's garden has much in

---

[27] Dimitri Merezhkovsky, *Atlantis/Europe: The Secret of the West* (New York: Rudolf Stei-ner Publications, 1971), p. 416; cf. also Critias's story of Atlantis in Plato's *Timaeus*: "There have been and will be many different calamities to destroy mankind, the greatest of them by fire and water ..." (Plato, *Timaeus* [Harmondsworth: Penguin, 1965], p. 35); cf. also M. Eliade, *The Myth of the Eternal Return or, Cosmos and History* (Princeton: Princeton Univ. Press, 1971), p. 125: "In the two Iranian systems—as, moreover, in all doctrines of cosmic cycles—the world will end by fire and water, *per pyrosim et cataclysmum,* as Firmicus Maternus was later to write."

[28] "Water and fire, mutually antagonistic energies of nature, are both conspicuous for their ambivalent effects. At once life-sustaining and destructive (much more obviously so than the two other elements, air and earth), they represent the whole realm and force of the extrahuman world and its creating and dissolving, at once propitious and disastrous, character. They repre-sent the totality of life energy and the whole of the life process, the constant action and interac-tion of conflicting opposites." (Zimmer, p. 36). While the presence of these two elements is un-disputable in *Under the Volcano,* it has to be admitted that alcohol is nowhere referred to in the book as "fiery water". Nevertheless, in view of its clear associations with both water and fire which, just like drinking, are mainly shown through their destructive aspects, the interpretation of alcohol as "fiery water" seems justifiable.

common with the Garden of Eden; and when neglected, it represents, in Lowry's Cabbalistic symbolism, the misuse of wine which in turn implies the misuse of magical powers (*Letters*, p. 71). Just like Atlantis—which according to legend perished because of unlawful magical practices,[29] and where Donnelly places the ancient paradise of humanity[30]—the Consul's little garden is visited by a flood. Although mentioned only briefly, the flood seems to reflect what is happening elsewhere in the novel and suggests the deluge myth of the Old Testament which, as Donnelly maintains, is only one of a number of mythical narratives recording the catastrophe of Atlantis.[31] According to the Biblical account, the waters of the flood came from above (cf. Laruelle's towers threatened to be engulfed by torrential rains) as well as from below. "All the fountains of the great deep were broken up", tells us the Book of Genesis (7:11). Interestingly enough, the significance of the Biblical watery depths throws light on the abyss under the volcano:

Great deep, in the original text: *thehom rabba. Thehom* is the primal flood, savouring of the weird, darkly chaotic, losing itself in dreadful darkness (Greek *abyssos*). *Thehom* is the totality of all nocturnal powers of Chaos, which in the form of the dragon Leviathan had to be thrust by Jahve in the primeval world conflict . . .[32]

In Lowry's novel the great deep is situated under the volcano, as the abyss of the barranca: "the eternal horror of opposites" (p. 130), "the city Moloch" (p. 15), the "general Tartarus and gigantic jakes" (p. 131). It is not entirely certain whether "the fountains of the barranca were broken up" and the Consul's property inundated by its cloacal waters, but the way he describes the event strongly suggests that possibility. "And the flood: the drains of Quauhnahuac visited us and left us with something that smelt like the Cosmic Egg" (p. 66). The cosmic egg, the common symbol of fertility, is here obviously in a state of putrefaction. This implies an emphasis on the destructive aspect of the flood from which no survival seems to be indicated. True, the Consul evinces a particular interest in Noah and his Mexican counterpart Coxcox,[33] to whom he wants to devote some space in his mysterious book on Atlantis (p. 86). Yet the word "Coxcox" undergoes a peculiar change in his mind since it becomes a curse he flings at his fascist persecutors. Does the Consul mean that the evil powers are the only survivors from catastrophe? Perhaps. The epithet "You

[29] See Spence, *The Occult Sciences in Atlantis,* pp. 58—59, 88, 102.

[30] See Donnelly, *Atlantis*, part IV, chapter 5.

[31] See ibid., part II, "The Deluge".

[32] Rudolf Frieling, *Hidden Treasure in the Psalms* (London: The Christian Community Press, 1967), p. 69.

[33] The Mexican story of Coxcox and his wife is a striking parallel to the Biblical account of Noah. See Spence, *The Myths of Mexico and Peru,* pp. 122—23; Donnelly, *Atlantis*, p. 99.

poxboxes. You coxcoxes" (p. 371) is certainly not a salutation to Coxcox, or Noah, who commits the sin of drunkenness. Symbolic of a mystical transgression (as we shall see in the next chapter), this ill-boding event occured after the deluge.

Alcohol, as has been pointed out, consists of water and also of fire; "the fine old healthful throat-smarting fire" of whisky (p. 70), or the fire of the tequila that Laruelle so distinctly feels running down his spine like lightning (p. 215). Even though Lowry develops this comparison into a metaphor in which the lightning strikes "a tree which thereupon, miraculously, blossoms" (p. 215), and even though the Consul talks about the sacred fire of the Hindu god Agni (p. 307), both fire and lightning are in the book presented in their destructive aspects. Flashes of lightning, as we remember, accompany the death of the protagonists, and fire, as we shall see, indicates disintegration and dying.

A great rock, the image of the union between Yvonne and Geoffrey, is said to have been destroyed by forest fires. What is more, "the violence of the fire which split the rock apart had also incited the destruction of each separate rock, cancelling the power that might have held them unities" (p. 55). The image of the rock, which for the moment affects Yvonne much more than the Consul, is a prefiguration of a destruction by fire that is to come later. During the search for the Consul in the dark forest Yvonne becomes now and then conscious of laughing unnaturally to herself: a laugh oddly associated with a feeling that something is smoldering within herself, that she is on fire:

But no, it was not herself that was on fire. It was the house of her spirit. It was her dream. It was the farm, it was Orion, the Pleiades, it was their house by the sea. But where was the fire? It was the Consul who had been the first to notice it. What were these crazy thoughts, thoughts without form or logic? (pp. 326–27)

The crazy thoughts will soon approach reality when Yvonne, struck by the horse, experiences the ebbing of her consciousness as the burning of the little house by the beach she has so much dreamed of, the house that was to be a new beginning, a new life, a reunion and salvation for herself and Geoffrey. Dying, she becomes conscious of the ultimate collapse of her dearest dream, of a death in which not only fire but water and darkness also take part:

Geoffrey's old chair was burning, his desk, and now his book, his book was burning, the pages were burning, burning, burning, whirling up from the fire they were scattered, burning, along the beach, and now it was growing darker and the tide coming in, the tide washed under the ruined house, the pleasure boats that had ferried song upstream sailed home silently over the dark waters of Eridanus. Their house was dying, only an agony went there now. (p. 336)

In this chapter we have not explored all the consequences and ramifications of drinking, for the Consul's addiction is only an epicentre from which the whole spiritual earthquake of *Under the Volcano* radiates. As we shall see in the following chapter, Geoffrey's drunkenness is symbolically embedded in the motif of black magic which pervades the novel as the quality of "infernal paradise". Thus all the significant events and images are not without at least some connection with drinking. Alcohol is always in one way or another responsible for the irreconcilable dualism between ascent and fall, light and darkness, regeneration by water and death by flood, and so forth. It seems, moreover, invariably to contribute to the victory of the "dark side", the second element in each pair of opposites. Consequently, the theme of every chapter in this dissertation may be regarded as having its origin—though sometimes indirectly— in Geoffrey's alcoholic deluge. Lowry's novel is, in other words, literally permeated with the Consul's sickness which has by innumerable connections penetrated to almost every motif and image. This allows for a number of generalizations with regard to the significance of drinking: all of them more or less valid, all of them somehow contained in the universe of *Under the Volcano*. In the letter to Cape, Lowry himself indicates one such general interpretation hinting, however, at the depths and final meanings yet to be discovered by the reader:

The drunkenness of the Consul is used on one plane to symbolize the universal drunkenness of mankind during the war, or during the period immediately preceding it, which is almost the same thing, and what profundity and final meaning there is in his fate should be seen also in its universal relationship to the ultimate fate of mankind. (*Letters*, p. 66)[34]

In discussing the *Draught of Immortality* we have chiefly confined ourselves to the most conspicuous and dramatic polarities that the Consul's drinking implies. We have seen how thirst and drought are set against images of regeneration: an abundance of water and "nature out-doing itself in extravagant fructification" (p. 320). Regeneration through nature, however, proves to be beyond the Consul's reach. Suffering the tortures of Tantalus, he partakes of alcohol holding it to be the nectar of the gods, and willingly confusing his cantina Farolito with a fountain of the water of life. And if alcohol is not always effective as a draught of immortality, it is at least supposed to heighten "metaphysical consciousness". Yet the alcoholic consciousness turns out to be greatly limited and deceptive. Divorced from conscience, it disowns relations with other people and what has been removed from an illusory feeling of omniscience returns in a magnified form as

[34] It might be pointed out in this context that not only the Consul has confused ecstatic intoxication with heightened consciousness, sobriety, and a state of being fully awake. "*Deutschland erwache!*——Germany awake! the Fuehrer shouted, at the very moment when he was plunging his people into the nightmare of collective hypnosis." Denis de Rougemont, *The Devil's Share* (New York: Pantheon Books, 1944), p. 194.

suffering and evil. Drinking itself shows a demonic face and cantinas seem to be nothing better than outposts of hell. The most infernal of them is Geoffrey's beloved Farolito. Situated so close to the fearful chasm of the barranca, it remains under the patronage of the nearby fascist headquarters. Finally, alcohol, instead of quenching the Consul's thirst for the living water of paradise, brings the waters of deluge and fires of hell.

Once, at least, the confusion of regeneration and destruction is clearly delimited. While searching for the Consul, Yvonne and Hugh come to a crossroads where their path divides in two. The choice that thus presents itself is between "*a la Cascada*" and "*a Parián*" (p. 318).[35] Such a dramatic alternative is emblematic of Geoffrey's drinking. While mescal brings him to a sense of eternity, it makes the earthly transitoriness completely senseless. It creates a Manichean polarization of the world and eternity where the world is not only insufficient unto itself but fundamentally unredeemable. As a realm of evil powers, the world has to be totally negated and denied:

But without mescal, he imagined, he had forgotten eternity, forgotten their world's voyage, that the earth was a ship, lashed by the Horn's tail, doomed never to make her Valparaiso. Or that is was like a golf ball, launched at Hercules' Butterfly, wildly hooked by a giant out of an asylum window in hell. Or that it was a bus, making its erratic journey to Tomalín and nothing. (p. 287)

We are now going to deal more closely with the kind of eternity that makes the Consul a prisoner on earth, and examine his magical mysticism by which he tries to reach eternity to the exclusion of the here and now.

[35] Cf. *Letters*, p. 85: 'Parián, as I have said, has represented death all along ..."

Chapter 4
Eternity

"The best writing of our contemporaries is not
an act of creation, but an act of evocation,
peculiarly saturated with reminiscences."

Harry Levin[1]

In this chapter we are going to examine the Consul's mysticism and try to indicate the way in which he seeks God and eternity. The task is difficult because
Lowry seems to avoid any unequivocal description of his protagonist's occult
beliefs and practices. Instead he operates chiefly by means of evocations
grounded in myth and esoteric lore. Moreover, the occult allusions and
references do not, in my opinion, allow us to establish beyond doubt the
extent of Geoffrey's commitment to any of the secret sciences mentioned or
alluded to in *Under the Volcano*. We shall therefore refrain from pursuing all
the cryptic hints and from actualizing in any systematic way the host of
evocations scattered all over the novel. I shall, however, utilize their suggestive potential in order to present the most general and significant features of
the Consul's mystical strivings. Thus his transcendental search will be revealed mainly through its inversion manifested in the confusion of heaven and
hell and epitomized, as I shall maintain, in the archetypal figure of the black
magician.

We have already seen ascent confused with fall, light with darkness, draught
of immortality with perdition. In this chapter we are going to trace the mythical
source of all this *concordia discors*. Certainly the confusion of the infernal with
the paradisal is intimately bound with the Consul's drinking, but drinking is so
saturated with mythical and esoteric overtones that it comes to signify much
more than just a "case" of chronic drunkenness. Indeed, we shall see that it
symbolizes the abuse of mystical powers and consequent betrayal of divine
mysteries; an act which, mythologically speaking, often leads to black magic.
But before we finally establish the symbolic value of drinking, we shall consider
a number of myths referred to in *Under the Volcano* and related to the Consul;

[1] *James Joyce: A Critical Introduction*, p. 182.

64

myths which deal with various legendary figures who have made themselves guilty of black magic; who, like the Consul, have reached for a god-like existence but, abusing their mystical powers, allied themselves with the forces of evil.

Having regarded the Consul as a black magician we shall stop to ask whether this is indeed the case; whether drinking is not, as is sometimes claimed, a legitimate way to seek eternity, and whether his descent into hell is not undertaken for some noble and lofty purpose. I shall try to demonstrate, however, that his journey down the abyss does not in fact bear any likeness to Dante's remedial vision of the infernal circles or Christ's harrowing of hell. It will be seen that the Consul is not journeying but falling into the underworld: falling as a result of his betrayal of mysteries.

We shall then proceed to deal with the more earthbound level of the Consul's betrayal and observe how his mystical way inevitably leads him into flight from the world and his fellow human beings. In conclusion we shall point out that Geoffrey's mysticism is, like Faustus' magic, an escape from the concerns of the world into the delights of secret knowledge; that it remains within the Renaissance tradition of "science without conscience" which is a manifestation of the archetypal idea of black magic.

The term "eternity" has been chosen here to designate those strivings and goals of the Consul which may be described as metaphysical, mystical, occult, esoteric, or religious. The choice of this broad category has been, first of all, conditioned by the vague contours of the "mystical dimension" of *Under the Volcano*. Lowry never tells us whether his hero actually practises hermetic arts, dabbles in them, or merely considers them a philosophical possibility. We do not learn what kind of mysticism the Consul adheres to, to what extent he takes magic seriously, or whether the Cabbala is for him a matter of mystical speculation or magical practices.[2] Nor is it always quite clear how the several references to Christianity fit into the Consul's commitment to transcendence. Therefore the distinction that Douglas Day makes between the magical and the religious level of the novel seems to me somewhat strained.[3] True enough, in twentieth-century Christianity, especially in Protestantism, the distance between religion and magic is almost infinite but it tends to disappear in various forms of mystical religion.[4] So, too, in *Under the Volcano* the distinction often

---

[2] For the distinction between speculative and practical Cabbala see Gershom Scholem, *Major Trends in Jewish Mysticism,* pp. 144, 259.

[3] See *Biography* pp. 327–350.

[4] "Everyone knows that Hinduism is permeated through and through with magic; and it is, quite naturally, this magical element, as exhibited in the Tantras and the Yoga techniques, that

cannot hold since the meanings that can be construed as religious (Christian) are—as we shall see—by and large compatible with the magical elements. Moreover, Lowry gives us no reason to suppose that these latter, as Douglas Day would have it, are merely symbols or allegories of existential psychological realities.[5]

Thus the whole mystical dimension of *Under the Volcano* is doubly elusive: it is based on secret knowledge which, transmitted by religious undercurrents and often opposed to and banned by orthodoxy, has deliberately disguised itself in obscurity and very seldom received systematic and unequivocal codification characteristic of great world religions; and, in a like spirit, it is handled by Lowry by means of cryptic allusions and subtle indications. One such indication is the monumental work on Secret Knowledge that the Consul apparently is writing. The book, concerned—among other things—with Alchemy and Atlantis (p. 86), deals with "such questions as: Is there any ultimate reality, external, conscious and ever-present etc. etc. that can be realized by any such means that may be acceptable to all creeds and religions and suitable to all climes and countries?" (p. 39).

Now this formulation suggests a quest for what Aldous Huxley has called the "Highest Common Factor" of all religions; a quest characteristic of the *philosophia perennis* of which Huxley and an eminent Indian thinker Ananada Coomaraswamy have been leading exponents in our time.[6] This philosophy claims to derive from the experience and insights of religious mystics of all times and faiths. It maintains that "the ultimate truths about God and the Universe cannot be directly expressed in words, that these truths are necessarily everywhere and always the same, and that ... the truth itself is that experienced by the mystics whose unity of thought and language is said to speak for itself".[7] Furthermore, mystical experience, in almost all of its varieties, is commonly known to provide a release from space and time which, when transcended, disappear in "the timeless now of the divine Spirit."[8] The mystic, in other words, experiences an irruption of eternity into his time-bound existence: he realizes what lies at the core of practically every religion. Kether, the goal of the Cabbalistic mystical journey, represents not only light but also

---

has attracted the attention of the psychologist." R. C. Zaehner, *Mysticism Sacred and Profane: An Inquiry into Some Varieties of Praeternatural Experience* (London, Oxford, New York: Oxford Univ. Press, 1961), pp. 129–30.

[5] See *Biography,* p. 347.

[6] See Aldous Huxley, *The Perennial Philosophy* (London: Collins, 1958), p. 9; and Zaehner, p. 30.

[7] Zaehner, p. 27.

[8] Huxley, *Perennial Philosophy,* p. 192; cf. also Zaehner, p. 6.

eternity and infinity.[9] Christ is not only the Light of the world, but the messenger of the Kingdom of God and dispenser of eternal life. Thus eternity may be conveniently taken to represent the Consul's metaphysical commitment regardless of its extent and specific contents. Mystic or magician, philosopher or believer, he is, so to speak, anyhow bound for eternity.

According to Douglas Day "Geoffrey is—or had been, before the gods turned against him—an adept in a number of esoteric cults; he had been a magus, a dark magician who was privy to the innermost secrets of alchemy, Rosicrucianism, Swedenborgianism, and—most importantly—the Cabbala".[10] It cannot, however, be sufficiently emphasized that this "mystical portrait" of the Consul is a result of speculation and guesswork. For all the scattered references to the occult sciences testify to Geoffrey's acquaintance with them but not necessarily to his being an adept in esoteric cults. To mention the angels (p. 37) of which Swedenborg speaks in his *Heaven and Its Wonders and Hell,* or to write a chapter on the alchemists in a treatise on secret knowledge, does not have to mean that one is "privy to the innermost secrets" of Swedenborgianism and alchemy. Nor does the possession of an occult library make one a magician. Likewise, allusions to the Cabbala do not necessarily make the Consul a Cabbalist and *Under the Volcano* a thoroughly Cabbalistic fable, as Perle Epstein is trying to make out.[11] It is one thing to agree with Lowry that the Cabbala functions as the deepest mythical layer of the novel (see *Letters,* pp. 65, 86), but quite another to reduce all the multiple meanings of the book to the concepts and emblems of Cabbalistic lore. Such a reductionist tendency is a constant danger besetting those who grapple with interpretation of symbols in literature. As Harry Levin observes in his essay on "Symbolism and Fiction":

Part of the difficulty would seem to spring from the critic's addiction to the copula . . . Suggestive allusions tend to become flat assertions. Something, instead of suggesting some other thing, somehow *is* that other thing; it cannot mean, it must be. Everything must be stated as an equation, without recognizing degrees of relationship or the differences between allusion and fact.[12]

Thus it seems clear to Epstein that because of "references to Marlowe, Goethe, Dante, Aztec legend, the Cabbala, Swedenborg, Rosicrucianism, astrology, and alchemy" in Lowry's correspondence, because of his interest in oc-

[9] See Leo Schaya, *The Universal Meaning of the Kabbalah* (Baltimore: Penguin Books Inc., 1973), pp. 35—38.

[10] *Biography,* p. 344.

[11] Epstein, *The Private Labyrinth of Malcolm Lowry.*

[12] Harry Levin, *Contexts of Criticism* (Cambridge, Mass.: Harvard Univ. Press, 1957), p. 193.

cultism and use of occult sources in writing his book, *Under the Volcano* "is consciously intended by its author to depict the ritual of mystic initiation."[13] In support of her argument she quotes a portion of Lowry's letter to Cape, in which a general esoteric and Cabbalistic import of the novel is indicated. But there is not a word on ritual initiation in this letter. Nor does Lowry's short exposition of the occult symbolic significance of the number twelve[14] entitle one to claim with assurance that "each of the twelve chapters is really one degree in the twelve stages of initiation, as Lowry attests in his explanatory letter to Jonathan Cape."[15] For, in point of fact, Lowry does nothing of the kind, unless by some cryptic allusion which Epstein, however, does not disclose.

On the other hand, it can seldom be categorically excluded that Lowry alludes to an esoteric meaning, hidden away in some occult sources, which becomes available only when extracted from them by the interpreter. Moreover, the more poetic a work of literature is (and *Under the Volcano* is eminently poetic) the looser and more varied the relations between different units of meaning. Words tend to have a connotative rather that denotative function; often they are, so to speak, hurled at the reader rather than organized in an orderly sequence. They evoke meanings rather than serve them in an unequivocal fashion.[16] This does not, however, give us absolute freedom to read anything into the text. It may happen that a particular context, while not radically excluding a recondite allusion, will assign it to an inferior position. This occurs when the immediate meaning (or meanings) is so obvious and strong, so solid by virtue of its relations to other meanings, that it effectively suppresses the concealed reference.

Let us by way of example consider Yvonne's moment of hesitation just before she goes with Hugh for a walk, taking advantage of Geoffrey being asleep. "Yvonne glanced hastily around, as if fearful Geoff might come catapulting out of the window, bed and all" (p. 98). According to Epstein, this is an allusion to "the common power of magicians to make sudden and surprise appearances."[17] Granted that magicians indeed commonly possess that power, it is rather uncommon that they should manifest it by catapulting

---

[13] Epstein, p. 6.

[14] "Twelve is a universal unit. To say nothing of the 12 labours of Hercules, there are 12 hours in a day, and the book is concerned with a single day as well as, though very incidentally, with time: there are 12 months in a year, and the novel is enclosed by a year; while the deeply buried layer of the novel or poem that attaches itself to myth, does so to the Jewish Cabbala where the number 12 is of the highest symbolic importance." *Letters,* p. 65.

[15] Epstein, p. 47.

[16] See Daiches, *A Study of Literature,* Chapter 7: "The Nature of Poetry".

[17] Epstein, p. 98.

themselves out of the window, bed and all. To do so is not an established attribute of magicians; it is not traditionally associated with them as, for instance, flying on broomsticks is with witches. The important thing, however, is the context of the situation which tends to rule out this rather unconvincing interpretation, simply because it conceals the alleged allusion under much more apparent meanings. For what counts here above all is not the "esoteric physiology" of the situation but its human content. Not the magical acumen of the Consul but Yvonne's fear derived evidently from her feeling of guilt towards the man she has betrayed several times. To be sure, she is merely going for a walk with Hugh, but the reader has already witnessed her unusual reaction at the sight of Laruelle's house; her apprehension at the merest indication of her guilt and betrayal. The "sudden appearance" theory is but one example of Epstein's, as Day puts it, "ingenious yet persistently wrong-headed and reductive interpretation"[18] in which Cabbalistic and other esoteric meanings overshadow and sometimes replace universally human ones, where love, hate, guilt, responsibility, or fear are allowed to come into play.

It remains true, nonetheless, that the mystical dimension in general, and the Cabbala in particular, are of paramount importance in *Under the Volcano*. It is, as we shall presently see, a "mythical correlative" of the novel, sometimes an indispensable source of its deepest significance. While not always essential by themselves, all the bits and pieces of esoteric lore often amplify or make intelligible the major themes of the novel. "The Cabbala", says Lowry, "is used for poetical purposes because it represents man's spiritual aspirations" (*Letters*, p. 65). And the esoteric element "does not of course matter two hoots in a hollow if the whole thing is not good art" (*Letters* p. 86). It is thus very probable that many occult hints, which are avidly seized by the initiated but passed unnoticed by the profane reader, will only have a subordinate function. Especially when dependent on involved speculation, they will be screened and dominated by the more principal concerns of the book. Naturally so, since the novel

is concerned principally ... with the forces in man which cause him to be terrified of himself. It is also concerned with the guilt of man, with his remorse, with his ceaseless struggling toward the light under the weight of the past, and with his doom. The allegory is that of the Garden of Eden, the Garden representing the world ... (*Letters*, p. 66)

What matters then are the universally human themes, but transposed through mythic motifs and imagery into which magic and esoteric detail may often be incorporated.

---

[18] *Biography*, p. 295.

"In Lowry's novel", observes Stephen Spender, "the myths and symbols are not mysterious centres of a tradition which lies outside this time so much as usable devices, guides, signposts indicative of the times."[19] This distinguishes Lowry from Eliot or Joyce who have made use of mythical themes and imagery at least just as extensively. But whereas they often give precedence to the exigencies of myth and mythical consciousness over the individual, Lowry has tried to subordinate myth to individual consciousness:

> The fact is that, though all three writers may use myths and symbolism and be concerned with the crisis of the modern world, the aims and methods of Lowry are the opposite of those of Joyce and Eliot. Joyce and Eliot use particular instances of modern people in order to move towards, enter into, the greater universality of a tradition of which modern life is only a fragmentary part. They use myths and symbols to get outside "the times" into the past of the tradition. Lowry uses them to exemplify "the times", to describe the Consul as illustration almost. Symbol and myth are used in *Ulysses* in order to absorb the characters at certain moments into a kind of cosmic consciousness. Lowry uses them with opposite effect in order to create the interior world of the Consul. Stephen Dedalus and Bloom tend to disappear into the cosmos. We finish *Under the Volcano* feeling that the Consul with all his defects is the cosmos . . .[20]

It has to be pointed out, however, that the interior world of the Consul is confined neither to purely psychological realities, nor to "the times" of which Spender speaks. It is not a world of emotion, lyrical or dramatic, but a veritable cosmos, or a universal plane of human existence, where the powers of evil contend with those of good.

It may seem that our general discussion on symbolic interpretation of literature is rather remote from the Consul's search for eternity. Nevertheless, by throwing light on the characteristic difficulties and pitfalls inherent in an esoteric reading of *Under the Volcano,* the discussion prepares the ground for further considerations. For it is precisely because its mystical dimension is so elusive that an appreciation of this aspect of the novel cannot afford to ignore the problems involved in its unravelling.

Let us now try to lift a little the veil of esoteric allusions covering the Consul's mysticism. Let us try to see what kind of occult path he is taking. Is he a Cabbalist? Probably. We know that at a certain stage of his life he "could dodge about the rigging of the Cabbala like a St. Jago's monkey" (p. 82). In the unsent letter to Yvonne we encounter references to unmistakably Cabbalistic terms: Chesed and Binah (Mercy and Understanding) and the Qliphoth. We realize that the Consul wants to see himself between Chesed and Binah, and to keep the precarious equilibrium. He confesses, however,

[19] Stephen Spender, Introduction to *Under the Volcano,* p. xiii.
[20] Ibid., p. xii.

that his place is really in the domain of Qliphoth. In other words, he is obliquely referring to a miscarried mystical ascent up the Cabbalistic Tree of Life, Mercy and Understanding being its upper parts, Qliphoth, the "extremely unpleasant abyss some way above the middle" (*Letters*, p. 65). Geoffrey is also in possession of works that could be described as Cabbalistic: *Ritual de la Haute Magie* by Éliphas Lévi[21] who identifies the doctrine of Transcendental Magic with that of the Cabbala,[22] Jacob Boehme whose thought is strikingly close to the Cabbala,[23] and the *"Elementaries of the Cabbala, reprinted from the text of the Abbé de Villars"* (p. 185). Then, on p. 89, we discover a reference to "that jewelled gate the desperate neophyte, Yesod-bound, projects for the thousandth time on the heavens to permit passage of his astral body". Yesod—we can easily find in any book on the Cabbala—is one of the ten Sephirot, the divine emanations which make up the Tree of Life. This is perhaps as far as "positive knowledge" can take us to the "paths and spheres of the Holy Cabbala", as Lowry puts it tangentially in another comparison (p. 84). Otherwise, the Cabbalistic substance of *Under the Volcano* rests on speculation around allusions and hints, most of which are either too vague or too general to manifest an unalloyed Cabbalistic significance.

The reference on p. 236 to the twenty-two paths is an instance in point. While the paths clearly seem to indicate the Cabbalistic idea of the twenty-two paths to God,[24] the precise esoteric meaning is too vague or too deeply hidden to signify more than a dim and passing allusion to the Jewish mystical lore.[25] A fairly general Cabbalistic significance, on the other hand, can be found in the Consul's speculation on the legend of the Garden of Eden. He suggests that Adam was not really banished from paradise. In fact, his punishment consisted

[21] Translated as *Transcendental Magic: Its Doctrine and Ritual* (London: Rider, 1923).

[22] Éliphas Lévi, *The History of Magic*, p. 41.

[23] See Scholem, *Major Trends in Jewish Mysticism*, p. 237.

[24] Cf. A. E. Waite, *The Secret Doctrine in Israel, p. 38*.

[25] Even Epstein does not try to explain which of the twenty-two paths Hugh and Yvonne have taken and why. In the Cabbala, however, this is by no means a matter of indifference since the paths are arranged hierarchically and every one of them has a particular significance. Moreover, there exist several interpretations of the paths, put forward by different schools throughout the ages (see Z'ev ben Shimon Halevi, *Tree of Life: An Introduction to the Cabala,* London: Rider, 1972, p. 95). If so, an attempt to explicate Lowry's allusion could easily lead to a semantic overcharge and a short circuit of contradictory meanings. In consequence, we would get a very rich but thoroughly indeterminate interpretation of what seems only a tangential allusion. It is one of the many cases in *Under the Volcano* where the tracing of an allusion would release a meaning in which the potential element dominates over the actual and does not allow it to crystallize.

"in his having to *go on living there*, alone, of course—suffering, unseen, cut off from God" (p. 133). This theory accords with a Zoharic[26] interpretation[27] but in the overall context of Lowry's novel it merely corresponds to a very potent and universally valid theme of separation and estrangement.

In one of his letters Lowry states *expressis verbis* that the Consul has been a Cabbalist (see *Letters*, p. 199). Yet in the novel he never commits himself to such an unequivocal statement. Why? Certainly not by accident. In a book where everything seems to be contrived and nothing fortuitous, such significant accidents are difficult to imagine. Therefore there must be an essential reason for the indeterminacy of the Consul's Cabbalism and the enigmatic character of all his mystical strivings. Two interpretations are here possible: one esoteric, the other aesthetic.

The esoteric theory would probably account for the obscurity by directing our attention to the fact that it is precisely "secret knowledge" we are dealing with; a knowledge which by definition has to remain veiled from our sight. It might also be argued that esoteric authors have invariably concealed their meanings, often to the point of deliberately leading the readers astray—a measure calculated to guard the secrets against the vulgar and the profane. In that case, however, it would remain to prove that *Under the Volcano* is primarily an esoteric treatise whose *raison d'être* is to impart knowledge. Admittedly, such proof would not be simple since Lowry himself testifies to the limited significance of the Cabbalistic layer of the book. In a letter to his friend David Markson he plays down the Cabbala to the point of contradicting himself. He admits that what he has said about *Under the Volcano* and the Cabbala in the preface to the French edition of the novel[28] (which in that respect does not differ much from the letter to Cape) is

quite misleading and probably not a little juvenile, and which was no doubt suggested by the magnificently abyssal and heavenly motions of one of your bauxite freighters on which the preface was written, rather than in strict fact ... It is true that the Kabbala played a part, through scarcely anterior to the fact of writing the book; I mean I didn't group it *consciously* around any of the correspondences within that unresting and dynamic filing cabinet-cum-tree of knowledge. But that I ran into a Kabbalist at a critical and coincidental moment in the writing of the book: that is true ...[29]

[26] *Zohar*—"The Book of Splendour", the most important literary work of the Cabbala, one of the most influential (often considered authoritative)sources of the Jewish esoteric wisdom.
[27] Waite relates that "it was not the Lord God who drove out Adam but rather that the latter expelled the Divine Being, presumably from his own heart and also, as a manifest Presence, from that world which man had ravaged by his tresspass." (*Secret Doctrine*, p. 105.)
[28] Malcolm Lowry, "Preface to a Novel", *Canadian Literature*, No. 9, (Summer 1961) pp. 27–28.
[29] Letter to David Markson, *Canadian Literature*, No. 44, (Spring 1970), p. 54. R. H. Costa, who has investigated Lowry's drafts and manuscripts, confirms the writer's admission. Arguing

Lowry's contradictions seem to show that the Cabbala provided him with a general mythical framework rather than specific guidelines for the novel. This is one of the reasons why *Under the Volcano* can hardly be treated as a Cabbalistic treatise or fable.

So much for the esoteric approach. The aesthetic interpretation, on the other hand, will follow Lowry in assuming that *Under the Volcano* is primarily a work of art, and as such subject mainly to aesthetic exigencies (see *Letters*, p. 85). Consequently, it will tend to account for the obscurity of Geoffrey's mysticism by trying to explain it in terms of the novel itself. If the mystical dimension of the novel remains by and large undetermined, then the elements that go to make it up—all the occult allusions and references as well as such broader themes as *Ascent, Light,* or *Salvation*—have a chiefly evocative function. They suggest and intimate but do not define. All this creates a peculiar impression of semantic irridescence. The Consul, while not being actually a Cabbalist, astrologer, magus, alchemist, or mystic, is nevertheless potentially all of these together. As much is suggested by *Under the Volcano*. It is as if the esoteric portrait that Lowry has painted were constantly changing colours: all possible combinations of hues and shades crowding on to the canvas, few of them able to stay for any length of time. The end result of such variegated evocation is an archetypal figure of a mystic, a Cabbalist, or a magus; in short, a man who searches for God and eternity by means of some secret practices inaccessible to the average believer and church-goer. His occult path is all the more nebulous because, when we meet him, he is no longer ascending into the light but falling into the abyss of darkness. How are we going to trace his mysticism if he has betrayed the Mysteries and is now courting damnation (p. 289)? Certainly not by deciphering systematically every one of the esoteric allusions, for they will not yield the Consul's secret unless we turn to the most accessible aspect of his mystical search, namely, its demonic inversion. Let us then inquire into Geoffrey's damnation, into his mystical fall, epitomized, as I shall try to show, by an archetypal figure of the black magician.

One of the key myths informing the Consul's magico-mystical universe, a melodic line joining—directly and indirectly— with every theme of the novel, is the Faustus legend.[30] In chapter 1 above we saw how it is woven into the im-

---

with Epstein's "Cabbalistic theory" of the novel, he points out that "Lowry had barely heard of the Cabbala when he composed the essential drafts of *Volcano* in Mexico, drafts containing, although clearly undeveloped, most of the major talismans which Mrs. Epstein claims to be Cabbalistically oriented." (*Journal of Modern Literature,* September 1971, p.3.)

[30] Myth is here not taken in its strictly religious sense, i.e. "a traditional narration which relates to events that happened at the beginning of time and which has the purpose of providing

ages of the Consul's fall and how he is in some measure identified with Faustus. In his letter to Cape Lowry goes so far as to say that the Consul seems like Faust who has sold his soul to the devil (see *Letters*, p. 70). Even if we do not follow Lowry in visualizing Geoffrey's pact with the evil one, we know at least that his death is conceived in Faustian terms. "Dies Faustus", the end is foreshadowed in the middle of the book, when the Consul finds himself in a state of extraordinary drunkenness. But he apparently chooses to take the portentous words in their Latin meaning[31] and enjoy a happy day: "the longest day in his entire experience, a lifetime [with] plenty of time for more drinks" (p. 220). Such is the ambivalence of drinking, incorporated here into the Faustus theme. The delights of a heightened consciousness, or even ecstasy, go hand in hand with a lurking awareness of something being amiss. "Dies Faustus", it flashes across the Consul's mind as he looks at his watch. It is not the first nor the last

grounds for the ritual actions of man" (Paul Ricoeur, *The Symbolism of Evil*, Boston: Beacon Press, 1967, p. 5), but as "a story or a complex of story elements taken as expressing, and therefore as implicity symbolizing, certain deep-lying aspects of human and transhuman existence." (Philip Wheelwright, an article in *Princeton Encyclopedia of Poetry and Poetics*. Ed. Alex Preminger, Princeton: Princeton Univ. Press, 1972, p. 538). Thus the Faustus myth may be regarded as a paradigmatic story symbolizing the post-Renaissance development of Western civilization. Cf. also Karl Jaspers' threefold definition of myth:

"(1) The myth tells a story and expresses intuitive insights, rather than universal concepts. The myth is historical, both in the form of its thinking and in its content. It is not a cloak or disguise put over a general idea, which can be better and more directly grasped intellectually. It explains in terms of historical origin rather than in terms of a necessity conceived as universal law.

(2) The myth deals with sacred stories and visions, with stories about gods rather than with empirical realities.

(3) The myth is a carrier of meanings which can be expressed only in the language of myth. The mythical figures are symbols which, by their very nature, are untranslatable into other language. They are accessible only in the mythical element, they are irreplaceable, unique. They cannot be interpreted rationally; they are interpreted only by new myths, by being transformed. Myths interpret each other." (Karl Jaspers and Rudolf Bultmann, *Myth and Christianity*, New York: The Noonday Press, 1958, pp. 15—16.)

See also: Martin Buber, *Good and Evil* (New York: Scribner, 1953), "The Truth of the Myths", pp. 115—120; Ernst Cassirer, *An Essay on Man* (New York: Doubleday, 1956), chapter 7; Ernst Cassier, *Language and Myth* (New York: Dover Publications Inc., 1953), chapter 1; Mircea Eliade, *The Sacred and the Profane*, pp. 95—104; H. and H. A. Frankfort, John A. Wilson, Thorkild Jacobsen, *Before Philosophy* (Harmondsworth: Penguin Books, 1949), chapter 1, "Myth and Reality"; Susanne K. Langer, *Philosophy in a New Key* (New York: The New American Library, 1948), chapter 7; Denis de Rougemont, *Love in the Western World* (New York, Harper, 1974), pp. 18—19; Paul Ricoeur, *The Symbolism of Evil*, pp. 3—10; Alan Watts, *Myth and Ritual in Christianity*, pp. 7, 63; Philip Wheelwright, *The Burning Fountain* (Bloomington: Indiana Univ. Press, 1954), pp. 158—160.

[31] *Dies*=day, *faustus*=happy, blessed.

time on this Day of the Dead that he becomes apprehensive of the passage of time. Perhaps he has an intimation of the fateful moment drawing inexorably near; the inevitable disaster that must come at the close of the day.[32]

The stars move still, time runs, the clock will strike,
The Devil will come, and Faustus must be damn'd.

(Faustus, xix, 143—44)

And so the blessed and longest day, measured by an infinite number of drinks, merges with a threat of passing time. Happiness is inextricably bound with calamity, just as the inner voice of temptation is accompanied by the corrective whisper of salvation. The frequent appearance of the Consul's familiars as well as Faustus' good and bad angels marks the coexistence of contending opposites always present in the soul of the hero.

The tension of contradictions seems to spring from the already mentioned confusion of hell with Elysium which is rooted in a miscarried attempt to reach that which lies beyond ordinary human limitations. "Ye shall be as gods", the devil tells Adam and Eve, and we may imagine the same promptings being whispered to Doctor Faustus and Geoffrey Firmin. They reach high but their undertaking fails because in their strivings they ally themselves with the impure and destructive powers of magic. In a sense they repeat the fall of man by taking a shorter and illusory road to divinity.[33] Faustus by availing himself of the good offices of Mephostophilis who makes him into a demi-god ("A sound magician is a demi-god", *Faustus*, i, 61), and the Consul by drinking which heightens his metaphysical consciousness and puts him in touch with eternity (cf. p. 287).

At the same time they renounce their "chiefest bliss" (*Faustus*, i, 27): salvation in the Christian scheme of the Elizabethan, or, in the more comprehensive outlook of the modern, man's spiritual aspirations. Faustus abjures God and gives both his soul and body to the devil, and the Consul, as it seems, betrays and abuses the true mystic way. "Give me back my purity, the knowledge of the Mysteries, that I have betrayed and lost", he prays to the Virgin Mary (p. 289). Does it imply that he has in some distant past made great progress on the occult path? Has he been granted initiation into the secrets of divinity and the universe; has he perhaps attained great mystical heights? We cannot be sure. The esoteric aura of *Under the Volcano* and the capital "M" of the Mysteries suggest this but without necessity or force. The Mysteries remain hidden. Al-

---

[32] And also at the close of the book. Insisting on having his twelve chapters in *Under the Volcano*, Lowry says: "it is as if I hear a clock slowly striking midnight for Faust" (*Letters*, pp. 65—66).

[33] Cf. de Rougemont, *The Devil's Share, p. 32.*

though never definitely settled in the novel, their meaning is not left unmodified by the immediate context which suggests a universal rather than narrowly esoteric import. The Mysteries, juxtaposed with purity, true suffering, love, honest prayer, and happiness, seem to signify man's true path in life. Their violation is, moreover, reflected in the betrayal theme persistent throughout the novel. We shall now consider the mythical aspect of the theme and follow it through various myths and legends alluded to in *Under the Volcano*. We shall see in this way how the mythical evocations enrich and broaden the ultimate significance of betrayal. The betrayal of the Mysteries will in effect signify an abuse of man's mystical powers as well as a disclosure of divine secrets; it will imply man's hubris in his attempt to become god-like and betrayal of his highest responsibilities both towards God and towards his fellow human beings. In other words, man betrays the Mysteries not necessarily by revealing hidden knowledge but by turning away from God and abusing the gifts of heaven. Man's divine faculties are thus turned to ends contrary to God's design and hence evil. If the legitimate use of these faculties may be described as white magic, their abuse implies necromancy, or black magic.

The act of betrayal may be committed not in an avowedly evil purpose but with the best and highest intentions. The end may be to reach heaven but, if the means are inadequate, man will inevitably fall. Not as a result of ill will but of aiming too high, Faustus' "waxen wings did mount above his reach" (*Faustus*, Prol. 21) in a burning desire to know the secrets of heaven and earth. So also Noah—the Noah of Cabbalistic exegesis—tried to fathom a mystery of wisdom without being equal to the task. After the flood he planted a vineyard and pressed the grapes, an action symbolic of sounding the depths of knowledge. He partook, however, of the juice and, becoming drunk, repeated the sin of Eve who, according to certain Cabbalistic traditions, obtained forbidden knowledge not by eating the apple but by pressing the grapes and drinking their intoxicating juice. According to the *Zohar*, Noah failed in the noble purpose to disentangle the mystery of the sin which had caused the fall of man:

His intention was to find a cure for the world, "in place of Eve and her poison"; but he became drunken by laying bare the Divine Essence without having the intellectual strength to fathom it. This is why Scripture says that he was drunken and was uncovered within his tent. The meaning is that he raised a corner of the veil concerning that breach of the world which ought always to remain secret.[34]

This Zoharic legend well illustrates one of the more important suggestions Lowry provides in the letter to Cape: in fact a Cabbalistic key to the

[34] Waite, *Secret Doctrine*, p. 112. Cf. also Lévi, *The History of Magic*, pp. 59–60.

significance of drinking. "In the Cabbala", he explains, "the misuse of magical powers is compared to drunkenness or the misuse of wine" (*Letters*, p. 71). Thus, in as far as the Consul is a Cabbalist and a drunkard, he may be said to misuse magical powers. And since, mythologically speaking, misuse of magical powers is often tantamount to black magic—black magic being always provided by evil powers—Geoffrey's drunkeneness is directly analogous to Faustus' pact with the Devil.

As we saw in the previous chapter, the Consul's drunkenness is projected in the image of a Tower of Babel which, crashing down to the earth, forever buries his true self. Drunkeness is thus associated with a disaster brought about by man's arrogance and unlawful magical practices. According to a Cabbalistic legend, the builders of Babel were in possession of a book containing deep mysteries of wisdom. The book is said to have belonged to the wicked generation of the Deluge, which intended to escape the divine chastisement and to make war with God by resorting to their magical sciences. The builders of Babel followed in their footsteps. Having great skill in magic, they set about constructing "a citadel built against floods and tempests, a promontory from the elevation of which the deified people would soar above the atmosphere and its commotions."[35] But the ambitious project failed because the builders lacked sufficient knowledge and wisdom[36]. For, as the Psalmist warns, "Except the Lord build the house, they labour in vain to build it" (Ps. 127). Once they had abandoned the way of the Lord, yet desiring to become like gods, the designers of Babel must have leagued themselves with the powers of evil which always welcome man on his shortcut to divinity.[37] The magic of their mysteries became black and they decided to abandon heaven for hell and to rebuild the celestial realm according to their evil designs.[38] An embodiment of hubris and apostasy, the Biblical magician-builders whom Waite compares to the giants of Genesis,[39] could well have inspired the late medieval Faustus whose rejection of God, as the first German Faustbook tells us,

was nothing more nor less than his pride and arrogance, despair, audacity and insolence, like unto those giants of whom the poets sing that they carried the mountains together and were fain to make war on God, yea like unto that evil angel who opposed God, and was cast off by God on account of his arrogance and presumption.[40]

[35] Lévi, ibid., p. 109; cf. Laruelle's tower and the Cholula pyramid in chapter 1 above.

[36] See Waite, *Secret Doctrine*, p. 114.

[37] Cf. de Rougemont, p. 146. *The Devil's Share*.

[38] See Waite's footnote to Lévi, op. cit., p. 108, n. 2 (cf. also Waite's *Secret Doctrine*, p. 114).

[39] See ibid., p. 108, n. 2.

[40] Quoted after E. M. Butler, *The Fortunes of Faust* (Cambridge: Cambridge Univ. Press, 1962), p. 5.

Likewise, the insolent Titans of the Greek tradition are known for their struggle against the supreme deity, and through Prometheus they are associated with sciences and secret knowledge.[41] Like the fallen angles of Cabbalistic legend,[42] Prometheus rose against the gods, stole the divine fire of arts and sciences, and for his trickery was bound with indestructible chains to Mount Caucasus.[43] Probably because of his kinship with the fallen angels, he has in *Under the Volcano* lost the popular glamour of mankind's benefactor. As a "cloacal Prometheus" he inhabits the depths of the infernal barranca (p. 131). His dwelling and the company of Ixion (p. 219), who was in Tartarus bound to an ever turning wheel, suggest an affinity to the tortures of the fallen angels.[44] This in turn implies a reversal of the customary significance of Prometheus. His fire is no longer an unmixed blessing, "the succour of succours, or the help of helps, which infinite ways affords aid and assistance to all labours and mechanical arts, and to the sciences themselves", as Francis Bacon said nearly four hundred years ago.[45] His fire is a magic art, betrayed and misused, "the help of helps" in man's deification. For "who was the first man to bring fire?", asks the Russian symbolist writer and scholar Dimitri Merezhkovsky in his interpretation of Prometheus. "*Homo sapiens*, the Intelligent Being, *Homo faber*, the Skilful? No, *Homo magus*, The Sorcerer Fire-father of magic: man possessed God in possessing flame. . ."[46]

We must not, of course, overestimate the role of Prometheus in *Under the Volcano*, where he makes only a few appearances. Yet the image is striking because it so obviously lacks the common "Promethean" attributes and because it substantially contributes to the principal theme of the black magician. No

---

[41] Cf. Spence, *The Occult Sciences in Atlantis*, p. 21, and Ricoeur, *The Symbolism of Evil*, p. 210.

[42] According to the *Zohar* and to an occult tradition derived from the apocryphal *Book of Enoch*, the angels instructed men in the forbidden arts of magic; they taught them the secrets of roots, the art of adorning themselves, the art of forging weapons and waging war. Having betrayed God's secrets to men, some of them were chained on the "Mountains of Darkness", where people repaired to receive instruction in black arts. See Lévi, *The History of Magic*, pp. 55–56; Merezhkovsky, *Atlantis/Europe*, chapter 5; Spence, *The Occult Sciences in Atlantis*, p. 21; *Enoch or the Hebrew Book of Enoch*, ed. Hugo Odenberg (Cambridge: Cambridge Univ. Press, 1928), pp. 10–12; Scholem, *Major Trends in Jewish Mysticism*, p. 365; Waite, *Secret Doctrine*, p. 85.

[43] See *New Larousse Encyclopedia of Mythology* (London, New York, Sydney, Toronto: Hamlyn, 1968), p. 95.

[44] Cf. Watts, *Myth and Ritual in Christianity*, p. 65.

[45] Francis Bacon, *The Essays: The Wisdom of the Ancients, New Atlantis* (London: Cassel, 1907), p. 262.

[46] Merezhkovsky, p. 167.

true benefactor, the Greek Titan is a profaner of divine mysteries, cast into darkness and chained to a moutain. At the same time he is also something of a Faustus, an originator and representative of a culture dedicated to the magic of science and technology.[47] He also resembles the Consul, a "Faustian gent" (*Letters*, p.199) and a betrayer of mysteries. The Consul is even compared to Prometheus, if we grant that the "poor fool who was bringing light to the world [and] hung upside down over it" refers to the fire thief of the Greek mythology (p. 222).

Profanation of divine mysteries and Titanic pride also brought about the downfall of Atlantis.[48] An occult tradition derives the Greek Titans as well as the Biblical giants of Genesis from a much more ancient legend describing the rebellion of the lower caste on the lost continent. They are said to have practised witchcraft and led the more civilized inhabitants into evil sorceries.[49] Again black magic is responsible for a fall, the fall of the antediluvian humanity destroyed by fire and water. As we saw in the previous chapter, in *Under the Volcano* the catastrophe of Atlantis is associated with Geoffrey's drinking. It is significant that the image of the calamity contains an allusion to unlawful magical practices precisely when the Consul makes up his mind to go to his fatal cantina. He has just rejected Dr. Vigil's offer to travel with him to the beautiful city of Guanajuato. Instead, he has decided on Tomalín, Parián and the Farolito which the doctor describes as "un infierno" (p. 147). Immediately after the decision has been made, the conversation is interrupted by sudden explosions and gunfire. An impression of a dislocation of time is created and Geoffrey, turning to Vigil, paraphrases a few lines from Shelley's *Alastor* in such a way as to connect an evil sorcerer with the end of the world and Atlantis:

somewhere a clock was striking nineteen. Twelve o'clock, and the Consul said to the doctor: "Ah, that the dream of dark magician in his visioned cave, even while his hand—that's the bit I like—shakes in its last decay, were the true end of this so lovely world. Jesus. Do you know, compañero, I sometimes have the feeling that it's actually

---

[47] For an interpretation of Prometheus as an originator of science who gave man "the faculty of mastering nature, shaping his environment, setting out on rational undertakings", see Karl Jaspers, *Philosophical Faith and Revelation* (London: Collins, 1967), pp. 305—306. Se also Oswald Spengler, *Man and Technics* (New York and London: A. Knopf/Allen and Unwin, 1963), part V, for the concept of the "Faustian culture", whose leading idea is "*to enslave and harness* [Nature's] *very forces* so as to multiply [man's] strength" (p. 84). "To build a world *oneself*, to be *oneself* God—that is the Faustian inventor's dream, and from it has sprung all our designing and re-designing of machines to approximate as nearly as possible to the unattainable limit of perpetual motion" (p. 85).

[48] See Merezhkovsky, pp. 95, 190.

[49] See above, chapter 3, n. 29.

sinking, like Atlantis, beneath my feet. Down, down to the frightful 'poulps'. Meropis of Theopompus . . . And the *ignivome* mountains." And the doctor who was nodding gloomily said: "Sí, that is tequila." (pp. 147—48).[50]

In Chapter Seven, waiting for his drink, the Consul repeats the paraphrased quotation from Shelley, substituting this time "lousy" for "lovely" world (p. 202).[51]

As I have mentioned several times before, Geoffrey himself appears to be aware of the dark side of drinking. Almost every draught bespeaks death and annihilation, while holding at the same time the promise of eternity and know-ledge. Evidently, drinking is charged with the archetypal contents of the fall of man which in the Judeo-Christian tradition implies the punishment of death following the temptation of becoming god-like. "Man wants to be on a level with God, and in so doing to become independent of Him", writes the well known contemporary Protestant theologian Emil Brunner.[52] Also in the Cab-bala sin implies the self-seeking of man.[53] By eating the apple, Adam destroys man's unbroken communion with the Godhead which consists in the contemplation of the divine and its mysteries, and in consequence falls into a state of profound isolation and separation from God.[54] And what is pertinent to our theme, this act of apostasy bears fruit in man's magical presumptions.[55] In the Zohar "magic is represented as a faculty first manifested in the fall of Adam and originating in the corruption of man".[56] Thus Adam, in a manner of speaking, is humanity's first black magician.

---

[50] Theopompus, a Greek historian (400 B.C.) who described an imaginary land by the name of Meropis, supposed later to be Atlantis. (See Donnelly, *Atlantis*, pp. 27, 171; Spence, *The Problem of Atlantis*, London: Rider, 1924, pp. 8—9.)

[51] . . . O, that the dream/Of dark magician in his visioned cave,/Raking the cinders of a crucible/For life and power, even when his feeble hand/Shakes in its last decay, were the true law/Of this so lovely world! ("Alastor", pp. 93—94, in *Poems of Shelley*, London: Thomas Nelson & Sons, no date.)

[52] Emil Brunner, *The Christian Doctrine of Creation and Redemption* (London: Lutterworth Press, 1952), p. 92. For an interpretation of the Biblical idea of sin in terms of alienation and estrangement see also Paul Tillich, *Systematic Theology* (Chicago: The Univ. of Chicago Press, 1957), part III, pp. 44—78; and Paul Ricoeur, pp. 73, 89.

[53] See Scholem, *Major Trends in Jewish Mysticism*, pp. 236—37.

[54] See Scholem, "On Sin and Punishment", in *Myths and Symbols: Studies in Honor of Mircea Eliade* (Chicago: The Univ. of Chicago Press, 1969), pp. 175—76.

[55] See Scholem, *Major Trends*, p. 237.

[56] Scholem, *On the Kabbalah and Its Symbolism* (New York: Schocken Books, 1969), p. 175. Cf. also Scholem, *Major Trends*, p. 405, note 106; Waite, *Secret Doctrine*, p. 274: "The source of all magical power, howsoever it may be derived through individual persons, is the first serpent, who is the impure spirit. . ."

In his *History of Magic* Eliphas Lévi ascribes the sin of Adam, the fall of the angels alluded to in the Genesis story of the antediluvian giants, the flood, and the intoxication of Noah to one and the same cause: the profanation and betrayal of divine mysteries.[57] Thus the betrayal of mysteries, usually rooted in an attempt to reach divinity, may be said to result in an alliance with the evil powers and the practices of black magic. All the mythical figures we have so far considered—Adam, Noah, the builders of Babel, Enoch's fallen angels and giants, Prometheus, Faustus, and the Atlantean sorcerers are overreachers who have betrayed divine mysteries either by misusing their divine powers or by disclosure of deep occult secrets. In other words, they have betrayed both God and man. Their evil practices have brought about different kinds of punishment, including in the case of Atlantis a cataclysm striking a whole civilization through the submergence in the deluge waters.[58]

All these myths are more or less openly alluded to in *Under the Volcano* and related to the Consul. Geoffrey is identified with Faustus, Adam, and compared to Prometheus who is, in turn, shown dwelling in the barranca, the inverted goal of Geoffrey's life journey. The barranca, inhabited by *Hurakan,* the god of storm, has some curious connection with Atlantis, the sinking of which the Consul so palpably feels, presumably thanks to tequila and mescal. Drinking assumes the form of a Tower of Babel, and is Cabbalistically associated with Noah whom the Consul intends to discuss in his book on secret knowledge. There are many more such connections and cross references. In this chapter we have touched only upon the most direct and obvious associations between the Consul and the mythical variations on the theme of the black magician. The involved polyphony of the novel, however, through which themes and images are constantly interrelated, allows for a great many more connections to be made. It seems clear that all the principal themes of the novel—in as much as they represent the quality of "infernal paradise"—are aspects of the great archetypal figure of the white magician turned black;[59] a figure evoked by all the mythical parallels so far considered, skilfully if somewhat loosely embodied in the Consul.

---

[57] See Lévi, *The History of Magic*, pp. 55—56, 59—60.

[58] See Merezhkovsky, p. 95.

[59] "In Magic, that is to say, the science of the Control of the Secret Forces of Nature, there have always been two great schools, the one great in Good, the other in Evil; the former the Magic of Light, the latter of Darkness; the former usually depending on the knowledge and invocation of the Angelic natures, the latter on the method of evocation of the Demonic races. Usually the former is termed White Magic, as opposed to the latter, or Black Magic." S. L. MacGregor Mathers, *The Book of the Sacred Magic of Abra-Melin the Mage* (London: J. Watkins, 1956), p. xxv.

Is the Consul a black magician then? Yes, but only in as much as the archetypal figure conjured up by the mythical allusions displays a fairly coherent significance, and in so far as it relates to the Consul. Evidently we are invited to treat Geoffrey *in terms of* the black magician: terms precisely as broad as the indeterminacy of the allusive context suggests. In this way the black magician becomes a hermeneutic concept but one provided by *Under the Volcano* itself, a legitimate key to one of the novel's most significant dimensions. Hence it could hardly be said of the Consul that he is a black magician in actual fact. Obviously he is no Elizabethan Faustus. Unlike Marlowe, Lowry does not show his protagonist concluding an agreement with the devil. But that does not prevent him, as we have seen, from suggesting in a variety of ways that the Consul is nevertheless a black magician. The pact with the evil one and the various antics performed through the supernatural powers are of course of secondary importance. Black magic and alliance with the forces of darkness—whether conceived literally or metaphorically—have always provided the opportunity to touch upon some of the most significant human issues of universal appeal. Although modern man no longer believes in black magic, modern reality often lends itself to interpretations in terms of the old myth which still haunts the artistic imagination. Thomas Mann in his *Doktor Faustus* has chosen black magic to portray the decline of twentieth-century culture and civilization; a decline which has given rise to Nazism and the barbarities of the Second World War. And Lowry, writing before and during the war, chose a Faustus-like hero to portray approaching catastrophe caused by man's confusion of heaven and hell; a confusion which leads to his constantly renewed alliance with the dark forces of destruction. These forces and the diabolic magic, it might be pointed out, reside chiefly in alcohol and are merely creations, however imaginative, of the Consul's unusual states of drunkenness. Yet in actual fact *Under the Volcano*, as Stephen Spender aptly remarks, "is no more *about* drinking than *King Lear* is *about* senility" (Introduction, p. ix). It is—to recall Lowry's words quoted earlier on in this chapter—"concerned principally ... with the forces in man which cause him to be terrified of himself" (*Letters*, p. 66). It is about black magic conceived not through its external supernatural trappings but through its far-reaching consequences for the human condition.[60]

The profanation of mysteries and the practice of necromantic arts brings, as we have seen, punishment and suffering. Would it imply then that the Consul's

[60] I owe my interpretation of the Consul as a black magician to hints and suggestions contained in the letters to Cape and to Derek Pethic (*Letters,* pp. 197—202). It may also be mentioned that among Lowry critics Day, Dodson, Epstein, and Kilgallin have accepted the Consul as a black magician figure.

suffering—an overwhelming theme independent of any esoteric props—is intimately bound up with an occult transgression and black magic? Such indeed seems to be the case. The agonies of the mystic who has abused his powers, writes Lowry, are a perfect poetic analogue of the agonies of the drunkard (*Letters*, p. 71). Not without reason is drinking thus interwoven with the Babel image and the Atlantis theme, juxtaposed with the dark magician mentioned by the Consul, and associated with Noah. Drinking, the alleged source of spiritual enlightenment is, then, the black magic of *Under the Volcano*, the inverted way to seek God and eternity.

It has been claimed, however, that drinking may be a direct and legitimate way to acquire mystical powers[61], that divinity has often revealed itself to man in alcohol and drugs. "For the Brahmins who pressed and drank soma, its name was Indra", writes Aldous Huxley, "for the hemp-eating yogis, Siva. The gods of Mexico inhabited the peyotl. The Persian Sufis discovered Allah in the wine of Shiraz, the shamans of the Samoyedes ate toadstools and were filled with the spirit of Num."[62] It is true that alcoholic and narcotic ecstasies have been very similar to the experiences of many a mystic, but the similarity, as R. C. Zaehner has convincingly demonstrated, is deceptive and misleading. "Do not mistake elation for grace", he imagines St. Paul cautioning his followers. "Elation or exaltation is a state that is common to saints and sinners alike: it can be produced by alcohol or drugs, but do not confuse it with the grace that is infused into you at our *agape*."[63] Apparently the Consul persists in precisely such a confusion. So obviously unable to love, yet urged on by his thirst for eternity, he regards drink as an eternal sacrament and takes it to be the nectar of immortality. Suffering the tortures of thirst at the same time, he is only a Tantalus who has betrayed Zeus' secrets and stolen the divine food from the Olympus. Also the resemblance to this ancient betrayer of divine mysteries places the Consul in the gallery of the dark magicians alluded to in *Under the Volcano*. He belongs, in the words of Baudelaire, to "these unfortunates who have neither fasted nor prayed and who have refused redemption by work, [asking] from black magic the means of raising themselves, at one fell swoop, to a supernatural existence. Magic dupes them and kindles for them a false happiness and a false light."[64]

The Consul, as we recall, seeks happiness in the Farolito, the Lighthouse, which through drink offers him heigthened metaphysical consciousness. But

---

[61] Among the critics of *Under the Volcano* P. Epstein and A. Albaum are often close to such a point of view.

[62] *Point Counter Point* (Harmondsworth: Penguin Books, 1955), p. 228.

[63] Zaehner, p. 26.

[64] Baudelaire, *Oeuvres Complètes,* quoted after Zaehner, p. 104.

the magic of alcoholic mysticism is just as deceptive as the magic of Faustus, Lowry appears to imply through a somewhat involved juxtaposition. "Your Faust man", Laurelle tries to make the Consul realize the distortions of his vision, "saw the Carthaginians fighting on his big toe-nail. That's the kind of clear seeing you indulge in. Everything seems perfectly clear, because indeed it is perfectly clear, in terms of the toe-nail" (p. 217). The metaphysical consciousness is exclusively confined to drinking; all the rest of the Consul's life, so wilfully neglected, is being taken over by "the legionnaires of damnation" (p. 139):

"Erekia, the one who tears asunder; and they who shriek with a long drawn cry, Illirikim; the misleaders or turners aside; and those who attack their prey by tremulous motion, Dresop; ah, and the distressful painbringing ones, Arekesoli; and one must not forget, either, Burasin, the destroyers by stifling smoky breath; nor Glesi, the one who glistens horribly like an insect; nor Effrigis, the one who quivers in a horrible manner [. . .] nor yet the Mames, those who move by backward motion, nor the movers with a particular creeping motion, Ramisen [. . .] The flesh inclothed and the evil questioners." (pp. 185—86)[65]

Unlike Faustus, the Consul is paying for the fruits of his magic here and now. Suffering "the tortures of the damned", he feels the infernal reality progressively enclosing him until he is actually cast into the abyss. He has become almost like Marlowe's Mephostophilis, or like Milton's Satan who confess to being always in the infernal regions: "Which way I flie is Hell; my self am Hell."[66]

But is the comparison justified? Perhaps, neither a demon nor a damned soul, the Consul is a Dante; "a great explorer who has discovered some extraordinary land from which he can never return to give his knowledge to the world: but the name of this land is hell" (p. 36). He knows that there is a mysterious path in hell, beyond which appear vistas of a new life. "To discover the secret path is to discover that as the center implies circumference, so Hell implies Heaven, and Satan implies the Lord", writes Alan Watts in his mythological interpretation of *The Divine Comedy*.[67] But the Consul knows that he may neither take the path nor find his way back from the inferno. Unlike Dante, who has been offered a remedial vision of Hell, the Consul is claimed by the in-

---

[65] All these demons that Lowry (as P. Epstein has pointed out in *The Private Labyrinth of Malcolm Lowry*, p. 127) has taken from *The Book of the Sacred Magic of Abra-Melin the Mage* (see note 59) are said to be servitors of Amaymon, a very potent spirit of violence and vehemence (pp. 111, 122). They are not, as far as I have been able to establish, mentioned in any other source.

[66] John Milton, *Paradise Lost*, Book IV, 75. Cf. also the words of Mephostophilis: "Why, this is hell, nor am I out of it." (*Faustus,* iii, 79.)

[67] *The Two Hands of God* (New York: Collier Books, 1969), p. 167.

fernal forces.[68] It is above all his inability to love, and the suffering he causes others, that condemns him to "an ultimate hell on earth" (p. 367). This alone throws light on the direction of his mystical strivings, his search for God and eternity. Is it possible that the man who knows "the final moments of the retiring of the human heart, and the final entrance of the fiendish" (p. 136)[69] is, as Epstein and other commentators would have it, a messiah figure?[70] Is it possible that he is carrying on a task of redemption which—many religious and mystical traditions are unanimous on this point—requires extraordinary purity, goodness, and love?

His esoteric search alone does not make him into a redeemer, for the devil as well as God has his own contemplatives and mystics.[71] It would not be difficult to see the devil's hand in Geoffrey's quest for paradise. For the Consul, says Lowry commenting on Chapter Ten of *Under the Volcano*, has become "a man that is all destruction—in fact he has almost ceased to be a man altogether, and his human feelings merely make matters more agonizing for him, but don't alter things in the least; he is thus in hell" (*Letters*, p. 200). True, the hell often appears to him so blissful that it is easily taken for paradise but that is precisely due to the devil's genius to simulate. The Catholic Church and the Sufis (the mystics of Islam) have always recognized the devil's ability to counterfeit mystical states.[72] The Cabbalists, too, have been aware of the demonic *Imitatio Dei*. "The Spirit of Evil imitates the Spirit of Good, and that which it occasions below in malice the spirit of good fulfils in holiness above."[73] Moreover, the infernal regions are held to be a mirror replica of the heavenly: the seven hells are dark manifestations of the seven luminous emanations of God: inverted images of transcendent archetypes.[74]

---

[68] "We must be careful to distinguish between Hell itself, taken literally, and *the vision of Hell* which is offered to Dante. Hell itself is not remedial; the dead who have chosen the 'eternal exile' from God, and who thus experience the reality of their choice, cannot profit by that experience. In that sense, no living soul can enter Hell, since, however great the sin, repentance is always possible while there is life, even to the very moment of dying. But the *vision of Hell*, which is remedial, is the soul's self-knowledge in all its evil potentialities—'the revelation of the nature of impenitent sin'". Dorothy Sayers in a commentary to her translation of Dante's *Divine Comedy* (Harmondsworth: Penguin Books, 1949), p. 68.

[69] Cf. De Quincey, "On the Knocking at the Gate in *Macbeth*", in *A Book of English Essays*, selected by W. E. Williams (Harmondsworth: Penguin Books, 1951), p. 169.

[70] Albaum, Barnes, Costa, Dodson, and Kilgallin have all, with varying degrees of emphasis, indicated the Consul's messianic role.

[71] See Zaehner, p. 67.

[72] See ibid., p. 43.

[73] Waite, *Secret Doctrine*, p. 96.

[74] See Schaya, *The Universal Meaning of the Kabbalah*, pp. 111, 69, 115; Waite, p. 259.

Understandably, both Faustus and the Consul "confound hell with Elysium": the former by Mephostophilis' wordly magic, the latter by the transcendental magic of alcoholic contemplation. That the devil can have his own contemplatives has not escaped William James's attention, the same William James who, as we remember, ascribes mystical faculties to alcohol. "In delusional insanity", he says, "paranoia, as they sometimes call it, we may have *diabolical* mysticism, a sort of religious mysticism turned upside down."[75] Interestingly enough, the same quotation from James has been chosen by R. C. Zaehner to illustrate his discussion of the devil's ability to counterfeit mystical states, and by Douglas Day to throw light on the personality of Geoffrey Firmin.[76] The Consul's life has become all destruction, his search for eternity has turned into diabolic mysticism because, as I have tried to suggest, by betraying the Mysteries he has betrayed his highest human calling.

Like Prometheus, Tantalus, or Noah, the Consul has appropriated secrets of heaven without being able to make proper use of them. Dying, he suddenly realizes that his life has been a fraud: "And it was as if, for a moment, he had become the pelado, the thief—yes, the pilferer of meaningless muddled ideas out of which his rejection of life had grown" (p. 374). Indeed, his mystical pursuits have been radically severed from people, and from the moral problems besetting the world. The mention of the Indian murdered by the "vigilante hombres" and a need to be wholly awake, apparently make the Consul withdraw to his holy place, the toilet. An odd place for a sanctuary, to be sure, but one that no doubt stresses the irony of Geoffrey's attempts to reach eternity. Earlier on in his house he sat in the bathroom "in an attitude like a grotesque parody of an old attitude in meditation" (p. 145). Now in the Salón Ofélia the situation is more or less repeated:

They had been discussing the man by the roadside and the thief in the bus, then: "Excusado" [Spanish for toilet]. And this, this grey final Consulate, this Franklin Island of his soul, was the excusado. Set apart from the bathing places, convenient yet hidden from view [. . .] Why was he here? Why was he always more or less, here? [. . .] Nothing but stone [. . .] Perhaps this was the eternity that he'd been making so much fuss about, eternity already, of the Svidrigailov variety, only instead of a bath house in the country full of spiders, here it turned out to be a stone monastic cell wherein sat—strange! who but himself? (pp. 294—95)

A "stone monastic cell" faintly suggests some monk who has perhaps offered his life to the contemplation of God and eternal life, but the suggestion is almost entirely overshadowed by the Svidrigailov eternity. The monastic cell is associated with the bath house in the country: an image of eternity as Svidri-

---

[75] William James, *The Varieties of Religious Experience,* p. 410.
[76] See Zaehner, p. 43, and *Biography,* p. 335.

gailov pictures it; not grand and ineffable but limited and dingy: a tiny room with spiders in every corner.[77] The Consul's sanctuary reveals here a sinister aspect. Instead of the sublimity of mystical contemplation, it spells the disgust of despairing imagination. And yet the Consul is always drawn into the sphere of the dark and dingy. He may compare his sanctuary to a tomb (p. 294), but he loves the tomb all the same. How happy he feels when, after the vicissitudes of the day, he has found refuge in the sanctuary of the Farolito, "the paradise of his despair" (p. 338).

The modern Faustus, as we can see, gains paradise in return for despair. His expanded consciousness, his eternity, has to be paid for by hopelessness, suffering, and evil. The connection between evil and sanctuary is intimated at the beginning of the novel by a poster which announces the film about the *Hands of Orlac*. As Lowry comments, "the man with the bloody hands in the poster, via the German origin on the picture, symbolizes the *guilt* of mankind, which relates him also to M. Laurelle and the Consul again, while he is also more particularly a foreshadowing of the thief who takes the money from the dying man by the roadside in Chapter VIII, and whose hands are also covered with blood" (*Letters* p. 69). Called the "hieroglyphic of the times", the poster is said to tell a tale of "tyranny and sanctuary" (p. 25). This implies that tyranny is the corollary of Geoffrey's sanctuary, his inverted way of seeking eternity through magic. There is yet another connection between tyranny and black magic, for it is faintly suggested that Hitler was a black magician, since he wished to destroy the Jews in order to obtain their occult knowledge (cf. p. 186).[78]

Sanctuary also appears in Geoffrey's dreamy vision of Tlaxcala: "a white beautiful cathedral city toward which the Consul's soul yearned" (p. 302). Its extraordinary whiteness could perhaps suggest innocence and purity, were it not for the nightmarish emptiness which creates an impression of lifelessness and ruin. The white sanctuary of the Church in Ocotlàn, earlier on associated by a subtle juxtaposition with the Farolito (p. 299), the white towers with a white clock, the cold white sheets and the white bottles in the hotel, the white cantinas—all this indicates some peculiar frozen condition where neither life nor death holds sway. Indeed, the tower clock is timeless, and in the innumerable empty cantinas where the wind is blowing through the open doors, one can perpetually drink on credit. Such is the eternity of Tlaxcala which, Lowry

---

[77] Cf. Dostoevsky, *Crime and Punishment* (Harmondsworth: Penguin Books, 1966), p. 305.

[78] Cf. Lowry's letter to Cape: "And Hitler was another pseudo black magician out of the same drawer as Amfortas in the *Parsifal* he so much admired, and who has had the same inevitable fate. And if you don't believe that a British general actually told me that the real reason why Hitler destroyed the Polish Jews was to prevent their cabbalistic knowledge being used against him you can let me have my point on poetical grounds ..." (*Letters*, p. 76).

writes to Cape, "just like Parián, is death" (*Letters,* p. 82). For Parián, already related to the abyss of the barranca, owes its existence to the Tlaxcalans. "Originally settled by a scattering of those fierce forbears of Cervates who had succeeded in making Mexico great even in her betrayal, the traitorous Tlaxcalans" (p. 285), Parián is now known for the headquarters of the fascist Unión Militar.[79] Through Tlaxcala and Parián, sanctuary is again associated with tyranny and incorporated into the betrayal theme.

In *Under the Volcano* Tlaxcala rises to a universal symbol of betrayal. Not only is its role in Mexican history persistently emphasized, but through a free association the Consul situates it in a completely different time and space. He relates it to Taxila[80] whose king entered an alliance with a foreign conqueror in order to undo his rival. Treason, such as this, implies a more or less deliberate action undertaken for an evil end. But in a wider sense treason may refer to a trap set by external or internal enemies on a path transcending man's everyday existence. It may become a pitfall waiting for those who, like the Consul, fail in their striving upwards. "Tlaxcala is on the way to Vera Cruz, Hugh, the true cross", ambiguously remarks the Consul when he wants to combine his trip to Tlaxcala with Hugh's journey to the Mexican port. Accordingly, the purpose of Geoffrey's trip is to have more drinks, Hugh's, to sail on a ship bringing relief to the hard-pressed Spanish Loyalists, with every chance of dying in the adventure. The treason theme becomes still more pregnant if we keep in mind the references to Judas (pp. 111, 122) and remember that the motif of the Indian killed by the roadside is a transposition of the Biblical story of the Good Samaritan and represents, in fact, a betrayal of the brotherhood of man. In this light the Christian chords struck in the Tlaxcala theme should not be surprising. The Tlaxcalans together with the conquerors, Lowry delicately implies, are guilty of betraying Christ once again.

"Was this the face that launched five hundred ships, and betrayed Christ into being in the Western hemisphere?" (p. 287),[81] the Consul asks himself, looking at a Tlaxcaltecan fighting cock. The bird, a herald of dawn, symbolic

---

[79] Tlaxcalans were Mexico's traitors. Hostile to the Aztecs, they "heartily assisted Cortés in his invasion of the Aztec capital, Tenochtitlan, or Mexico." Spence, *The Myths of Mexico and Peru,* p. 26. Cf. also the tourist folder of Tlaxcala: "In this town was built and tried in a dike the ship used for the conquerors in the attack to Tenochtitlán the great capital of Moctezuma's Empire" (p. 300).

[80] An archeological site in West Pakistan containing ruins of three successive cities on the same site.

[81] This is a paraphrase of Faustus' words expressing his admiration at the sight of Helen of Troy: "Was this the face that launch'd a thousand ships and burnt the topless towers of Ilium?" (*Faustus,* xviii, 99.)

of vigilance and resurrection,[82] here represents "the vicious little man-made battles, cruel and destructive" (p. 287). It suggests the conquest of Mexico, military and religious, accomplished with the help of Tlaxcala where, as we read in *Under the Volcano*, the first Indian was baptized (p. 301). Thus was Christ betrayed in the Western hemisphere, Lowry seems to suggest: heralded to the natives of the New World and yet treacherously abandoned through the destruction and cruelty brought by the conquest.

Firmly rooted in the reality of the novel, the theme of Tlaxcala substantiates the evocation of the magus figure as the betrayer of divine mysteries. It is the more earthbound aspect of the whole betrayal theme. As a second yet suggestive voice, the Tlaxcala theme accompanies the Consul's prayer for a recovery of his purity and of the knowledge of the Mysteries that he has betrayed and lost. It seems to be the only response to his dramatic supplication, which the Virgin appears not to have heard. Scarcely has the Consul finished praying, when Cervantes, the Tlaxcaltecan owner and trainer of the fighting cock, apparently for no reason at all opens a drawer full of books, including the History of Tlaxcala in ten volumes. It is the same Cervantes whom Geoffrey later on suspects of betrayal, solely on the grounds that the Tlaxcaltecan is simply unable to resist it (p. 303). And so the theme of betrayal expands in ever-widening circles. The mystic betrays his holy mysteries, Christ is betrayed by Judas, the brotherhood of man by indifference and egoism, justice surrendered to power through political treason, the Spanish republicans betrayed by the European nations, the Consul betrayed by his wife, his half-brother, and his closest friend. By abandoning his highest goals, his aspirations to goodness and a nobler life, man betrays himself.

Not surprisingly, the "excusado", the toilet to which the Consul retreats in search of eternity and away from the world, is called "a purely Tlaxcaltecan fantasy" (p. 294). For the Consul commits betrayal precisely because he evades the world and shuns the responsibility he owes to himself and others. He finds himself in constant flight because, as Douglas Day points out, he is "terrified of life, terrified of human responsibility, terrified of what he sees in himself".[83] It is a deeply rooted unwillingness to face himself, manifested in a persistent—though often unconscious—refusal to cope with the problems of his life otherwise than by alcohol. In chapter 2 above we saw how the Consul escapes from the light because he is unable to face the dark horrors of his life. But is he not himself responsible for the horrors? Is he not, like Faustus, trying to escape from the wrath of God for his transgression? Here we come

---

[82] Cf. Cirlot, *Dictionary of Symbols*, p. 49, and Spence, *An Encyclopaedia of Occultism* (London: Routledge, 1920), pp. 105–106.

[83] *Biography*, p. 348.

to the vicious circle of his flight. He flees from the terror and the suffering, but these—it may well be supposed—have been in the first place caused by some fundamental temptation to run away from the world and people into the magical bliss of alcoholic eternity. On the other hand, the theme of escape is so replete with meaning, so all-embracing and full of ambiguities, that we cannot be certain about the origin of Geoffrey's sickness. Is it moral escapism that has led him into drinking, or vice versa? Is it some unspecified universal guilt, or is it the betrayal of the Mysteries that makes him live "in continual terror of his life" (p. 30)?

Be that as it may, the restless polyphony of the theme, while admitting all these possibilities, suggests a circular, continuous movement of escape, arrested only in the Farolito, where the Consul is—ironically—actually advised to flee. But it is evidently too late. He has relinquished Yvonne's love for a succubus, "a calamity, a fiendish apparatus for calamitous sickening sensation" (p. 349). Without conscience he has already done the irrevocable. Like Faustus, who has signed the pact with the devil, [84] the Consul rejects all thought of escape, and the decision soon leads to his death, the culminating point of which is the flight into the abyss of the barranca. Now Laurelle's misreading of Marlowe acquires additional and more profound reverberations. To substitute *fly* for *run* in Faustus' "Then will I headlong run into the earth" (*Faustus*, xix, 155) points not only to the Consul's "hellish fall" but connects it with his escape, with his "downward flight". In other words, to fly into magic is to fall: doubtless an echo of the mystic's great sin of betrayal. And to fall into black magic is to fly from the world, for both Faustus and the Consul, because they avoid human responsibility, are equally indifferent to mundane concerns. Granted that their aims are different, their basic attitudes are essentially alike: both use a "technical" device for the achievement of selfish ends, both avail themselves, to recall Levin's words, of "science without conscience". In the Renaissance it was a matter of gaining the world by magic, today heaven is often gained through the "instant religion" of narcotic

---

[84] See *Faustus*, v, 74—81.

[85] "That humanity at large will ever be able to dispense with Artificial Paradises seems very unlikely. Most men and women lead lives at the worst so painful, at the best so monotonous, poor, and limited that the urge to escape, the longing to transcend themselves if only for a few moments, is and has always been one of the principal appetites of the soul" (*The Doors of Perception*, Harmondsworth: Penguin Books, 1959, p. 51)—writes Aldous Huxley, a man who has familiarized us with "synthetic transcendence" produced by drugs. It is characteristic that the mescalin-induced bliss experienced by Aldous Huxley should leave "no room, so to speak, for the ordinary, the necessary concerns of human existence, above all for concerns involving persons" (ibid., p. 31). How very much like the Consul's mescal experience which shuts off human voices, and in which the world seems to be "a golf ball, launched at Hercules' Butterfly, wildly hooked by a giant out of an asylum window in hell." Cf. also Zaehner, pp. 12—13.

experiences.[85] Yet man loses his soul all the same. Inhabiting a world of despair and lovelessness, both Dr. Faustus and Geoffrey Firmin are on the way to damnation.

The Consul's fall often seems inevitable, if only because he has started his ascent under the "Faustian auspices". Dying, he imagines himself setting out for the grand climb of Popocatepetl. But even the slope of the foothills at the beginning of the climb is too difficult and painful for him. After a few steps, ex-hausted and helpless, the Consul sinks to the ground, utterly weighed down by his equipment, provisions, and the information from Hotel Fausto. He dies, without anyone really coming to his rescue. As it seems, the Faustian magic has thus betrayed and undone him; through it he has estranged himself from the world and his fellow human beings, and run away from love—"the only thing which gives meaning to our poor ways on earth", as he confesses in the letter to Yvonne (p. 40).

Chapter 5
Love

"No se puede vivir sin amar"—one cannot live without love. The dying Consul is impatiently waiting for these words to be spoken by his imaginary rescuers, words "which would explain everything" (p. 375). But his expectation is illusory and his sudden readiness to ask forgiveness proves useless. No Good Samaritan comes to help him. The vision of the completed ascent crumbles, the world collapses, and the Consul is falling into the volcano.

The Spanish words[1] perhaps "explain everything" in as much as their message has been so often ignored and betrayed by the inhabitants of Lowry's universe. Inscribed on Laurelle's house, they have been deliberately disregarded by Yvonne and the Consul, and ridiculed by the Frenchman. As a matter of fact it is because of his affair with Yvonne that their significance has been lost in an atmosphere of guilt, fear, and estrangement. Independently of each other, both Geoffrey and Yvonne recoil from the inscription which, associated with Laurelle, evokes betrayal and separation. This is yet another of the human dilemmas of *Under the Volcano*. Love is denied because it has once been denied. It appears impossible not because man is incapable of experiencing it but because it has been betrayed. The world Lowry depicts is in a state of disintegration and collapse yet it is not a world falling apart into nothingness but one fallen from grace. Man's essential nature has been more than deeply wounded but not dissolved, as in, for example, Proust where "the self is broken up into elements, sensations and thoughts, the image and likeness of God disappear and everything is enveloped, as it were, in mental cobwebs. The refinement of a soul which ceases to be the bearer of superpersonal values, of the divine principle, leads to dissociation and disintegration."[2] In Lowry's work, the consciousness of a split personality is portrayed not for its own sake since the fate of Geoffrey Firmin bears upon broad issues of the conflict of good and evil. Love, therefore, is much more rooted in man's metaphysical rather than his purely psychological being. It appears not as a subjective feeling, however

---

[1] A quotation from the Spanish religious writer and poet Frey Luis de Léon.
[2] Nicolas Berdyaev, *The Destiny of Man* (New York: Harper Torchbooks, 1960), p. 56.

profound, nor as an overwhelming passion, but as a sacred gift entrusted to man, an ultimate reality in which he participates through his choices.

There are perhaps few contemporary novels in which love is affirmed as much as in *Under the Volcano*. Affirmed, paradoxically, by its absence, but an absence which, through the spiritual dimension of the novel, lends to love enormous significance. Despite the profound estrangement dividing Yvonne and Geoffrey, they both feel the invisible, but nonetheless indissoluble and eternal, bond between them. To Yvonne love, their own love, is not an experience whose loss is merely painful, but an absolute and imperishable gift whose forfeiture is essentially tragic:

For my life is irrevocably and forever bound to yours. Never think that by releasing me you will be free. You would only condemn us to an ultimate hell on earth. You would only free something else to destroy us both. I am frightened, Geoffrey. Why do you not tell me what has happened? What do you need? And my God, what do you wait for? What release can be compared to the release of love? My thighs ache to embrace you [. . .] My tongue is dry in my mouth for the want of *our* speech. If you let anything happen to yourself you will be harming my flesh and mind. I am in your hands now. Save—(p. 367)

These are Yvonne's last words to appear in *Under the Volcano*. Her dramatic plea is interrupted by the incoherent babbling of the pimp who has already once prevented the possibility of Geoffrey's reunion with Yvonne by procuring the succubus Maria. His voice, which has been said to be the only voice rising above the confusion of tongues in the Farolito, is in turn supressed by the radio, for the second time urgently asking the same question: "Quiere usted la salvación de Méjico? Quiere usted que Cristo sea nuestro Rey?" (pp. 365—66, 367, 368).[3] For the second time (there will be a third one) the answer spoken by an anonymous voice or voices is "no".

This denial of Christ is not without reason juxtaposed with an ultimate breach with Yvonne, for Geoffrey's intercourse with the succubus has cancelled the hope of any new life together not only "for brutal hygienic reasons alone" (353). An "ultimate contamination" (354), the very essence of the calamity of his own life (cf. 350), it has been at least as decisive a "consummatum" as that of Faustus who before singing the pact has to "abjure the scriptures and his saviour Christ" (*Faustus*, iii, 50). The Consul abjures, to borrow Marlowe's expression, his unity with Yvonne, the unity, as he puts it, "we once knew and Christ alone knows must still exist somewhere" (p. 40). If Christ, the perfect man, the second Adam, is thus associated with the new self Yvonne and Geoffrey have created through their love, the calling of his name suggests more than a gesture of emotional emphasis. "I am dying without

[3] Do you want the salvation of Mexico? Do you want Christ to be our King?

you", confesses the Consul, "For Christ Jesus sake Yvonne come back to me, hear me, it is a cry, come back to me, Yvonne, if only for a day . . ."(p. 41), he writes in the unsent letter. As if to confirm a Christian truth, lovelessness has in the Consul's life associated itself with dying.[4]

Again Christ is evoked in the only moment in the novel when Geoffrey, without his dark glasses on, trembling and sweating, seems genuinely willing to forego his drunken infernal paradise and start a new life with Yvonne. "Let's for Jesus Christ's sweet sake get away. A thousand, a million times away, Yvonne, anywhere, so long as it's away [. . .] Away from all this. Christ, from this" (p. 277). In Christian terms Christ represents the new creation achieved through love: ". . . the reality in which the separated is united. . . . He represents and mediates the power of the New Being because he represents and mediates the power of an undisrupted union."[5] Despite the abyss that divides them, Yvonne and Geoffrey cannot help feeling that their separation is an absurdity. For in some fundamental way their love exists: it has only turned away from its true path. Confined within their souls, it has retained its spiritual strength, its intensity, and its power of renewal. It is a destiny, a calling they have wilfully neglected. "And yet", asks the Consul, "do we not owe it to ourselves, to that self we created, apart from us, to try again? Alas, what has happened to the love and understanding we once had! What is going to happen to it– what is going to happen to our hearts?" (p. 40). Yvonne, too, is unwilling to relinquish the hidden potential of their love:

I cannot, I will not believe that you have ceased to love me, have forgotten me. Or can it be that you have some misguided idea that I am better off without you, that you are sacrificing yourself that I may find happiness with someone else? Darling, sweetheart, don't you realize that is impossible? We can give each other so much more than most people can, we can marry again, we can build forward . . ." (p. 366)

The affirmations of love expressed by Yvonne and Geoffrey and their awareness of its transcendental value appear, as we can see, in a "mythical glow". They evoke not only Christian but also Cabbalistic overtones.

I suggested in the previous chapter that Geoffrey's rejection of life has grown out of his search for eternity; that his estrangement from the world is bound up with an act of betrayal symbolized by the misuse of mystical powers, represented by drinking, and evoked by the myth of the black magician. The myth, moreover, was seen to be governed by the archetype of man's fall, in so far as the betrayal of the mysteries implies a failed attempt to reach divinity

---

[4] Cf. I John 3:9—18.

[5] Paul Tillich, *The Boundaries of Our Being* (London: Collins, 1973), p. 168; cf. also Dietrich Bonhoeffer, *Ethics* (London: SCM Press Ltd., 1955), chapter "Love", pp. 32—37.

and a subsequent disruption of the essential unity with God. This cosmic cleavage is, as we saw, particularly emphasized in the Cabbala. We might now add that Adam's sin not only destroys the communion with God but it causes the exile of the Divine Presence, the *Shekhinah*, that is, it effects the separation of the masculine and feminine principles in God.[6] The *Shekhinah*, "driven out of the Garden of Eden with Adam, like a wife sent away by her husband",[7] will have been fully reunited to God when the task of redemption is completed. Meanwhile one of the ways to redeem man's fall, the primal betrayal of divine powers, leads through a union of man and woman. For the Cabbalists "every true marriage is a symbolical realization of the union of God and the *Shekhinah*."[8] Not a concession to the weakness of the body but one of the most sacred mysteries, marriage can bring about a unity of man.[9] Although aware of the unity that their marriage implies, Yvonne and Geoffrey are in actual fact very far from it.

Divorced and despite all their efforts incapable of reunion, they are, to borrow a Zoharic phrase, "divided in two". "Without you I am cast out, severed. I am an outcast from myself, a shadow—" (p. 364), writes Yvonne. "Nothing can ever take the place of the unity we once knew", admits the Consul (p. 40), just as he admits the necessity of love for his own survival:

I have been deliberately struggling against my love for you. I dared not submit to it. I have grasped at every root and branch which would help me across this abyss in my life by myself but I can deceive myself no longer. If I am to survive I need your help. Otherwise, sooner or later, I shall fall. (p. 38)

The separation from Yvonne, the Consul implies here, has opened an abyss in his life. In the Farolito he will mentally trace the "abysmal path" of the barranca to the cleft rock symbolizing the broken union with Yvonne (cf. p. 339). Not for nothing, it appears, has the abyss of the barranca been called "the frightful cleft, the eternal horror of opposites!" (p. 130). But this is certainly not the only way in which it comes to represent separation. The metaphysical gutter of

[6] See Scholem, *On the Kabbalah and Its Symbolism*, p. 108; see also Waite, *Secret Doctrine,* chapter XVI.

[7] Waite, p. 204.

[8] Scholem, *Major Trends in Jewish Mysticism,* p. 235.

[9] See ibid., p. 235. See also Scholem, ed., *Zohar: The Book of Splendor* (New York: Schocken Books, 1963), pp. 115—16: "When is 'one' said of a man? When he is male together with female and is highly sanctified and zealous for sanctification . . . Hence a man and his wife should have a single inclination at the hour of their union, and the man should be glad with his wife, attaching her to himself in affection. So conjoined, they make one soul and one body... whereas, and this we have learned, if a man is not wedded, he is, we may say, divided in two."

Under the Volcano is capable of absorbing almost every motif, of associating with almost every image, and in a variety of ways. "Darkness of the sundering" was an image belonging to the dialectics of light. Transposed, it can be just as well discovered in the barranca: "It was dark to see the bottom, but: here was finality indeed, and cleavage!" (p. 15).

The cleavage between Yvonne and Geoffrey is sharply marked by the fact that their letters are doomed to miss each other. Their desperate messages, their dramatic pleas for help, their confessions and affirmations of love eternally enduring but gone astray, are divided by an abyss of space and time. The Consul's letter to Yvonne, written five months after she has left him and some six months before the action of the novel begins, never posted and abandoned in a book of Elizabethan plays, is quite by chance discovered by Laurelle precisely a year after the tragic Day of the Dead. Yvonne's letters, posted and delivered but apparently lost and forgotten, are accidentally restored to the Consul only at his point of no return in the Farolito. Here, Yvonne's hopeful words prove powerless. As a matter of fact, they have been powerless ever since the Consul received the letters for, apparently more in love with his own misery than anything else, he has never really wanted to read them. Too painful and heartbreaking, they came too late to break the spell of his despair:

Alas, but why have I not pretended at least that I had read them, accepted some meed of retraction in the fact that they were sent? And why did I not send a telegram or some word immediately? Ah, why not, why not, why not? For I suppose you would have come back in due course if I had asked you. But this is what it is to live in hell. I could not, cannot ask you. I could not, cannot send a telegram. I have stood here, and in Mexico City, in the Compãnia Telegráfica Mexicana, and in Oaxaca, trembling and sweltering in the post office and writing telegrams all afternoon, when I had drunk enough to steady my hand, without having sent one. (pp. 38–39)

Geoffrey's paralysis of will, his physical and spiritual impotence, stand in the way of breaking the barrier of estrangement with Yvonne. The act of love becomes incapable of fulfilment because, despite the hopes for "one shared instant beautiful as trumpets out of a clear sky" (p. 89), it has not been really wanted, and because it is overshadowed by the Consul's greater yearning for a drink:

But he could feel now, too, trying the prelude, the preparatory nostalgic phrases on his wife's senses, the image of his possession [. . .] fading, and slowly, inexorably, that of a cantina, when in dead silence and peace it first opens in the morning, taking its place [. . .] But now, now he wanted to go, passionately he wanted to go, aware that the peace of the cantina was changing to its first fevered preoccupation of the morning . . . (p. 89–90)

Overwhelmed by the image of the cantina, the Consul eventually breaks the prelude and with "Sorry, it isn't any good I'm afraid" (90) rushes out of the room. Outside he grabs a bottle of whisky and drinks fiercely from it, without, however, forgetting the antidote supplied on doctor's prescription by the well-meaning Hugh. The strychnine, the Consul consoles himself, is an aphrodisiac which might take immediate effect.[10] Indeed, soon afterwards he grips the whisky bottle murmuring "I love you" (91). Meanwhile Yvonne is crying behind in the room. Presently one of the familiars breaks into Geoffrey's thoughts pointing out that Yvonne is weeping not merely because of what has just happened but because he has never cared to answer her letters. Absent-mindedly he takes another sip of whisky and immediately becomes faced with a hallucination of a dead man with a large sombrero over his head: clearly a foreshadowing of the Indian dying by the roadside. With the apparition gone, the Consul experiences an upsurge of self-confidence. Convinced that he will soon sober up, he persuades himself that his impotence is only a sign of fidelity and that his inability to rush and get drunk in the Bella Vista bar (caused, in fact, by his no longer having a car) proves his loyalty to Yvonne. Besides, alcohol is both a food and an aphrodisiac, he argues with himself. No, the Consul is not escaping from anything. He is staying at home and drinking in order to be better able to, as he puts it, "perform his marital duties" (p. 92). After all, "The will of man is unconquerable. Even God cannot conquer it", he tells himself (p. 93). On the pure horizon appear the two mountains, Ixtaccihuatl and Popocatepetl, the two legendary lovers, the image of the perfect marriage. Soon after, they are succeeded by joyous clouds telling Geoffrey that to live is to drink, and then by hovering vultures faintly redolent of the floating wisps of ashes from the Consul's burnt letter, his great confession of love. Thus his hopes and the image of an ideal slowly melt away. As if in ironic conclusion to Geoffrey's spurious self-confidence, the chapter ends here with an alcoholic blackout: "The shadow of an immense weariness stole over him . . . The Consul fell asleep with a crash" (p. 93).

There are many more similar situations in *Under the Volcano*. In spite of his intense suffering, Geoffrey is never able to carry into effect his impulse to reunite with Yvonne. His love seems too deeply hidden to be even expressed. "Haven't you got any tenderness or love left for me at all", suddenly asks Yvonne, and the Consul, unable to react spontaneously, at first merely thinks his painfully entangled answer: "Yes, I do love you, I have all the love in the world left for you, only that love seems so far away from me and so strange too, for it is as though I could almost hear it, a droning or a weeping, but far, far away, and a sad lost sound, it might be either approaching or receding, I can't tell which" (p. 197).

---

[10] Strychnine is used chiefly as an antidote for poisoning by depressant drugs because of its stimulating effect on the central nervous system, and to increase appetite.

The Consul's love has been banished and replaced by drinking which has dominated his life. The image of "the sweet beginnings" (p. 39) of their marriage in Granada gives way to a vision of the falling tower, the imaginary Babel composed of glasses and bottles. Later in the same chapter (Chapter Ten) Yvonne's eyes no longer evoke Granada to the Consul. Its place will be taken by Tlaxcala, a town of infinite drinking and a symbol of betrayal, false eternity and death. Their marriage, too much of a triumph at the beginning, has soon become impossible to bear. Too precious to lose, perhaps too formidable a gift, it has turned into its own foreboding that it could not last, a foreboding leading the Consul through all the cantinas and the Farolito to "a place where even love could not penetrate" (p. 201). And yet Geoffrey is all the time drawn to his inferno not because of its lovelessness but, on the contrary, because the prospect of going there fills him with an almost healing love (cf. p. 200). Indeed, his longing is sometimes as great as that of the mariner who after a long voyage waits to embrace his wife (cf. p. 201). His yearning for the "healing love" can be fulfilled only in the inferno of the Farolito, even though, as we shall presently see, in an inverted demonic way.

While reading Yvonne's letters for the first time in the Farolito, the Consul realizes for a moment that everything is not yet lost, that perhaps it is not too late to begin again. Her words seem to bring a hopeful message. "If we could rise from our misery", she writes, "seek each other once more, and find again the solace of each other's lips and eyes. Who is to stand between? Who can prevent?" (p. 346). As if suddenly struck by the open possibility lying before him, the Consul leaves the letter, falling into an expectant reverie. "Who indeed was to stand between? [. . .] Who indeed, even now, was to stand between? he thought desperately. Who indeed even now could prevent? He wanted Yvonne at this moment, to take her in his arms, wanted more than ever before to be forgiven, and to forgive: but where should he go? Where would he find her now?" (p. 347). On the one hand Geoffrey knows very well that his love could be recovered only outside the infernal cantina, and on the other he does not want to leave the Farolito: "He was safe here; this was the place he loved—sanctuary, the paradise of his despair" (p. 338). Hence his wavering: "miserably he wanted Yvonne and did not want her" (p. 347). His rising hopes and his desire are soon fulfilled but because of the indecision which firmly holds him within the infernal realm of the Farolito, instead of Yvonne a prostitute offers herself. The Consul, powerless to refuse, led by "the constricted power of aching flesh alone, of pathetic trembling yet brutal lust" (p. 347), accepts the services of the prostitute who draws him into an ultimate act of rejection. For a while she curiously resembles Yvonne but the illusion is short-lived. Geoffrey soon discovers that "her body was nothing, an abstraction merely [. . .] it was disaster, it was the horror of waking up in the morning in Oaxaca" (p. 349).

98

Oaxaca, already mentioned in relation to thirst and indicated as the symbol of the sundering between Geoffrey and Yvonne, is at the same time a place where they have found each other, where they have been happy. Recalling Oaxaca soon after she has met the Consul for the first time since their separation, Yvonne remembers the cries of love at night "rising into the ancient fragrant Mayan air, heard only by ghosts" (p. 49). But the recollection of their love leads her back to the present reality of the divorce: "it was as though their love were wandering over some desolate cactus plain, far from here, lost, stumbling and falling, attacked by wild beasts, calling for help—dying" (p. 49). Like Parián, Oaxaca used to have a huge monastery and, like Parián, it boasts a sorrowful and evil cantina with a telling name. El Infierno, associated firmly in the Consul's mind with the Farolito, is likewise a refuge, an ultimate goal of his escape. In his dramatic inner monologue which accompanies the counterfeit act of love with the prostitute, the theme of escape, as though gathering force and resounding througout the novel, reaches its culmination.

The girl's body, as we have seen, is identified with "the horror of waking up in the morning in Oaxaca" (p. 349) where the Consul, suffering and newly separated from Yvonne, has gone, searching perhaps for some traces of their happiness, or perhaps pretending to himself that she was still there. But in their old hotel room he finds only "horrors portioned to a giant nerve" (p. 36). At night, yearning for a drink, he is overwhelmed by a desire to escape to El Infierno. Just as he cannot face the light turned into tormenting darkness, the love become horror is too much of a burden for him. Hence the flight to the infernal cantinas which offer the alcoholic peace of lovelessness. For alcohol, as we remember, while opening the gates of eternity, provides release from earthly concerns. Yet the eternity he finds in the Farolito is too much like an action infinitely suspended by a paralysed will. Eternally, powerlessly, the calendar is saying their wedding anniversary, just as powerless has been Yvonne's invocation of their anniversary in her letters. Having run away to the Farolito, the Consul has no power to reject the succubus, despite the pleas for love found in Yvonne's forgotten letters. Lying with the Mexican girl he realizes that he has already reached a calamity, an ultimate point of his life: "[. . .] how alike are the groans of love to those of the dying, how alike, those of love, to those of the dying" (p. 349). The acute awareness of the calamity is accompanied by the reminiscences of Oaxaca: the desperate escape from the haunting memories of happy love to El Infierno, almost obsessively compared and juxtaposed with the Farolito. Thus escape becomes a thematic correlative of the intercourse with the prostitute.

The sordid adventure releases in Geoffrey's consciousness a whirl of thoughts centred round escape. We can suppose that, like the mysterious inscription on Faustus' arm ("Homo fuge!", v, 77), they warn him against the imminent danger of damnation and threaten with despair. But at the same time they pulsate with the essential rythm of his whole life, as though bringing home to him that he has run away from love and human relations. Inexorably they convey a sense of what is happening at this very moment; they remind the Consul that, through the act of betrayal with the prostitute, he is ultimately completing his escape and terminating the wayward course of his life. His delirious monologue ends with a dramatic confession of bad faith as well as a premonition of death awaiting him after the final transgression. Having successfully escaped to El Infierno, the Consul finds himself

talking to beggars, the early workers, the dirty prostitutes, the pimps, the debris and detritus of the streets and the bottom of the earth, but who were yet so much higher than he, drinking just as he had drunk here in the Farolito, and telling lies, lying—the escape, still the escape!—until the lilac-shaded dawn that should have brought death, and he should have died now too; what have I done? (p. 351)

Let us recapitulate: the Consul escapes from his love for Yvonne and from the horrors into which this love, betrayed and unfulfilled, has turned. By the same token he escapes from his better self and from the threat of conscience. He flees also from time, from the clock striking the fatal hour for Faustus, into the ecstasies of alcoholic eternity but these only increase and intensify his estrangement, all too often causing such suffering that he has to run still further away. Thus from the horrors that have already become infernal he escapes into the loveless paradise of El Infierno and the Farolito. Then, escaping the consequences of his escape, he lets himself be drawn into the adventure with the prostitute. He ignores the warnings of his consciousness, thus foregoing a possible chance to avoid the ultimate rift, and escapes still deeper, as if fulfilling his fundamental denial of life. Soon after, his life will end with a flight into the abyss of the barranca.

It is clear that Geoffrey's evasion of life, bound up with his drinking and search for eternity, has been mainly responsible for the severance from Yvonne. But it would be misleading to suppose that their love has been squandered and brought to ruin without Yvonne contributing to the tragedy. After all she has betrayed him both with Laruelle and Hugh even though the Consul—through his own faults—might have indirectly caused it (cf. p. 78). It is true on the other hand that, despite the breach and despite the anguish of separation, Yvonne has not been able to stop loving him:

How many times in the misery of the last year had Yvonne not tried to free herself of her love for Geoffrey by rationalizing it away, by analyzing it away, by telling herself—Christ, after she'd waited, and written, at first hopefully, with all her heart, then urgently, frantically, at last despairingly, waited and watched every day for the letter—ah, that daily crucifixion of the post! (p. 259)

It is also true that Yvonne returns to Quauhnahuac quite spontaneously, led by her love for the Consul, by a desire to end the absurdity of their separation, finally, to save him. But already into her innocent appearance Lowry weaves a dark warning: a foreshadowing, in fact, of the novel's final tragic act in the Farolito. "Suprise party. I've come back ... My plane got in an hour ago", are Yvonne's first words to the Consul. "—when Alabama comes through we ask nobody any questions", unwittingly echoes a voice from the other side of the glass partition in the bar where Geoffrey and Yvonne meet (p. 47). The voice will return in the last chapter, and we shall then recognize it as belonging to the ammunition smuggler by the name of Weber: a fascist and a member of the Foreign Legion, a man who could probably have saved the Consul had he been sober enough to will it. And so Yvonne's coming stands in the shadow of destructive forces represented by a man whose destination is Parián, a fascist by conviction whose voice insinuates itself through juxtaposition into her annunciation of return and the hopes of a reunion.[11]

Besides the ominous adumbrations carried by Weber's voice, the scene of Yvonne's arrival reveals her essential weakness which casts a doubt on her efforts to restore the lost unity with Geoffrey. Unable to acknowledge her own guilt and the extent of his downfall, she refuses to face the negative side of their fate. Despite her determination to drink with Geoffrey, to accompany him on his downward alcoholic path, Yvonne cannot bring herself to touch a drink. This does not make it any easier for the Consul who feels misunderstood and rejected. Yvonne, moreover, seems to demand that Geoffrey should immediately stop drinking, feeling that this alone could still save their ruined marriage. Yet this is precisely what a person who has been so dependent on alcohol cannot do. There is no question of the Consul simply beginning a new, sober, sane, and pure life. Yvonne, however, impatient to renew their happiness and afraid to assume the hardships of a more thoroughgoing sacrifice, will not accept Geoffrey until he mends his ways. The reality of guilt and evil is just as loathsome to her as it is to the Consul (see p. 207). She truly longs to be with him but away from the disturbing traces of her betrayal and apart from the unbearable reality of drinking. Loving the Consul deeply she seems incapable of helping him genuinely for, like him, she is basically unwilling to redeem their misery. Instead she prefers to escape into her beautiful dreams of a new life together. I shall have more to say on the character of Yvonne, her weakness and her fundamental lack of faith, when discussing the theme of salvation in chapter 7. Let us for the time being consider love in its aspect of *agape,* that is to say, love as help, compassion, or forgiveness.

---

[11] Cf. D. Edmonds, *"Under the Volcano:* A Reading of the 'Immediate Level'", *Tulane Studies in English,* 16, (1968), 82.

One of the greatest obstacles on the way to reunion is Geoffrey's inability to forgive. "We're together again, it's *us*. Can't you see that? ", asks Yvonne. "Yes, I can see", answers the Consul. "Only he couldn't see [. . .] I do love you", he assures Yvonne. "Only—I can never forgive you deeply enough", he adds voicelessly to himself (p. 197). For in a curious way he is sustained by Yvonne's guilt and his own sufferings on which his soul seems to thrive. As we shall see more fully in chapter 8, the Consul often deliberately seeks pain and misery, not, however, in order to take upon himself the sufferings of the world on a redemptive journey to the underworld but through an obsessive preoccupation with guilt and an inability to free himself from the grip of the past. Imprisoned in his own wretchedness, he lacks the power to forgive and cannot help feeling hatred when confronted with recollections of his suffering, caused by Yvonne's betrayal with Laruelle. Under the Frenchman's pillow he secretly places the belated postcard: a sign of love and a proof of the senselessness of their separation and his sufferings. Far from being able to redeem the past—"and conscience has been given man to regret it only in so far as that might change the future" (p. 108)—the Consul experiences a fit of anger at the thought of Laurelle sleeping with Yvonne.

Nor is he able to forgive Hugh. He announces his good will and readiness to forgive but the words never reach his half-brother. The Consul—who in search of a drink has guiltily escaped from home where Yvonne has just returned—is only in a drunken reverie, lying face downwards on a deserted street, enacting his imaginary conversation with Hugh. And the willingness to make amends is overshadowed by Geoffrey's harping on Hugh's guilt and by implying, in fact, that merely because of his own conscience Hugh is going to suffer horribly in any case. Moreover, the Consul's readiness to forgive is based on admission of his own guilt and not on an act of reconciliation and acceptance. In other words, there is no question of changing the future since the magical circle of the past has not been broken. The same holds true of Yvonne whose preoccupation with the future is so overpowering that she deliberately avoids facing the past. Unable to accept Geoffrey as he is, she often appears to him merely as the accuser exhorting him to stop drinking. She undermines thus the confidence to rebuild and plunges the Consul back into his despairing loneliness.

Despite the overriding awareness of guilt and injury, resulting in a desire to hurt, Geoffrey realizes that "forgiveness alone could save the day" (p. 198). Just like love, forgiveness is in *Under the Volcano* affirmed through the contrast between an acute sense of its absence and scattered premonitions of its essential value. It is called a miracle, something fantastic and unimaginable for which no logical explanation can be found. Hugh's life, which has already seemed to him irretrievably lost, is suddenly saved through a sheer act of forgiveness. Hence forgiveness becomes here coloured by the idea of rescue.

The connection is further strengthened by the fact that Hugh's recollection of the miraculous event is suddenly interrupted by Geoffrey's call for help (cf. p. 173). A measure of identification between forgiveness and help is thus achieved, suggesting at the same time the Christian aspect of love in relations between people.

Christian love, however, finds no fulfilment in the world of *Under the Volcano*. It either appears on a merely superficial level, or, denied, turns into its own opposite. Actually, the Consul's sense of guilt springs chiefly from a failure to act compassionately towards foes. During the First World War some German officers, taken prisoners of war, were burned alive in the furnaces of the ship commanded by the Consul. We do not know exactly how it happened: Geoffrey may not have been directly involved in this act of cruelty but, naturally, he was held responsible for what happened under his command. On returning to England he was court-martialled and—probably because of lack of concrete evidence—acquitted. And yet it was easy to regard the Consul, Jaques Laruelle thinks, "as a kind of more lachrymose pseudo 'Lord Jim' living in a self-imposed exile, brooding [. . .] over his lost honour, his secret, and imagining that a stigma would cling to him because of it throughout his whole life" (p. 33). Sometimes the Consul went even so far as to maintain his sole responsibility for the deed. But this, according to Laurelle, was a "quixotic oral fiction" (ib.), a pretext to drown the guilt in yet another bottle of mescal.

Be that as it may, the extent of Geoffrey's involvement in the inhuman act seems irrelevant for the novel's symbolic ends. True, it may seem somewhat incongruous that such a concrete, almost "sensational" piece of plot should be so loose and indeterminate but a realistic, tightly-knit design would make it perhaps more difficult for more universal and mythical significances to emerge. Indistinct as they are, Geoffrey's transgression and guilt assume fairly general, even archetypal overtones, especially by virtue of their connections with the themes of love and estrangement. Hence the act of burning the German prisoners of war may be regarded as a paradigmatic offence against humanity, on a par with the betrayal of the Mysteries. As we have seen, the mystical transgression, discussed in the previous chapter, entails a disruption of the union with God. Its analogue, the betrayal of the brotherhood of man, breaks the union both in the sphere of *Agape* and *Eros*. Associated with the Consul's primal guilt from the war time, it leads to lovelessness: to his estrangement from his fellow human beings as well as from the woman he deeply loves.

Mythologically, estrangement and alienation are in Western culture symbolized by man's exile from paradise following his first transgression.[12] Accord-

---

[12] See Ricoeur, *The Symbolism of Evil*, p. 18.

ing to the Cabbala, Adam becomes through his sin alienated from God and condemns to exile not only himself but the Divine Presence, the transcendent feminine principle. On a different plane the Consul seems to be following in Adam's footsteps. He banishes his wife (in her letters Yvonne speaks of being „sent away" by Geoffrey, p. 365) and in a sense exiles himself from the world; all because his attempt to become god-like, his search for eternity, pushes him into ever more profound personal isolation. By betraying divine powers he betrays human unity at the same time. Therefore the primal guilt focused in the incident of murdering the enemy may be taken as a correlative of the mystical transgression, for it both epitomizes estrangement and leads to exile. After the court-martial the Consul never returns to England. His diplomatic job being merely a retreat, Geoffrey has been descending into ever more remote consulships, "and finally into the sinecure in Quauhnahuac as a position where he was least likely to prove a nuisance to the Empire" (p. 31). Anticipating our discussion of the garden symbol in the next chapter, we may mention that in the Cabbala exile is compared to a "garden that has been abandoned by its gardener so that weeds have sprung all over it",[13] a description which strikingly fits the Consul's own neglected garden.

What adds special poignancy to Geoffrey's guilt and subsequent exile is both the character and the name of the ship on which the Germans were burned. The s.s. *Samaritan* was a Q-boat, that is to say, a man-of-war camouflaged as a freighter. Everything about the ship was a ruse. So innocently did she look and behave that on encountering a German submarine she simply hove to. "An unarmed merchantman, the *Samaritan* put up no fight", Laurelle relates the incident. "Before the boarding party from the submarine reached her, however, she suddenly changed her temper. As if by magic the sheep turned to a dragon belching fire. The U-boat did not even have time to dive. Her entire crew was captured" (p. 32). And the merciless treatment of the German officers has given the lie to the Biblical name of the British ship.

The ideal of the Good Samaritan is most emphatically denied in Chapter Eight which describes the bus trip to Tomalín. The trip, which to Hugh seems "the best of all possible ideas" (p. 236), starts in a good, cheerful atmosphere. A more or less ordinary and innocent distraction, this trip to see a bullthrowing appears to lend a certain, at least external, cohesion to the entangled relations between the protagonists. It seems to lead away from the great problems of the day: from Geoffrey's drinking, Yvonne's painful and so far failed efforts to restore their broken unity, Hugh's loss of spiritual bearings in the world, and the consciousness of betrayal which they all somehow share. The cheerful driver of

<hr>

[13] Scholem, "Kabbalah", an article in *Encyclopaedia Judaica* (Jerusalem, 1971), X, p. 619.

the bus carries two beautiful white pigeons, "little secret ambassadors of peace, of love" (p. 232). The bus, which belongs to the *Cooperación de la Cruz Roja,* seems so safe that one could easily transfer one's responsibilities to it (p. 240). It carries an atmosphere of the gaiety of the fiesta in which everybody participates on that day.

But the occasion is, as we remember, the Day of the Dead, and the Mexicans' joy is mixed with terror.[14] Likewise, the cheerfulness of the trip is from the beginning mixed with evil omens: the poster of *Las Manos de Orlac,* the undertakers' office with a sign inquiring "Quo Vadis", the clownish devil in the garden, a dead dog at the bottom of the barranca, the marks of volcanic eruptions, a burned church. All this suggests that the disaster, always present in the world of *Under the Volcano,* has only been lulled to sleep on the bus. Even Hugh, who in a superficially optimistic and somewhat fatuous way wants everybody to be happy, realizes dimly that "the naked realities of the situation, like the spokes of a wheel, were blurred in motion toward unreal high events" (p. 236).

And the "unreal high events" soon become fact. The bus comes to a crossroads where a man, his face covered by a wide sombrero, is lying on his back with his arms stretched towards a wayside cross. Nearby a horse, with number seven branded on its rump, is cropping the hedge. Soon it turns out that the man, unconscious and breathing heavily, has been cruelly wounded in the head. No doubt he needs help in order to survive. But this is precisely what cannot be given under the circumstances. Protected by the law the man cannot be touched; for naturally everyone is afraid of becoming an accessory after the fact. And so instead of actively helping, the passengers, who have got out of the bus to see what has happened, get involved in a long discussion about the likely causes of the incident and the possible ways of saving the man:

Was it robbery, attempted murder, or both? The Indian had probably ridden from market, where he'd sold his wares, with much more than that four or five pesos hidden by the hat, with mucho dinero, so that a good way to avoid suspicion of theft was to leave a little of the money, as had been done. Perhaps it wasn't robbery at all, he had only been thrown from his horse? Posseebly. Imposseebly.

Si, hombre, but hadn't the police been called? But clearly somebody was already going for help. Chingar. One of them now should go for help, for the police. An ambulance—the Cruz Roja—where was the nearest phone? (pp. 244–45)

Nobody daring to act, the discussion becomes more and more futile. These people have apparently realized that to help the Indian is in any case someone else's concern. "It is not my business, but, as it were, yours, they all said, as they shook their heads, and no, not yours either, but someone else's, their ob-

---

[14] Cf. Octavio Paz, *The Labyrinth of Solitude* (London: Allen Lane, 1967), p. 53.

jections becoming more and more involved, more and more theoretical, till at last the discussion began to take a political turn" (pp. 245—46). Finally the case is declared hopeless and the bus is about to leave. Neither the Consul nor Hugh have been capable of doing anything. Yvonne, unable to stand the sight of blood, has not even seen the Indian. Two expensive cars with the sign "Diplomático" have surged quickly past, despite Hugh's attempts to stop them.

The whole world seems to turn away from the wounded Indian dying by the roadside. Ironically enough, the only people to remain with him are the "vigilante hombres", the fascist policemen who finally arrive on the scene. And so the place of the Good Samaritan is assumed by the very people who, as we shall learn later in the book, have been involved in the robbery: the "thieves, which stripped him of his raiment, and wounded him, and departed, leaving him half dead" (Luke 10:30). Later in the Farolito the Consul will discover the man's horse, already in the possession of one of the Unión Militar chiefs. The sight of the horse, this obvious evidence of guilt, will suddenly make the Consul aware of what has actually happened that afternoon. But as usual with him, awareness of truth, however acute, does not lead anywhere. Moreover, the insight into the evil scheming of the Unión Militar people will prove not only ineffective but, through a strange fate, destructive. Released by Geoffrey in a desperate attempt to do something good, the stolen horse, scared by the raging storm, plunges into the dark forest where it will kill Yvonne who has almost completed her search for the Consul. Hence her death is an indirect result of the failure to show compassion to the Indian; had he been helped, the horse probably would not have fallen into the hands of the fascists.[15]

Lowry's version of the story of the Good Samaritan signifies more than a failure to help a man abandoned by the roadside. In a sense the Indian is a symbol of a new life, of joy, of goodness. Encountering him for the first time earlier on, in town, riding gaily and singing, the Consul is seized by a curious nostalgia. "Ah, to have a horse, and gallop away, singing to someone you loved perhaps, into the heart of all the simplicity and peace in the world" (p. 213). It is also suggested that the Indian might have been a bank messenger of the *Banco Ejidal* which finances collective effort in the countryside (cf. 297). If so, he might have been attacked and robbed not for the money alone but as a representative of Cardenas' land reforms which aimed at improving the lot of the poorest. In this case his death would mean the victory of the dark forces over what Lowry calls "a human cause" (p. 107).

[15] Cf. D. Markson, "Malcolm Lowry: A Study of Theme and Symbol in *Under the Volcano*", (M. A. Thesis: Columbia Univ., 1952) p. 85.

That the dark forces are gaining the upper hand is also conveyed by the fact that the Indian is robbed twice, first of the saddle bags in which he might have carried the bank's money and then—still without anybody protesting—of the handful of silver pesos and centavos that have been left by his head. The second petty robbery is shamelessly carried out by one of the bus passengers, a man earlier on referred to by the Consul as a "pelado". "Pelado", a term of abuse, is a word, according to the Consul, "that had actually been distilled out of conquest, suggesting as it did, on the one hand thief, on the other exploiter" (p. 235). And the description fits the man. An exploiter and a petty thief at the same time, his person presents a sad picture of ruin and degeneration, except for the huge rapacious hands, the hands of the conquistador. The times having changed, this contemporary incarnation of the conquerors is said to have some connections with the local fascists. Characteristically for Lowry's sense of irony, the man who will so unscrupulously rob the Indian of the little blood-smeared pile of money, appears on the scene together with an evocation of the love of loves. El Amor de los Amores is the name of the fascist joint out of which we see him coming just before he boards the bus to Tomalín. At the end of the journey, when the bus has reached its destination, the pelado, a fatuous smile on his face, will disappear into another cantina, this time appropriately called Todos Contentos y Yo También: "everybody happy including me" (p. 253). The name of the cantina and the suggestion that the pelado is probably going to make some kind of a deal and share the stolen money with the bus driver seem to provide an ironic comment on the common acceptance of the theft that has been committed; an acceptance certainly not without connection with the general agreement to leave a man dying by the roadside. "It was a recognized thing, like Abyssinia", remarks Hugh to himself (p. 252). Without in the least trying to hide the Indian's money the pelado is almost boasting of his exploit. He knows only too well that nobody will do anything, nobody will move, just as nobody has tried to help the wounded man. For under the circumstances the only firm conviction the other passengers could act upon expresses itself in an attitude of resigned prudence: "it is better to stay where you are [. . .] They weren't sure of anything save that it was foolish to get mixed up with the police, especially if they weren't proper police" (p. 249). In other words, fear of the police paralyses these people into complete inability to aid one's neighbour.

This is the development of the theme of impotence, transferred here from the strictly personal to the generally ethical plane; from the sphere of *Eros* to that of *Agape*. In Lowry's world impotence, so often manifested in an inability to help, seems to reign supreme. In a sense everyone is left alone: the Indian, the Consul, republican Spain losing to Franco's forces, abandoned by European nations (cf. p. 153). All have their Good Samaritans but the Samaritans, themselves insecure and spiritually wounded, can never truly help. Their efforts are usually half-hearted, their willingness to aid others too much bound up with selfishness and dependent on some self-deception.

Preoccupied with a better future for the world, with doing good for humanity, Hugh fails to be effectively compassionate in individual cases. Despite his efforts, he is able to help neither Geoffrey nor Yvonne, nor the man by the roadside. His enthusiasm and good will urge him to sit "on top of a shipload of dynamite bound for the hard-pressed Loyalist armies" (p. 152) but do not suffice for more prosaic, less desperate situations. Twice does Hugh betray the brotherhood of man, even though he readily admits the reality of love and with all his being yearns for brotherly relations between men. "Christ, why can't we be simple, Christ Jesus why may we not be simple, why may we not all be brothers?" (p. 240). Ironically, this "spiritual manifesto" presents itself to Hugh just before the bus comes across the wounded Indian. For despite the idealistic pronouncements, Hugh fails to be a brother to the dying man, just as he has failed to be a brother to Geoffrey, first by betraying him with Yvonne, and then by being innocently unconcerned about the extent of Geoffrey's sickness, his slow spiritual death (cf. *Letters*, p. 75). Hugh has quite energetically tried to "straighten out" the Consul but without the slightest effort to penetrate more deeply into his half-brother's dramatic perdicament. As he explains to Yvonne:

"My attitude toward Geoff was simply the one I'd take toward some brother scribe with a godawful hangover. But while I've been in Mexico City I've been saying to myself: Cui bono? What's the good? Just sobering him up for a day or two's not going to help. Good God, if our civilization were to sober up for a couple of days it'd die of remorse on the third—" (p. 117).

No wonder Hugh's apparent indifference hardly encourages Yvonne whose helplessness and inability to assist Geoffrey in a genuine way have already been touched upon. Also Jaques Laruelle attempts to do something about Geoffrey's drunkenness but he either becomes the Good Samaritan when drunk himself, or provides the Consul with the advice which, however sensible in itself, appears too harsh and too hostile to be effective.[16] And so the Consul, on a different plane and in a different sense, is as much left to his own fate as the Indian dying by the wayside cross.

There is no charity in the world of *Under the Volcano*, unless we are deceived by gestures; forgiveness is thwarted and love remains tragically unfulfilled. For this world is, as it were, contaminated with estrangement. The

---

[16] Cf. Edmonds, p. 75.

Consul, by his escape into the magical search for eternity, cuts himself off from other human beings and the world. In so far as he is Everyman, he represents humanity's attempt to deify itself by betraying divine mysteries and taking possession of unlawful magical knowledge; an attempt which surrenders human life to the powers of estrangement since it brings about a breach in some fundamental unity, plunging man deeply into separation from God, from himself, and from his fellow men. Gradually, the Consul's estrangement reaches an ultimate point as it leads him to the hell of the Farolito where he meets death at the hands of the Mexican fascists, representatives of the world's evil forces. His death is, moreover, described in such a way as to suggest a universal catastrophe involving all mankind. Adapting T. S. Eliot, we might say that the world of *Under the Volcano* "ends with a bang, not with a whimper". For despite the life-corroding spiritual aridity, this world is not devoid of a tragic greatness: its evil does not merely bring general decomposition but it destroys man, condemning him to damnation. This is mainly due to the spiritual dimension of the novel; to the fact that the hell of *Under the Volcano* would not have been possible without the heaven implied by the rare flashes of insight into the wonder of love, forgiveness and compassion; that, theologically speaking, God is not absent from Lowry's universe but hidden under his wrathful aspect, precisely because man has rejected love.[17] Nor does the devil seem to be absent from this world since the metamorphosis of good into evil that we constantly witness, the pretence that falling is ascending or that darkness is light, for example, is an unmistakably demonic feature.

As we have seen, the Farolito is a place of reversed transfiguration; a sort of alchemical crucible in which a transmutation of the noble into the base occurs. Geoffrey's love for Yvonne turns into the sordid and calamitous affair with the succubus Maria and releases a chain of events which lead up to his being shot by the Unión Militar people. The Consul, profoundly moved by the sudden recovery of Yvonne's letters, spontaneously draws a little map of Spain in the liquor spilled on the bar. Spain was where they met, where their love began, where they were happy. But for the people gathered in the Farolito, Spain arouses hostile suspicion since it merely signifies communist trouble. "You make a the map of the Spain? You Bolsheviki prick? You member of the Brigade Internationale and stir up trouble?", the Consul is asked by one of the policemen (p. 357). Finally Geoffrey will be shot as a communist, a Spanish anarchist, a Jew, and a spy. His protestations will of course be irrelevant for the blood- and power-thirsty policemen since the clue he has unwittingly given them is sufficient to condemn him. As a sign of love the invocation of Spain no

[17] Cf. P. Tillich, *Systematic Theology,* II, pp. 76—78.

longer has any benevolent power. On the contrary, this gesture born of the Consul's sudden longing for Yvonne will soon lead to the ultimate consummation of his estrangement. For in the atmosphere of the Farolito love is bound to become death. The inversion of love described in this chapter testifies to a world turned upside down by the black magic of Geoffrey's drinking, a world permeated by the quality of "infernal paradise".

Chapter 6
Life

As we have seen, the Consul's death is in a sense only an ultimate consequence of his denial of life. This fact is important for it brings to light a meaningful though tragic coherence of human life. In Lowry's universe death is not a senseless eruption of nothingness, a blind force of general disintegration, but a phenomenon endowed with moral significance. As I hope to show in the concluding chapter, the Consul's "sickness unto death" is by and large a matter of choice. In this way *Under the Volcano* is closer to the Judeo-Christian emphasis on man's freedom and responsibility than to the secular despair rooted in the modern fear of annihilation. "I have set before you life and death, blessing and cursing: therefore choose life, that both Thou and thy seed may live", says God to man in the Bible (Deut. 30:19). In *Under the Volcano* the Consul is faced with just such a choice: a choice inherent in the Mexican setting itself.

Mexico, the stage on which the action of Lowry's novel is set, is a meeting point of extremes. It is as though life and death were contending there with one another, trying to gain ascendancy in this land of paradisal beauty, where the soft exuberant nature is interspersed with the hardness of desert-like stretches. Chapter One gives us a taste of the Mexican scene whose essential mood reflects the tragedy taking place on the human plane:

The leaves of cacti attracted with their freshness; green trees shot by evening sunlight might have been weeping willows tossing in the gusty wind which had sprung up; a lake of yellow sunlight appeared in the distance below pretty hills like loaves. [. . .] How continually, how startlingly, the landscape changed! Now the fields were full of stones: there was a row of dead trees [. . .] another planet [. . .] but beautiful, there was no denying its beauty, fatal or cleansing as it happened to be, the beauty of the Earthly Paradise itself. (pp. 9—10)

In the world of *Under the Volcano* Mexico becomes the archetypal land entrusted to man; a gift as precious as love, bestowed on man and left to his powers of creation or destruction. The minor theme of the imperial couple of Maximilian and Carlotta, a foreshortened transposition of the fates of Geoffrey and Yvonne, suggests an affinity between the paradisal significance of Mexico and the meaning of love. Mexico was where destiny brought them, in

111

Mexico they were meant to find their love and happiness: "Look at this rolling glorious country, its hills, its valleys, its volcanoes beautiful beyond belief. And to think that it is ours! Let us be good and constructive and make ourselves worthy of it!" (p. 14).

Yet the gift of the earthly paradise and of love is squandered, despite the beauty of the country and despite the bonds of love. Perhaps because Maximilian and Carlotta, as well as Geoffrey and Yvonne, were already exiles, branded with estrangement? "And yet, how they must have loved this land, these two lonely empurpled exiles, human beings finally, lovers out of their element—their Eden, without either knowing quite why, beginning to turn under their noses into a prison and smell like a brewery, their only majesty at last that of tragedy" (p. 14). These words, which pass through Laruelle's mind, refer to Maximilian and Carlotta, but they could be just as well applied to Geoffrey and Yvonne. Not only are their fates similar, but the voice of Maximilian that Laruelle hears in his reverie in the Emperor's ruined palace merges imperceptibly with the Consul's voice.

In this chapter we shall see how the exuberant life forces are superseded by destruction and disintegration, how once again the paradisal gives way to the infernal. If Mexico sets the tone for the opposition of life and death, the garden theme brings into relief and emphasizes the transition from one to the other. Just like Mexico, the Consul's garden is likened to paradise, but its neglect and ruin are a more dramatic sign of man's wilful choice of death than the Mexican setting, which merely establishes his options. Symbolically, the garden is for Geoffrey and Yvonne what Mexico was for Maximilian and Carlotta: a gift of love set in the earthly paradise. Their love, as Lowry emphasizes, was born in the gardens. In Granada their way led

through the gardens, gardens, gardens everywhere, up, up, to the marvellous traceries of the Alhambra [. . .] past the well where they had met, to the América Pensión; and up, up, now they were climbing themselves, up to the Generalife Gardens, and now from the Generalife Gardens to the Moorish tomb on the extreme summit of the hill; here they plighted their troth". (p. 292)

As we see, life is here contaminated with death. The ecstatic ascent towards love, past the well and through the gardens, leads to the Moorish tomb, and the troth on the summit contains a baleful foreboding. The way from the well to the tomb is emblematic of the Consul's life, a life spent, metaphorically speaking, on a magical transmutation in which living water becomes water of death. "Thou art the grave where buried love doth live", the Consul, as we may recall, addresses his swimming pool (p. 143). To him water and vegetation have associated themselves with ruin and dying, presumably ever since he neglected the garden. His little earthly paradise has become a wreck, a picture of desolation; hardly a sign of welcome for Yvonne and Geoffrey returning home together, for the first time since their separation:

The tragedy, proclaimed, as they made their way up the crescent of the drive, no less by the gaping potholes in it than by the tall exotic plants, livid and crepuscular through his dark glasses, perishing on every hand of unnecessary thirst, staggering, it almost appeared, against one another, yet struggling like dying voluptuaries in a vision to maintain some final attitude of potency, or of a collective desolate fecundity, the Consul thought distantly, seemed to be reviewed and interpreted by a person walking at his side suffering for him and saying: "Regard: see how strange, how sad, familiar things may be. Touch this tree, once your friend: alas, that that which you have known in the blood should ever seem so strange! Look up at that niche in the wall over there on the house where Christ is still, suffering, who would help you if you asked him: you cannot ask him. Consider the agony of the roses. See, on the lawn Concepta's coffee beans, you used to say they were María's, drying in the sun. Do you know their sweet aroma any more? Regard: the plantains with their queer familiar blooms, once emblematic of life, now of an evil phallic death. You do not know how to love these things any longer. All your love is the cantinas now: the feeble survival of a love of life now turned to poison, which only is not wholly poison, and poison has become your daily food, when in the tavern—" (p. 65)

The picture of the neglected garden is in many respects symbolic of the Consul's life and epitomizes the whole novel, since it contains a number of images which belong to the different principal themes of *Under the Volcano*. Geoffrey's sunglasses recall the interplay of light and darkness and indicate the fearful escape from the reality of his life. The "unnecessary thirst" echoes the theme of drinking and the Tantalus motif, suggesting that the ruin of the garden and the tragedy of the Consul's life have not been imposed by an inevitable fate decreed by gods or demons but spring from the hero's sins of omission. "The dying voluptuaries [who try] to maintain som final attitude of potency" are reminiscent both of the Consul and of the pelado, the thief from the bus, who counteract their downfall by maintaining an upright posture. The image of the voluptuaries also touches on the Consul's impotence, the spiritual aspect of which is soon suggested by the image of the suffering Christ. Christ would bring help, if only Geoffrey asked for it. But this he cannot bring himself to do, just as he has been unable to ask Yvonne for help, knowing at the same time that she would come, if only he said a word. "But this is what it is to live in hell. I could not, cannot ask you", he tells Yvonne in the letter that he has been powerless to post (p. 38). It is the inability to act, among other things, that has caused the desolation of the garden. The traces of its former fertility and the picture of its present ruin bespeak life turned into death. And the image of biological barrenness is immediately juxtaposed with an inability to love and with a transmutation of the love of life into poison in the cantinas. Finally, poison is said to have become the Consul's daily food.

Gathering so many of the essential concerns of the novel, the polyphonic image of the ruined garden surely serves as one of the most comprehensive symbols in *Under the Volcano*. Its inclusiveness becomes still more conspicuous owing to a Cabbalistic significance suggested by Lowry in the letter to Cape and in the preface to the French edition of the novel. According to Lowry's Cabbalistic gloss, the neglected garden implies the misuse of mystical powers, identified in turn with the misuse of wine, or drunkenness (*Letters*, p. 71).[1] Thus the garden image is linked with the central mythical correlative of the Consul's downfall and ruin, the symbolic cause of the disaster depicted by the novel. But is it legitimate to resort to a meaning supplied by the author outside of the text itself?

As is clear from the letter to Albert Erskine, Lowry's editor at Reynal & Hitchock, Lowry himself intended to append *Under the Volcano* with notes "which would help to elucidate such matters in the deeper layers as that the garden can be seen not only as the world, or the Garden of Eden, but legitimately as the Cabbala itself, and that the abuse of wine (*sōd*) is identified in the Cabbala with the abuse of magical powers" (*Letters*, p. 115). In other words, Lowry thought of providing his book with a key to the esoteric and outlandish terms and phrases he had used. This implies that *Under the Volcano* has been, at least partly, written in a language that in some respects falls outside the semantic system of English, and that requires elucidation and commentary in order to be properly understood. If so, Lowry's Cabbalistic gloss appears to be no more inappropriate than a Spanish dictionary used for the elucidation of the Spanish words and phrases encoutered in the novel.

Yet the matter is not as simple as that. For the very appearance of the Spanish is a sufficiently powerful signal of a different language being used. Moreover, its conspicuous obscurity in relation to the English context immediately calls for some special linguistic aids. A similar situation occurs when the incongruity is created not by means of a different ethnic language, like Spanish, but through a semantic frame of reference proper to some specialized discourse, such as the Cabbala, Mexican mythology and the like. Such was the case of "the culmination of the Pleiades" discussed in chapter 1.

The garden image, however, presents a somewhat different problem, since it is intelligible on its own terms, that is to say, its context does not demand any external source of significance. Nevertheless, the Cabbalistic meaning suggested by Lowry perfectly corresponds to the general import of the garden, such as has been indicated above. A comprehensive symbol pertaining to the destruction of Geoffrey's life, the garden reflects the mystical transgression represented by the abuse of alcohol. In other words, the Consul's downfall,

---

[1] See also Lowry, "Preface to a Novel", p. 27. Cf. also Leo Schaya, *The Universal Meaning of the Kabbalah*, p. 18.

caused by the misuse of mystical powers, is transposed in the polyphonic image of the ruined garden. Therefore we may admit Lowry's Cabbalistic gloss into our interpretation because it both harmonizes with the garden image and enriches it with overtones otherwise present in *Under the Volcano*.

There is an additional reason for breaking the literal surface of the garden image. As we have just seen, Lowry, in the letter to Cape, identifies the garden with the Cabbala itself. No flight of fancy, the identification rests on an old and widespread Jewish tradition. In the Cabbala, and in much subsequent Hebrew literature, the whole of divine knowledge is designated by the word *pardes*, meaning both garden and paradise. Acronimically, the four consonants of the word (PaRDeS) refer to the four levels of Biblical interpretation: literal, allegorical, ethical, and mystical.[2] This fourfold interpretation of the Scriptures bears a striking resemblance to the conceptions of Christian authors, widespread during the Middle Ages, and often utilized by poets, notably Dante.[3] This is not to say that Lowry's garden is necessarily to be interpreted in that fourfold manner. But the comprehensiveness of the image, so characteristic of the multiple significances which abound in *Under the Volcano*, strongly suggests the Cabbalistic *pardes* and invites an interpretation operating on at least more than one level.

We have said that the image of the garden brings into relief the transformation of life into death. This happens already on the immediate "biological" level. Full of "spectres of neglect" (p. 129), the garden is quite obviously dying. At the same time the image points to the loss of eternal life, symbolized by man's exile from the Garden of Eden. Geoffrey's speculation on the nature of Adam's punishment, suggesting that the first man was not really banished from paradise but remained in the Garden cut off from God, gives us a significant clue (cf. pp. 133—34). Associated and compared with paradise, the Consul's garden is at the same time the place of exile, reminiscent of the Mexican Eden where Maximilian and Carlotta, "these two lonely empurpled exiles" (p. 14), have found tragedy instead of happiness, since their paradise has turned into decay.

The effect of decay and neglect is reinforced by the Consul's encounter with Mr. Quincey, the owner of a beautiful and perfectly kept garden, abutting on his own ruined and disorderly estate. Moreover, Quincey—to whom the Consul expounds his theory of Adam's expulsion—is identified with God, even though in a humourous and ironic way. One thing is clear, however. The Consul,

[2] See ibid., p. 18, and also Scholem, *On the Kabbalah and Its Symbolism*, pp. 52—53, 57, 58, 60, 61, 63.

[3] See Dorothy Sayers' Introduction to her translation of Dante's *Divine Comedy*, and note on p. 217 (Part I: Hell).

shaken by the striking contrast between the two gardens, and also perhaps by the proximity of the barranca which he has just been contemplating, is suddenly gripped by an overpowering nostalgia for home. Quincey's lovely and smooth turf reminds him of England and releases a wave of reminiscences which end with a recollection of "those mysterious submarine catchers Q-boats, fake freighters turning into turreted men-of-war at a moment's notice" (p. 131). In a word, the immaculate garden of the neighbour reminds the Consul of his own exile and leads his thoughts back to the war experiences on board the fake *Samaritan*.

Now we arrive at the comprehensive mythical level of our theme, since the main elements of the Consul's reverie display mythical overtones which have a bearing on the whole of Lowry's novel. The s.s. *Samaritan* represents a primal guilt which leads, as we saw in the previous chapter, to his exile from England, and England is associated with the garden which has many Edenic attributes. Furthermore, the Consul's guilt from the past, the cause of both his exile and his gradual downfall, is interwoven with a longing for an immaculate garden, associated with home and suggesting some primal state of existence. And so the Consul, in Chapter One identified with Adam (p. 22), appears before us as Everyman who through some momentous transgression has been banished from paradise, yet condemned to go on living in the garden, ruined and contaminated with lifelessness. Nevertheless, the Consul's fall is related not only to the Old Testament conception of original sin rooted in man's expulsion from paradise at the beginning of time. It is equally charged with an abuse of the Gospel idea of Christian love. Geoffrey falls, as I have already had occasion to indicate, in two fundamental ways. By betraying divine Mysteries through a self-seeking magic he falls away from God, and by failing to act compassionately he falls into profound estrangement from his fellow men. In *Under the Volcano* man's original guilt is thus repeated through an inability to love, through a betrayal of both *Agape* and *Eros*.

The Consul, who, as we have seen, is constantly escaping from the reality of his downfall, tries to convince himself that his garden, made only more charming by the chaotic exuberance, in fact presents a little vision of order. But the vision of order turns out to be deceptive. It holds as long as Geoffrey's secret bottle of tequila remains hidden in the garden; as long as he does not feel discovered, hemmed in by the judicious Quincey and by a mysterious public garden threatening him with an ominous sign: "You like this garden? Why is it yours? We evict those who destroy!" (p. 128). It is as though the Consul's guilt were suddenly brought to light and to judgement; as though God called to him, hidden after the trespass among the trees of the garden: "Adam, where art thou?" (Gen. 3:9). But even before the Consul becomes fully aware of the deception, the little vision of order turns into "a strangely subaqueous view of

116

the plains and the volcanoes" (p. 128). The subaqueous view implies that the plains and the volcanoes, and thus almost the whole world, have become covered by water; an image redolent of the flood and the destruction of Atlantis, considered to be by many occult authorities the Garden of Eden of the human race.[4] Regarding this strange vision "without sorrow, even with a certain ecstasy" (p. 128), the Consul lights one of his *Alas* cigarettes, repeating the word "alas" aloud mechanically. Not only does he put an ironic question mark over the vision of order but, through the word play on "alas", he indicates his inverted ascent, that is to say, his fall. Certainly not by accident is the Consul's garden said to be descending steeply toward the barranca. Ruined and neglected, it stands for his life on its downward course towards the abyss.

In the Farolito, the garden theme will assume its ultimately ironic form. One of the chiefs of the Unión Militar, a man who appears to enjoy a position of power and who is therefore most responsible for Geoffrey's death, bears the title of Jefe de Jardineros, Chief of Gardeners, or, as the Consul translates it, Chief of Gardens. Thus the Consul's paradise is in a sense transferred to the infernal regions. While his own garden is dying without a gardener, in the Farolito he encounters the chief of gardens, called, moreover, Fructuoso Sanabria, which may be translated as "fruitful well-being".[5] No wonder, the infernal cantina seems to offer fertility, bliss, salvation. At the same time the Farolito is sufficiently infernal to veil its paradisal qualities. It may entice with promises of alcoholic bliss, but it will confront the Consul with merciless accusations. Here, where most of the novel's themes and strands are gathered, he is judged not only by the three infernal chiefs but he feels accused by the awareness of having wasted his life. Faced with Yvonne's letters, the Consul for the first time becomes fully conscious of his hopeless plight, "his own fruitless selfish ruin", as he puts it (p. 345).

The "fruitless ruin", or life denied its due, comes also to expression through images of a dead child and through the barrenness of Yvonne and Geoffrey. The causes of their childlessness have been psychological. As long as Yvonne wanted to pursue her career as a film star, she could not think of having children. But "her ambitions as an actress had always been somewhat spurious: they suffered in some sense from the dislocations of the functions—she saw this—of womanhood itself" (p. 264). In other words, some element of self-deception, an attempt to escape one's potentialities, has thwarted the life forces within her. Bound up with this betrayal of motherhood and new life is Yvonne's betrayal of Geoffrey and of the new self they have created

---

[4] See Donnelly, *Atlantis*, pp. 322, 328–30.
[5] See *Biography*, p. 333.

together. Her adulterous relationship with Laruelle is juxtaposed with images of wasted potentialities and enchained life. In Jacques' room, the very scene of betrayal, the Consul's attention is drawn to a collection of stone Mayan idols resembling bulbous infants chained together, and he laughs uneasily at "all this evidence of lost wild talents, at the thought of Yvonne confronted in the aftermath of her passion by a whole row of fettered babies" (p. 199).

While the Consul reproaches Yvonne for denying him children, he is far from accepting them himself; in one scene of the book he in fact deliberately avoids them. Admittedly, these are a particular group of Mexican children playing in the square of Quauhnahuac but, as we shall presently see, certain features of the context make their appearance undoubtedly symbolic. The children want money from the somewhat eccentric Englishman whose reeling gait provides them with a peculiar entertainment. Eventually they lose sight of the Consul who runs away from them, simply because he is afraid of drawing attention to himself. He wanders aimlessly through the fair on the plaza, walking past booths, tents, and roundabouts until, spotted again by the children, he boards the Máquina Infernal, a huge loop-the-loop machine on which he will suffer unspeakably horrifying sensations. But, as he calmly admits just before boarding the monster, this is the penalty for avoiding the children. Back on earth he will encounter the children again, compassionate and helpful now, sympathizing with his plight. His attitude towards them abruptly changes. His thoughts, in a curious counterpoint with a girl's exercise-book left on a bench, wander to his own problems. "Yvonne and he should have had children, would have had children, could have had children, should have ..." (p. 223).

Ironically, this sudden longing will be answered only in the Farolito. "Oh Geoffrey, how bitterly I regret it now", confesses Yvonne in one of her letters. "Is it too late? I want your children, soon, at once, I want them. I want your life filling and stirring me. I want your happiness beneath my heart and your sorrows in my eyes and your peace in the fingers of my hand—" (p. 346). It is too late, however. The Consul reaches for one of his *Alas* cigarettes and soon after come Yvonne's hopeful words ("Who is to stand between? Who can prevent?") which immediately find demonic fulfilment in the intercourse with the prostitute. The intercourse thus closes in a dramatic way the theme of childlessness of Yvonne and Geoffrey, a theme which has often appeared almost from the beginning of the novel.

"A corpse will be transported by express!" are the Consul's first words Yvonne hears on her arrival in Quauhnahuac. As we soon learn, Geoffrey is talking about a child's corpse. Seemingly irrelevant, the theme will meander throughout the chapter with an almost obsessive insistence. But within the context of childlessness, unfulfilled love, and ruined marriage, the disconnected sentences about the little corpse become more understandable. In a way they intimate the reality which meets the returning Yvonne. Her hopes and dreams stumble on signs of inner death. Life seems arrested by the ghosts of the past, the painful, tragic and unresolved problems of their relationship and of Geoffrey's plight. It is as though the moment she wanted to begin a new life with him contained its own negation; as though it reminded her of the deliberately wasted potentialities of their love, of her own unwillingness to create with Geoffrey a new physical life.[6] On the way home they meet a child's funeral, and having passed the little cortège walk on in silence, unable to look at each other. The theme of the dead child reappears in Chapter Three, in the Consul's reminiscences of Yvonne's past. There we learn for the first time about her child from the first unsuccessful marriage, who died of meningitis at the age of six months. Yvonne's dead child is again mentioned in Chapter Nine, in which her life story is related. Later on, we are reminded of the theme by Cervantes the Tlaxcaltecan who, besides showing the Consul the History of Tlaxcala in ten volumes, produces a photograph of his child lying in a coffin. Finally the theme is transposed through the image of the moon which conveys an idea of existence frozen and suspended, of life forces resting in eternal sleep. With her fascination for astronomy, Yvonne becomes aware of lunar geography whose poetic names, juxtaposed with the moon's lifelessness, bear a message of life's unfulfilment, death and cataclysm:

Far away to the southeast the low leaning horn of moon, their pale companion of the morning, was setting finally, and she watched it—the dead child of the earth!—with a strange hungry supplication.—The Sea of Fecundity, diamond-shaped, and the Sea of Nectar, pentagonal in form, and Frascatorius with its north wall broken down, the giant west wall of Endymion, ellipitical near the Western limb; the Leibnitz mountains at the Southern Horn, and east of Proclus, the Marsh of a Dream. Hercules and Atlas stood there, in the midst of cataclysm, beyond our knowledge—(p. 323)

The interplay of life and death is also manifested in the images of the dogs and horses. In Chapter Four these animals represent paradisal innocence: they are part of a sunny, smiling landscape, teeming with exuberant growth. The mares on which Hugh and Yvonne are riding, the two accompanying foals, the affectionate white woolly dog which not only guards the horses but often runs ahead, sniffing for snakes, seem to form "a caravan, carrying, for their greater security, a little world of love with them as they rode along" (p. 107). All this creates an atmosphere of an essentially peaceful world, lovingly sustained by benevolent forces of nature. Yet this peculiar happiness is, as Hugh realizes, a deception:

it is all a bloody lie, he thought: we have fallen inevitably into it, it is as if, upon this one day in the year the dead come to life, or so one was reliably informed on the bus, this

[6] Cf. Dodson, *Malcolm Lowry*, pp. 30–31.

day of visions and miracles, by some contrariety we have been allowed for one hour a glimpse of what never was at all, of what never can be since brotherhood was betrayed, the image of our happiness, of that it would be better to think could not have been. (p. 107)

Indeed, both the dog and the horse will turn out to be images of death. The paradisal state is merely an exception. Throughout the novel the Consul is shadowed by pariah dogs, loathsome and evil-looking creatures, one of which, dead, is seen nuzzling refuse at the bottom of the ravine. Another dead dog will be thrown after the Consul's body down the barranca. Likewise the horse, so innocuous in the paradisal atmosphere of Chapter Four, will gradually gather menacing overtones, untill it actually becomes an instrument of death. As we remember, the Consul's interest in the Indian's horse, taken to the Farolito by the "vigilante hombres", arouses suspicion and indirectly leads to his death and to Yvonne being trampled by the panic-stricken animal. But while the dog and the horse illustrate the transition from life to death, destruction is in a much more unequivocal manner represented by the image of the scorpion.

The scorpion appears for the first time in *Under the Volcano* amidst emblems of desolation in the ruined palace of Maximilian and Carlotta, whose love has not been able to nourish itself on the paradisal Mexican surroundings. A year after the Consul's death, when Laruelle visits the palace, the air of a bygone splendour, which used to pervade it, seems to have gone:

The broken pink pillars, in the half-light, might have been waiting to fall down on him: the pool, covered with green scum, its steps torn away and hanging by one rotting clamp, to close over his head. The shattered evil-smelling chapel, overgrown with weeds, the crumbling walls, splashed with urine, on which scorpions lurked—wrecked entablature, sad archivolt, slippery stones covered with excreta—this place, where love had once brooded, seemed part of a nightmare. (p. 14)

As we can see, this image of havoc also reflects the Consul's fate; his life and marriage mindlessly and wilfully destroyed. It is not surprising therefore that the scorpion motif should be woven into an image of guilt and remorse for these, unable to break the influence of the past and change the future, have a destructive suicidal effect on Geoffrey's life. Hence the animal that stings itself to death appears among a swarm of insects, the little biting creatures which in the novel represent remorse, and by which the Consul feels mortally threatened (cf. pp. 148—49, 218). To counteract the threat he has to drink, for alcohol is the best medicine under the circumstances, and if alcohol is not within reach, bay rum (a kind of after-shave lotion) is just as effective. "A charm against galloping cockroaches anyway", the Consul assures the astonished Hugh. "And the polygonous proustian stare of imaginary scorpions" (p. 174).

A familiar Faustian pattern emerges again. Threatened by conscience, the Consul escapes into the magic of alcohol but there lurks another scorpion. Setting out for the trip to Tomalín, which eventually leads him to Parián and the Farolito, Geoffrey discovers a scorpion on the wall. His comment, containing an allusion to the peon abandoned by the roadside, is a startling intimation of what is to happen. "A curious bird is the scorpion. He cares not for priest nor for poor peon . . . It's really a beautiful creature. Leave him be. He'll only sting himself to death anyway" (pp. 187—88). But before the Consul, scorpion-like, stings himself to death by a stubborn refusal to escape from the Farolito, the tragedy will be delicately anticipated in the penultimate chapter of the novel. There, Yvonne's lyrical thoughts on the celestial geography revolve in circles, the first of which begins and ends with "Scorpio, setting" (see pp. 321—22). Already at the beginning of the following chapter (Chapter Twelve) the scorpion will be dead, merely an insignificant piece of dirt to be casually brushed off. For the last time the sinister animal appears in the stinking mingitorio, where the Consul goes after the intercourse with the prostitute. A similar impression of total insignificance is created. Shivering, the Consul notices a dead scorpion in the runnel but even the corpse apparently ceases to exist: "a sparkle of phosphorescence and it had gone, or had never been there" (p. 352). Finally it may be mentioned that—as Lowry points out in one of his explanatory letters—the whole book takes place in the astrological sign of "Scorpio" (*Letters*, p. 198). Without going into the nuances of astrological interpretation, we may assume that the sign merely provides a significant key for the novel. Its significance is for the most part confined to suicide and death, the oppressive presence of which permeates the whole of *Under the Volcano*. Not without reason did Lowry intend to call the novel *The Valley of the Shadow of Death*.[7]

The action takes place on the Day of the Dead, amidst a multitude of its gruesome emblems. Clockwork skeletons, chocolate skulls, funeral wagons, processions of mourners in a festive mood point to the insignificance of life and human existence. "How merrily Mexico laughed away its tragic history, the past, the underlying death!" (p. 254). In a sense the fiesta on the first of November parallels Geoffrey's inebriation which in so many ways implies death. It seems, moreover, that *Under the Volcano* is so thoroughly imbued with the atmosphere of some universal Day of the Dead that the actual fiesta taking place in Mexico is only an element in the whole mosaic of dissolution. Not only the scorpion but also *The Hands of Orlac* exert a powerful influence. We are presented not only with a world of suicide represented by the Consul bent on destroying his life and its spiritual potentialities, but also with a world of murder and killing, represented by the Mexican fascists, war, and World War Two looming on the temporal horizon of the novel. It is a world where creation

[7] See D. Day, Preface to Lowry, *Dark as the Grave Wherein my Friend Is Laid*, p. 11.

has been transformed into destruction, where life forces have been turned to the service of annihilation. "Mass reflexes, but only the erections of guns, disseminating death", the Consul comments on the target practice going on in the outskirts of Quauhnahuac (p. 207).

The Hands of Orlac, an emblem of death and evil, "the hieroglyphic of the times", as Laruelle calls it (p. 25), has both metaphorically and literally penetrated the reality depicted in *Under the Volcano*. The film poster showing the blood-stained hands of the murderer seems to be ubiquitous. It has even found its way into the paradisal atmosphere of Chapter Four, though the calm and the happiness are not dispelled in any dramatic way. As if to maintain the paradisal deception, Lowry lets his characters benevolently underestimate the portents of death. That a pulquería should be called *La Sepultura* (The Grave) seems somewhat grim to Hugh, but he promptly decides that the name must doubtless have "some humorous connotation" (p. 109). Only the reader who is already acquainted with the whole book is able to make the right, and much less optimistic, connections. For propped against one of the walls of the pulquería sits an Indian, his broad sombrero almost covering his face, the very same Indian who, dead, has already appeared to the Consul in an alcoholic hallucination (pp. 91—92), the same one who will be wounded, robbed and left to die by the "vigilante hombres". There are, however, in the scene itself sinister clues which break the paradisal illusion created by Hugh and Yvonne and foreshadow the future bloodshed and death. The Indian's appearance is, as it were, enclosed within two suggestive signs: *La Sepultura* and *Las Manos de Orlac*.

Most of the indications of death—those contained in the images and symbols and those pertaining to the story—suggest an inevitability of the approaching catastrophe and dissolution. "Es inevitable la muerte del Papa", the Consul catches sight of a newspaper headline and, terrified, takes the words to refer to himself. A moment later he will be reassured, discovering that "it was only the poor Pope whose death was inevitable" (p. 213), but the chapter, the crucial Chapter Seven, ends with an apparently disconnected and anonymous statement: "Es inevitable la muerte del Papa" (p. 230). While the Consul is often acutely aware of his freedom of choice, his decisions most often turn against life, and the inevitability of death becomes even more dramatic. A state of suspension between his return to the calamity-bringing mescal and the final choice of hell is signalled by numerous indications of death. The state of suspension may be said to span the whole of Chapter Ten, but the momentous act of returning to mescal which opens the chapter releases a dream-like phantasmagoria filled with images and emblems of death. The train, hitherto connected with the corpse of a child, resumes here its role of portending death: "trains, trains, trains, each driven by a banshee playing a shrieking nose-organ

122

in D Minor [. . .] trains, trains, trains, trains, converging upon him from all sides of the horizon, each wailing for its demon lover" (pp. 282—83). And the shadows of the cars on the fences of the station are said to be "portents of doom, of the heart failing" (p. 284). Besides the trains, the atmosphere of dying is created by the apparently incoherent, dream-like references to a dark cemetery, forsaken by its gravedigger carrying his special tools of death.

Such and similar images could easily be multiplied since almost every page of *Under the Volcano* testifies to an overwhelming sense of dissolution, death, and approaching disaster. It has been impossible to assemble all the instances of this theme, all the images, symbols and indications of death in the chapter concerned mainly with the tranformation of life into death. They have been and will be treated in other chapters, for they belong to almost every theme of the novel.

Here we have attempted to trace the theme of death in opposition to life. While the Mexican scene provided the setting, the Consul's garden revealed life forces attacked and superseded by death. The themes of "fruitless ruin", childlessness, and the dead child carried the message of barrenness and life denied its due. The dog and the horse exemplified the ambiguity of the life-and-death opposition. They were shown on the one hand to belong to paradisal exuberance and serenity, and on the other as portents, or even instruments, of death. The scorpion, the Day of the Dead, *The Hands of Orlac* represented death as a destructive force ready to strike and annihilate life both in its physical and spiritual aspect. But why, it may be asked, are the life forces shown to be declining? Why has death become an all-pervading reality in *Under the Volcano?* The answer may be on one plane sought in the Consul's ability—in so far as he is a black magician—to effect an inversion of the world; to turn white into black, good into evil, or life into death. Not because the universe of Lowry's novel is necessarily under some mysterious and direct influence of the Consul's magic, but because it is by and large a reflection of his personality; a personality which is less of an individual character than Everyman (cf. *Letters*, p. 60). More specifically, however, we may look for the reasons of death's victory in the spuriousness of human efforts towards rebirth and salvation. But this is the subject of the following chapter.

Chapter 7
Salvation

We recall the wounded Indian, robbed and left to die by the roadside. We remember the mood of helplessness enveloping Lowry's transposition of the story of the Good Samaritan. Nobody helps the dying man since nobody, except the thief, dares to touch him. All the bus passengers know very well that it is better to stay where they are; better not to interfere with the course of events, somehow or other supervised by the almighty Unión Militar. Where fear reigns, charity is paralysed. But fear alone cannot account for the apparent prudence of the people on the bus. They refrain from helping the dying man also because "death, by the roadside, must not be allowed to interfere with one's plans for resurrection, in the cemetery" (p. 249). In other words, a religious ritual—a ritual, moreover, intended to bring about a new life—stands in the way of helping a dying man. This is an extreme case of the spuriousness that has crept into the human strivings towards rebirth and salvation but it is nonetheless symbolic of the entire theme of *Salvation* as it runs throughout *Under the Volcano*. All the protagonists have their cherished dreams of renewal but the dreams prove ineffective and, because they tend to bypass reality, harmful. Instead of saving, the misplaced ideals bring destruction.[1] This is true of all the main characters, though in different degree. There is no doubt that the Consul's self-deception is much more profound than that of the others. Yvonne, Hugh, and Laruelle are still far from his consummate confusion of salvation with damnation.

As we may have seen by now, salvation is for the Consul first of all bound up with his esoteric pursuits. In as far as he is a mystic, in as far as he finds himself in search of eternity and transcendence, he is seeking salvation. This is borne out by all the principal themes of the novel. *Ascent, Light, Draught of Immortality, Eternity, Love,* and *Life* are all expressive of Geoffrey's transcendental aspirations, of a desire to reach a higher world. Given their archetypal overtones, the themes also suggest man's strivings after what is in Christian terms known as Eternal Life and the Kingdom of God. In short, salvation represented by the Consul's mystical endeavours signifies the way of spiritual self-transcendence, towards eternity and God.

---

[1] Cf. Edmonds, *"Under the Volcano*: A Reading of the 'Immediate Level'", pp. 74—75.

But salvation also implies rescue and deliverance; in the Judeo-Christian tradition deliverance from man's fallen estate, and in *Under the Volcano* from the Consul's fall into drunkenness. Hence to save the Consul means—for those who want to undertake the task—to liberate him from his dipsomania. Yet by virtue of all the mythical references it involves a lot more. We have already had occasion to note the archetypal contents of Geoffrey's drunkenness which, on one level of meaning, symbolizes humanity's first sin. Nor is this all. The Consul's addiction also represents the breakdown of all his spiritual aspirations as well as the confusion of heaven and hell to which he has fallen prey. Consequently, salvation sought for on the mystical path undergoes a process of inversion. Once more the Consul's plight reveals the quality of "infernal paradise". While still apparently ascending towards light and immortality, he is in fact descending into darkness and death. When we meet him on the Day of the Dead, he is already a long way on the path of damnation. With one part of his mind he seems certain of heading heavenwards, but otherwise he recognizes his true predicament. At times he even realizes that, in order to survive and to escape an ultimate fall into the abyss, he needs deliverance. Such is the tenor of his thoughts in the unsent letter to Yvonne:

Lift up your eyes unto the hills, I seem to hear a voice saying. Sometimes, when I see the little red mail plane fly in from Acapulco at seven in the morning over the strange hills [. . .] I think that you will be on it, on that plane every morning as it goes by, and will have come to save me. Then the morning goes by and you have not come. But oh, I pray for this now, that you will come. (pp. 40—41)

The Consul's prayer (inspired by Psalm 121) does not remain unanswered. Intent on saving him, Yvonne does return to Quauhnahuac literally out of the blue. Yet her gesture, ultimately born of love for Geoffrey, and of a desire to end the anguish of separation and to begin all over again, has hardly any effect. The Consul does not respond the way she has expected him to.

After an eleven months long separation she decides to return to Geoffrey. She intends to save him, to drag him somehow out of his drunkenness, to begin a new healthy life, far away from the horrors of the present existence. The remedy, as Yvonne pictures it, is to leave Quauhnahuac and settle on a farm, preferably in Canada, where they would be able to live in love, simplicity and health:

They would buy all their food, just as Hugh said, from a store beyond the woods, and see nobody, save a few fishermen, whose white boats in winter they would see pitching at anchor in the bay. She would cook and clean and Geoffrey would chop the wood and bring the water from the well. And they would work and work on this book of Geoffrey's, which would bring him world fame. But absurdly they would not care about this; they would continue to live, in simplicity and love, in their home between the forest and the sea. And at half-tide they would look down from the pier and see, in

125

the shallow lucid water, turquoise and vermilion and purple starfish, and small brown velvet crabs sidling among barnacled stones brocaded like heart-shaped pincushions. While at week-ends, out on the inlet, every little while, ferryboats would pass, ferrying song upstream—(p. 271)

This beautiful dream, tenacious though it is, proves unable to take root in the sordid reality of the Consul's drunkenness. Partly because the Consul, for reasons which will become apparent later in the chapter, rejects Yvonne's scheme of salvation; and partly because Yvonne, wounded by his rejection, withdraws the cherished dream from the sphere of practical suggestions. She will return to it the moment Geoffrey becomes sober. She realizes, however, that this is not the way to handle him. After all she remembers her resolve to drink together with the Consul, to help him by meeting him on his own ground, as it were. She seems to be aware of the danger that her outright disapproval of drinking might cause; that what Geoffrey badly needs is unconditional acceptance. Indeed, her refusal to touch whisky before breakfast makes him immediately feel rejected, whereas her frank encouragement ("for Pete's sake have a decent drink", p. 70) leads to the breaking of the ice and results in the lyrical scene of their embrace.

Nevertheless, Yvonne's gesture of acceptance is too timid and reluctant to break the spell of alcohol's magic powers. The lyricism of the moment of reunion seems merely to evoke in the Consul the lyricism of his cantinas. His longing for drink turns out to be much stronger than Yvonne's groping attempt to effect reconciliation. For to help a person out of an abyss of alcoholic addiction, an abyss which is often in no uncertain terms identified with the dark pit of hell, requires a lot more than Yvonne is willing to give. It requires, above all, great faith and singleness of purpose, qualities which she conspicuously lacks. Yvonne knows what she wants—her dream does not seem to leave her mind for a moment—and, unlike Geoffrey, is capable of action but, haunted by a sense of meaninglessness, she is seldom convinced of doing the right thing. "What was the use of a will if you had no faith?", she has once asked herself (p. 268).

Having made up her mind to return to Geoffrey, Yvonne decides to make the trip from America to Mexico by boat, "because she would have time on board to persuade herself her journey was neither thoughtless nor precipitate" (p. 48). But on the plane which takes her from the port of Acapulco to Quauhnahuac, she completely loses her self-confidence. Asked by Geoffrey whether she has really come back or just to see him, she avoids a straightforward answer. Unable to decide what to do, uncertain of her own relationship with Geoffrey, and not a little frightened by the whole situation, Yvonne desperately seeks Hugh's protection, asking him not to leave before she has talked it all over with the Consul. Yet Hugh's continued presence can hardly help. Having in the past betrayed Geoffrey with his wife, he remains an intruder, a potentially disruptive force standing in the way of reunion between the former husband and wife. Despite that, Yvonne cannot help asking him, of all people, whether there is any hope for the Consul, and whether there is anything she can do.

That Hugh is still the "old snake in the grass", as the Consul calls him (p. 141), seems to have escaped Yvonne's awareness. Her lack of sensitivity is most probably deliberate, even if unconscious, for, as we have already observed, she feels unable to acknowledge her past guilt. She would rather forget the painful past than settle accounts with Geoffrey and begin anew with a clear conscience. Just as she is reluctant to come to terms with her own "dark side", she seems incapable of recognizing the full extent of Geoffrey's downfall. In both cases she appears unwilling to cope with the reality of evil and thus possibly to redeem it. Overburdened by the forces of the past, as Chapter Nine amply shows, she is unable to save the Consul.[2]

Nor does the Consul cooperate with Yvonne. Instead of welcoming his deliverance, instead of exposing himself to the beneficial influence of the spirit of reconciliation brought by Yvonne, he withdraws into himself. Remote and sometimes hostile, he gives an impression of being able to do without her help. For the Consul her miraculous arrival does not automatically cancel her past blame by which he feels curiously sustained (cf. p. 63). The past seems to have imprisoned both of them; Yvonne cannot come to terms with it, Geoffrey is not able to shake it off. So immersed is he in her guilt that he finds it too difficult to open himself to the present. In a sense she has not returned. Her physical presence and her good will seem to be a gift which the Consul feels powerless to touch. How agonizingly aware he is of his failure, despite his desperate waiting, to take the fate-given opportunity: "This was the moment then, yearned for under beds, sleeping in the corners of bars, at the edge of dark woods, lanes, bazaars, prisons, the moment when—but the moment, stillborn, was gone: and behind him the *ursa horribilis* of the night had moved nearer" (p. 70). Overwhelmed by the past and incapable of forgiveness, the Consul cannot face the miracle of Yvonne's sudden return. Lacking the courage to step out of his hermetically sealed self and meet her, he will lose her together with his perhaps only chance of salvation. He knows that when the right moment is gone and the opportunity lost, the *ursa horribilis*, the terrible bear, draws near.

Seemingly incongruous, the bear is no mere poetic flight of fancy. It seems to refer to none other than the Aztec god Tezcatlipoca, traditionally identified with the constellation of the Great Bear. Of terrifying aspect, the deity, who presides over darkness and the night, bears also the names of "Enemy" and

[2] For a discussion of Yvonne's selfishness see Edmonds, p. 103.

"Dreaded Enemy". Represented by a wizard stone from which tempests are believed to arise, painted black, and associated with cold and death, Tezcatlipoca is a god of black magic.[3] Furthermore, he is in central America identified with *Hurakan,*[4] the god of storm and destruction who has already appeared in *Under the Volcano* as the "spirit of the abyss". In this way *ursa horribilis* (if its identification with Tezcatlipoca is correct) carries a wealth of meanings associated with the Consul's downward path towards damnation. It suggests the darkness and the storm accompanying Geoffrey's death, the "enemies" or the diabolic forces involved in killing him, and it points to the black magic which has led the Consul to the edge of the abyss where he is claimed by its spirit, which is also a spirit of universal destruction.

The appearance of *ursa horribilis* in the Consul's consciousness has a double function: on the one hand it indicates the threat of perdition implicit in his inability to accept deliverance promised by Yvonne's arrival, and on the other, it links the Consul's plight with the metaphysical dimension of *Under the Volcano*. Precisely because of mythical parallels, of which *ursa horribilis* is but one example, the significance of salvation transcends the earthbound level. Yvonne comes not merely to rescue the Consul from the deplorable state caused by his excessive drinking, but to offer him through her love a possibility of spiritual integration.

Spiritual integration, or the unity of man, is, as we saw in chapter 5 above, bound up with love. Perceived through its Cabbalistic reverberations, the unity is brought about through the union of man and woman, a union which at the same time contributes to man's redemption from the fall. The idea that deliverance implies integration is fairly universal and by no means confined to the Cabbala. The Christians are also aware that to save means to heal and make whole. As the Protestant theologian and philosopher Paul Tillich points out, "the terms for 'salvation' in many languages are derived from roots like *salvus, saos,* whole, *heil,* which all designate health, the opposite of disintegration and disruption. Salvation is healing in the ultimate sense; it is final cosmic and individual healing".[5] Unlike the Jewish esoteric wisdom, however, the Christian tradition derives the integration process and the healing solely from Christ's redemptive love, regarding the union of man and woman for the most part as *remedium concupiscentiae*. But Lowry's poetic imagination is not concerned with doctrinal differences. The universe of *Under the Volcano*

[3] See Spence, *The Problem of Atlantis,* pp. 176–77, and Spence, *Atlantis in America* (London: E. Benn Ltd., 1925), p. 158.

[4] See Spence, *The Myths of Mexico and Peru,* pp. 209, 237, and Spence, *The Magic and Mysteries of Mexico* (London: Rider, 1930), p. 274.

[5] P. Tillich, *The Protestant Era* (Chicago: The Univ. of Chicago Press, 1957), p. 61.

contains, as we have seen, many a "merger" in which various disparate mythological elements are fused to suit the exigencies of the novel. And so the unity of Geoffrey and Yvonne, whatever its Cabbalistic overtones, is the unity that Christ alone knows (p. 40), the prospects of their new life together being likewise associated with Christ.

The association is made only once, however. The Consul invokes "Jesus Christ's sweet sake" (p. 277) only when he seems genuinely willing to accept the *vita nuova* proposed by Yvonne; only when, for the first and last time on that Day of the Dead, he openly expresses his love for her. It is doubtless significant that just in this context Yvonne should refer to their future deliverance as a rebirth. In Christianity, as we know, rebirth is bound up with salvation (cf. John 3:3—8). To be sure, Yvonne does not specifically allude to any Christian ideas; all this is rather a matter of subtle overtones carrying archetypal meanings. That these do strike Christian chords, however, is further suggested by the juxtaposition of rebirth and the baptism of the first Christian Indian (p. 301). Ironically, when the suggestion appears, the mood has already changed and the Consul no longer thinks of committing himself to any new life. Sitting in the dark toilet of the Salón Ofélia, he is listening to the echoes of the day whirling chaotically in his mind. Among them appears the theme of a new life, shortly to be lost, however, in the confused pageant of disconnected utterances: broken fragments of Geoffrey's consciousness held together by some principle of free association. What is more, the sequence of the floating recollections ends on a note of death ("A corpse will be transported by—", p. 301)—a death which within *Under the Volcano* does not suggest rebirth.

Despite the Consul's sudden and enormous efforts to overcome himself, despite the dramatic confession of love, and despite the mythical Christian aura surrounding the theme of rebirth, the possibility of a new life with Yvonne recedes from his consciousness. Gradually his usual weakness and the incapacity to accept the suggested deliverance change into an ultimate rejection. Towards the end of the day, just before his exit to the Farolito, the Consul, stammering and somewhat incoherent, delivers his final message to Hugh and Yvonne:

"True, I've been tempted to talk peace. I've been beguiled by your offers of a sober and non-alcoholic Paradise. At least I suppose that's what you've been working around towards all day. But now I've made up my melodramatic little mind, what's left of it, just enough to make up. Cervantes! That far from wanting it, thank you very much, on the contrary, I choose—Tlax—" Where was he? "Tlax—Tlax—" [...] "Tlax—" the Consul repeated. "I choose—" [...] "Hell", he finished absurdly. "Because—" [...] "I like it," [...] "I love hell. I can't wait to get back there. In fact I'm running, I'm almost back there already." (pp. 313—14)

This is the last Yvonne and Hugh see of the Consul. The next moment he is indeed running, running towards the dark forest where the familiar path will lead him to Parián and the Farolito, the "paradise of his despair".

In a sense the Consul chooses not between heaven and hell but between two paradises: one sober, implying a reunion with Yvonne, love and life; the other alcoholic, full of "palpitating loneliness" (p. 350), haunted by hate and death. Paradoxical though it may seem, most often it is the first alternative that fills Geoffrey with fear and loathing, while the second promises unlimited bliss. This is another reason why the Consul rejects Yvonne's plans for the future. Her arrival and her efforts to interfere in his life constitute an immediate threat to his alcoholic paradise. To her suggestion to get away from Quauhnahuac he reacts with alarm:

In the end the Consul scarcely heard what she was saying—calmly, sensibly, courageously—for his awareness of an extraordinary thing that was happening in his mind. He saw in a flash, as if these were ships on the horizon, under a black lateral abstract sky, the occasion for desperate celebration (it didn't matter he might be the only one to celebrate it) receding, while at the same time, coming closer, what could only be, what was—Good God!—his salvation ... (p. 83)

Geoffrey is quick to protest vehemently against Yvonne's ideas, declaring them to be "unfeasible". Assuming an attitude of self-assurance, "indicative of a final consular sanity" (p. 83), the Consul becomes impervious to the thought of non-alcoholic salvation. Thus fortified, he is prepared to repel the assault of conscience symbolized by Goethe's church bell.

Actually this is not the first appearance of the church bell, borrowed by Lowry from Goethe's poem "Die Wandelne Glocke".[6] It has pursued Geoffrey ever since he began feeling menaced by Yvonne's arrival. As he confesses to himself, "one dreaded the hour of anyone's arrival unless they were bringing liquor" (p. 73). Frightened by the possibility of there being no liquor in the house, the Consul hastily plans to circumvent the difficulty. While Yvonne slept he would sneak out to some tiny bar and celebrate her coming back by drinking all morning. But are not his plans seriously jeopardized by all the implications of her arrival? Dreading "the issue that was already bounding after him at the gait of Goethe's famous church bell in pursuit of the child truant from church" (p. 73), Geoffrey fears that Yvonne's schemes of salvation would prevent the expected celebration. He would be forced to mend his ways, just as the truant child from Goethe's poem is forced back to church from the fields.[7]

[6] See *Biography*, p. 68.

[7] Cf. J. W. Goethe, "Die Wandelne Glocke", in *Goethes Werke in sechs Bänden*, ed. Erich Schmidt (Leipzig: Insel-Verlag, 1910), p. 189.

No wonder the Consul dreads the moment of reconciliation with Yvonne. Her words of sympathy and endearment merely make him feel the menacing bell draw nearer. And so the bell, originally a force of salvation, as in Goethe's poem, for Geoffrey comes to represent perdition. When the opportunity for reconciliation has been missed and "the perfect inappropriate moment arrived [. . .] the awful bell would actually touch the doomed child with giant protruding tongue and hellish Wesleyan breath" (p. 74). Thus the paradisal is transmuted into the infernal by Geoffrey's "alcoholic alchemy".

Likewise the mysterious public garden abutting on the Consul's own property appears to him frightful and menacing, although it represents the Garden of Eden, as yet untouched by forces of destruction. What the Consul sees there, instead of soothing him, aggravates his fears:

unusual tools, a murderous machete, an oddly shaped fork, somehow nakedly im-paling the mind, with its twisted tines glittering in the sunlight, were leaning against the fence, as also was something else, a sign uprooted or new, whose oblong pallid face stared through the wire at him.¿Le gusta este jardin? it asked [. . .] The Consul stared back at the black words on the sign without moving. You like this garden? Why is it yours? We evict those who destroy! Simple words, simple and terrible words, words which one took to the very bottom of one's being [. . .](p. 128)

The Consul further associates the words with a final judgement and with his own fate. Instead of tempting, the paradisal sight presents a mortal threat and fills him with essentially the same kind of terror he experiences towards light or love. To take off the dark glasses or to let himself be drawn again into the relationship with Yvonne would be, as we have seen, too painful and unbeara-ble. It would lead to a change of life involving a renunciation of drinking and of the blissful states dispensed by the cantina Farolito.

The Consul, as we know, experiences a peculiar longing for the beauty and peace of the Farolito, for the light of the sunrise he would watch in the open door of the cantina, breathing "the sharp cool pure air of heaven" (p. 200). Despite his ups and downs, despite the efforts to forego the way of the drunkard, he seems never to lose his ultimate goal from sight. He knows that he is aiming for the Farolito and that, sooner or later on that Day of the Dead, he will reach it. The prospect, as we remember, fills him not only with im-measurable longing but also with healing love. The expectation no doubt throws light on his attempts to comfort the miserable starving pariah dog that bows and scrapes before him on the floor of Señora Gregorio's cantina. Paraphrasing Jesus' words spoken to one of the crucified thiefs, the Consul promises paradise to the dog: "Yet this day, pichicho, shalt thou be with me in —" (p. 229; cf. Luke, 23:43). But before the holy word is uttered, the dog flees in terror, as if knowing perfectly well that where the Consul is going is no paradise but hell.

Nowhere else but in his hell is the Consul able to see salvation most clearly. There is a path in hell, as Geoffrey tells Yvonne in the unsent letter, which he may not take but which reveals itself to him precisely when, having received the news of their divorce, he feels his soul dying:

I seem to see now, between mescals, this path, and beyond it strange vistas, like visions of a new life together we might somewhere lead. I seem to see us living in some northern country, of mountains and hills and blue water; our house is built on an inlet and one evening we are standing, happy in one another, on the balcony of this house, looking over the water.[. . .] and we face east, like Swedenborg's angels,[8] under a sky clear save where far to the northeast over distant mountains whose purple has faded, lies a mass of almost pure white clouds, suddenly as by a light in an alabaster lamp, illumined from within by gold lightning [. . .] silence, and then again, within the white distant alabaster thunderclouds beyond the mountains, the thunderless gold lightning in the blue evening, unearthly . . . (pp. 36—37)

A similar clarity of vision is granted the Consul shortly after the intercourse with the Mexican girl in the Farolito. But just as before, the vision is associated with death. A crowing cock which, according to an Indian belief, crows over a drowned body, turns his thoughts away from the Farolito to the remote British Columbia where he once accompanied a search party in a boat looking for a dead man's body. Suddenly the Consul realizes that he has an island there: "an undiscovered, perhaps undiscoverable Paradise, that might have been a solution, to return there, to build, if not on his island, somewhere there, a new life with Yvonne" (p. 353). He realizes also that this is exactly what Yvonne has been suggesting to him. Why hasn't he thought of it before, the Consul asks himself surprised. A moment later it occurs to him that he has indeed thought of it before, at the very spot where he is now standing. Obviously, the thought of salvation has not been alien to him but it has been strangely confined to the infernal precincts. Not surprisingly therefore, the Consul contemplates afresh his deliverance precisely when his damnation is, so to speak, looming round the corner. Paradoxical though it may seem, an ultimate contamination, as Lowry points out, bestows strength on the Consul (cf. p. 354). Fortified by the adventure with the succubus, he experiences no inner resistance to considering the prospect of his and Yvonne's salvation. In fact, nothing seems simpler or more obvious at the moment. In thought and imagination the Consul translates himself to his Canadian garden of Eden when it is already too late to return to earth, let alone paradise or heaven.

The confusion of deliverance with perdition is at times almost complete. While the infernal Farolito entices with alcoholic bliss and peaceful contempla-

[8] Cf. E. Swedenborg, *Heaven and Its Wonders and Hell*, pp. 100—103.

tion of a paradisal *vita nuova*, the prospects of genuine salvation terrify the Consul with the tortures of the damned. As I have indicated at the beginning of this chapter, the confusion is, at least in one sense, an ultimate case of the spuriousness of human strivings towards salvation and rebirth. We have already seen both Yvonne and Geoffrey submitting to their self-deceptions and, each in their own way, maintaining the illusion of a search for paradise. And if salvation is understood in a sufficiently general way, all the four protagonists will be seen to express its different aspects. The Consul, Yvonne, Hugh, and Laruelle are, in a manner of speaking, different melodic lines constituting a polyphonic theme which may be said to represent what is in modern psychology often called man's urge for self-transcendence.[9] The melodic lines often merge with one another but their distinctive characteristics are easily discernible. The Consul's way to deliverance and rebirth is spiritual and mystical, Yvonne's more personal, Hugh's almost exclusively political, and Laruelle's artistic.

In the letter to Cape, Lowry maintains that not only the four main characters are in fact aspects of the same man and represent the human spirit, but also that "Hugh and the Consul are the same person" (*Letters*, p. 60). The statement probably appears odd to readers accustomed to the traditional novel but, as Lowry hastens to add, *Under the Volcano* "obeys not the laws of other books, but those it creates as it goes along" (*Letters*, p. 75). Even if one is not prepared to accept this claim without reservations, it has to be admitted that there are enough similarities between the two half-brothers to suggest more than a superficial affinity. As regards salvation, it seems that Hugh and Geoffrey manifest its outer and inner aspects respectively. The earthbound Hugh represents a political salvation while the Consul's bent is, as we know, primarily mystical and transcendental. Hugh dreams of saving the world through revolutionary action, the Consul seeks personal salvation by way of inner activity aimed at mystical illumination. The opposition between these two attitudes, between world and transcendence, is part, as we shall see later in this chapter, of the "Manichean theme" of *Under the Volcano*.

Let us now turn to Hugh, in whom the vicissitudes of the human urge to salvation are very clearly exemplified. In many ways Hugh typifies the general theme of salvation as it runs throughout Lowry's novel, and reflects the other principal characters' efforts to change their lives and the world. He often resembles Geoffrey, Yvonne, or Laruelle, not only because of their actual failings but because of the spuriousness of their strivings.

[9] Cf., for example, Viktor Frankl, *The Will to Meaning* (New York: The New American Library, 1969); Frankling J. Shaw, *Reconciliation: A Theory of Man Transcending*, ed. Sydney M. Jourard and Dan C. Overlade (Princeton: D. van Nostrand Co. 1955).

To begin with, Hugh, despite his good intentions, is not able to help his half-brother and rescue him from the alcoholic addiction. His "salvage operations" consist chiefly in providing strychnine which at best relieves the symptoms of drunkenness. Just like Yvonne, the young man lacks meaning and direction in life, even though his emptiness is masked by youthful idealism and romantic left-wing enthusiasm. His first voyage as a deck-hand, conceived in the pretentious belief that he was "running away to sea" (p. 159), is compared to Yvonne's ideas of the farm. Pervaded by an air of unreality, both schemes suggest an escape from oneself; from a spiritual vacuum which often results in a breakdown or in some reckless, blind and irresponsible action. Hugh's impulse to ride the bull in the arena Tomalin is seen by Yvonne as an expression of "that absurd necessity he felt for action" (p. 275).

"—Nel mezzo del bloody cammin di nostra vita mi ritrovai in . . .", so begins Chapter Six of the novel, Hugh's chapter, in which the Consul's half-brother tries to come to terms with his life. "In the middle of our life, in the middle of the bloody road of our life . . ."[10], Hugh promptly translates the Dantean words, as if to emphasize the implied loss of bearings in the dark forest and consequently, his own lack of direction and purpose. And the meaninglessness of his life, twice compared to the life of Hitler ("another frustrated artist", p. 156), ironically contrasts with his dreams of bringing salvation to the world.

The dreams spring from an ardent revolutionary faith which, as Lowry implies, impressed itself on Hugh's mind quite early in his life simply for lack of any other values. However, Hugh was to forget his first ideals. He forgot "that a Christian smiles and whistles under all difficulties and that once a scout you were always a communist. Hugh only remembered to be prepared. So Hugh seduced Bolowski's wife" (p. 172). Later, he obviously recovered his left-wing faith, together with a certain amount of scout spirit and a vague sense of the Christian perspective on life. This seems to account for his absurd urge for action and for providing his communism with both romantic and religious overtones. Communism to him is not a system or a doctrine but a new spirit, like Christianity, capable of transforming the world. And like Christianity, it carries the idea of brotherhood and love between people. Unfortunately, Christianity, according to Hugh, has not been really understood or set aright. Passing a burned church he lectures Christ on the necessity of joining the right cause:

—The time has come for you to join your comrades, to aid the workers, he told Christ, who agreed. It had been His idea all the while, only until Hugh had rescued Him those hypocrites had kept Him shut up inside the burning church where He couldn't breathe. Hugh made a speech. Stalin gave him a medal and listened sympathetically while he

[10] Cf. chapter 2 above, note 5.

explained what was on his mind. "True . . . I wasn't in time to save the Ebro, but I did strike my blow—" He went off, the star of Lenin on his lapel; in his pocket a certificate; Hero of the Soviet Republic, and the True Church, pride and love in his heart— (pp. 239—40)

Somewhat ashamed of himself, Hugh promptly shakes off the fatuous daydreams, admitting nevertheless the reality of love. In a desperate plea for simplicity and brotherhood he even invokes Christ. A moment later, however, he will fail to act in the spirit of brotherhood, turning out to be as powerless as everybody else to save the dying Indian. Hugh's impatient outcry directed at Christ, "why may we not all be brothers?" (p. 240), is thus ironically answered by the approaching events and by his own helplessness.

The gulf between professed ideals and action results not only from the meaninglessness of Hugh's life but it is also indirectly linked with the "betrayal of mysteries". In chapter 4 above we saw how the theme of betrayal is related to the idea of the black magician; an idea which through varied and often complex evocations permeates *Under the Volcano*. Dealing with Lowry's treatment of love in the subsequent chapter we noted the connection between the betrayal of divine mysteries and betrayal of the brotherhood of man. We also had occasion to observe that Hugh, despite his ideals, fails to be brother not only to the dying man on the road but also to the Consul. In this way Hugh's betrayal of the brotherhood of man is related to the betrayal of mysteries.

He knows that the innocent ride with Yvonne in the paradisal atmosphere of the early morning is a deception. It is a miraculous illusion, "a glimpse of what never was at all, of what never can be since brotherhood was betrayed" (p. 107). Apparently Hugh feels guilty of betraying his brother, of taking Yvonne away from Geoffrey. And a moment later his awareness of guilt undermining the paradisal atmosphere of the ride will be extended to a more archetypal event: the betrayal of Jesus by Judas. Hugh actually compares himself to Judas whom he imagines riding somewhere on the morning of the Good Friday, thinking

how joyous all this could be, riding on like this under the dazzling sky of Jerusalem—and forgetting for an instant, so that it really *was* joyous—how splendid it all might be had I only not betrayed that man last night, even though I knew perfectly well I was going to, how good indeed, if only it had not happened though, if only it were not so absolutely necessary to go and hang oneself—(p. 111)

Overpowered by remorse, Hugh will seek redemption for Judas through participating in Yvonne's dreams of the future. With his idea of a shack by the sea he manages to inspire enthusiasm in Yvonne to begin all over again with the Consul. Joyful and in high spirits, Hugh and Yvonne return galloping from their ride. But their enthusiasm proves to be short-lived.

The landmarks soon break the spell, hinting at the futility of dreamed-up happiness. The first to foreshadow disaster is the barranca which they cross on their way back to Quauhnahuac. As soon as they pass the bridge over the ravine they find themselves in the ruined palace of Maximilian and Carlotta. As we recall, the story of the imperial couple represents high expectations come to nought: a new life in the Mexican paradise turned to ruin and disaster. The atmosphere of catastrophe hanging in the air becomes still more oppressive when Hugh draws Yvonne's attention to the moon, described as "a fragment blown out of the night by a cosmic storm". Although the lunar geography is rich in poetically suggestive names and although Yvonne is, as we know, an amateur astronomer, oddly enough the only name that she claims to remember at the moment is "the Marsh of Corruption". To which Hugh contributes two equally mirthless ones: "the Sea of Darkness" and "Sea of Tranquillity" (p. 124).

From the contemplation of the moon they turn to the view of the valley with the volcanoes, behind which storm clouds are gathering. The volcanoes in turn lead Hugh's thoughts to the island of Sokotra, his own symbol of a blessed life, and then to the Mexican landscape which seems to convey a special message for him. The message— "some youthful password of courage and pride"—brings Hugh to a sense of self-affirmation and reminds him of his desire to be and do good. And yet, although the youthful password is passionate, it is at the same time "nearly always hypocritical" (p. 124). It is therefore difficult to take for granted Hugh's readiness for sacrifice, apparently the most noble intention of his life. Not only is it so mingled with bravado and desperation that it seems pathetic, but it is inseparable from his profound craving for applause and publicity:

And yet is it nothing I am beginning to atone, to atone for my past, so largely negative, selfish, absurd, and dishonest? That I propose to sit on top of a shipload of dynamite bound for the hard-pressed Loyalist armies? Nothing that after all I am willing to give my life for humanity, if not in minute particulars? Nothing to ye that pass by? ... Though what on earth he expected it to be, if none of his friends knew he was going to do it, was not very clear. [And Hugh had to admit] that the whole stupid beauty of such a decision made by anyone at a time like this, must lie in that it *was* so futile, that it *was* too late, that the Loyalists had already lost, and that should that person emerge safe and sound, no one would be able to say of *him* that he had been carried away by the popular wave of enthusiasm for Spain, when even the Russians had given up, and the Internationals withdrawn. (pp. 152–53)

Aware of the futility of his action, Hugh wants nonetheless to believe in the value of his sacrifice. "Death and truth could rhyme at a pinch", he tells himself but this consolation does not appear very convincing. For Hugh's life, as Lowry often hints, by and large consists in "running away from himself and his responsibilities" (p. 153). Like Geoffrey, and like Yvonne, he has a tendency to evade the harsh reality of the world and to escape into a world of dreams.

136

Here again we meet the theme of escape, transposed this time through the context of salvation.

"What is the use of escaping [. . .] from ourselves", the Consul moralizes on Yvonne's suggestions of a new life together. By saying this he touches the very heart of the escape theme, letting its ironic ambiguities come to the surface. Unwittingly he questions the genuineness of Yvonne's scheme of salvation. We should find a real solution, he seems to imply, not merely escape from the place of misery. In view of what we know about Yvonne, this appears to be a justified response to her dream world, but the Consul is not really responding to her. He merely guards himself from any interference into his life that would deprive him of drinking. He may be hitting on Yvonne's lack of realism, but by pretending to condemn escape he merely tries to maintain the right to his fundamentally escapist life.

The irony of the whole situation becomes still more acute when we realize that the Consul is trapped in a labyrinth of escape ways. For even when he does apparently desire salvation and tries to check his flight into drinking, he does not come closer to the truth of his predicament. Aware of the unreality and the meaninglessness of Yvonne's dreams, he seeks refuge in their remoteness from the world. "Please let Yvonne have her dream—dream?—of a new life with me—please let me believe that all that is not an abominable self-deception", he prays to Virgin Mary. "Let us be happy again somewhere", he asks a little further on, "if it's only together, if it's only out of this terrible world. Destroy the world!" (p. 289). Obviously salvation and the world are mutually exclusive for the Consul. Thus he becomes a modern Manichean since salvation, within the Manichean scheme, is possible only beyond the world. As we know, Manicheanism and most gnostic systems of antiquity display a radical dualism between the world and transcendence. Because the world is both evil and unredeemable, it cannot be saved; man can only liberate himself from it, that is to say, escape into the realm of the godhead.

Clearly, the Consul's attitude is similar to that general gnostic pattern. In as much as he despairs of the world and seeks refuge in transcendence, he repeats the age-old dualism.[11] His utter hopelessness, which seems inextricably bound up with mescal-induced eternity (as we saw at the end of chapter 3 above), is

[11] To be sure, he is no Manichean in the strict sense of the term, but, as Hans Jonas has demonstrated, the Manichean, or generally gnostic, attitude can be conceived in a very general way. The second edition of his study of the gnostic religion contains a supplement entitled *Gnosticism, Nihilism and Existentialism* in which Jonas distills, so to speak, the essence of the ancient dualism from its historical background and sees it carried over into various trends of twentieth century existential philosophy. Hans Jonas, *The Gnostic Religion* (Boston: Beacon Press, 1963).

strongly reminiscent of the general Manichean pattern. The same pattern may be discerned in Lowry's juxtaposition of Geoffrey and Hugh: two personalities, similar in their basic urge to "strive upwards", and so radically dissimilar in their fundamental outlook upon the world. Hugh, as has been already indicated, is confined to his earthbound way, which the Consul rejects for the sake of purely transcendental pursuits. Apart from the juxtaposition with his half-brother, however, Hugh as well as Yvonne, are set within a dualistic pattern. Unlike the Manicheans, they do not consciously or deliberately dissociate themselves from earthly reality. They do it nevertheless in so far as their dreams tend to bypass the world of here and now. Thus they arrive at quite a radical opposition between dream and reality; arrive there first of all because they feel by and large unable to accept, or come to terms with, the reality of evil, guilt, or death. That is why their schemes of salvation often remain mere gestures.

Yvonne cannot save the Consul because she is unwilling to take into account her guilt from the past and the full extent of Geoffrey's addiction. She wants him to conform to her dreams, apart from all the painful problems that have arisen between them. In this way she finally vitiates her goals since the Consul, who easily sees through the futility of her dreams, turns away from the salvation he does not really believe in. Moreover, he responds to the spuriousness of Yvonne's efforts by letting himself ultimately sink into his alcoholic damnation.

In a similar manner Hugh contributes to the Consul's downfall. The kind of help he offers is so superficial and insignificant that it encounters Geoffrey's scorn. But then Hugh does not pretend he really wants to save his half-brother. Unlike Yvonne whose life is, after all, concentrated on the Consul, Hugh is busy trying to save the world. He has a number of noble intentions which turn out to be both futile and pathetic. Like Yvonne, he has a tendency to avoid looking reality in the face and to cover up his inner emptiness with dreams of a new life. Although Hugh is apparently working for the improvement of the human lot, he fails in simple charity. Committed to lost causes, his revolutionary zeal is powerless to bring salvation to the world.

But whereas Yvonne and Hugh may sadly fail in their efforts to bring about a *vita nuova*, they never go as far as the Consul and never see their failures as success. In the Consul's life, however, this diabolic inversion has become a dominant note. All the possibilities of genuine deliverance appear to him as a threat, while the cantina Farolito—where he is cut off from his fellow human beings as well as from the world and claimed by the infernal forces—appears to him as a sunlit portal of salvation. This grand deception, however, is broken towards the end of the novel. Accused of spying and told simply that spies are shot in Mexico, the Consul begins to realize that the end is near. The Farolito is showing him its true infernal face. But all is not yet lost. An insistent voice on the radio, suddenly turned full blast, seems to shout orders to the crew of a ship; the only orders that could save her from the approaching catastrophe:

Incalculable are the benefits civilization has brought us, incommensurable the productive power of all classes of riches originated by the inventions and discoveries of science. Inconceivable the marvellous creations of the human sex in order to make men more happy, more free, and more perfect. Without parallel the crystalline and fecund fountains of the new life which still remains closed to the thirsty lips of the people who follow in their griping and bestial tasks. (p. 371)

Immediately after the message ends the Consul, as if prompted by a sudden awareness of man's infinite potential, perhaps also of his own dignity, casts off his powerlessness and passivity and strikes at his persecutors. "What a piece of work is man", the radio voice seems to have pointed out and the Consul appears to be taking the message to heart. Brandishing a machete he is trying to win his own freedom, at the same time identifying himself with "the wretched of the earth" in a struggle against the forces of evil, represented here by the fascist policemen. Obviously he no longer supposes that just a glance at the Chief of Rostrums, one of the fascist policemen, is enough to "feel that mankind was on the point of being saved immediately" (p. 355). All of a sudden he sees through all their scheming, and, shouting words of accusation, he is making a desperate attempt to resist injustice and evil. Unfortunately it is already too late. The Consul has been so much absorbed by the forces of evil that there is no turning back. His powers of renewal and his capacity for resistance have been for too long consumed by the confusion of heaven and hell. In his infernal paradise salvation is impossible and the Consul-Faust must pay his price. And yet, as Lowry points out in the letter to Cape, "there is even a hint of redemption for the poor old Consul at the end, who realizes that he is after all part of humanity" (*Letters*, p. 85). Has he not broken the spell of isolation and sided with humanity against the powers of evil? As if to acknowledge the fact and bring relief to the dying Consul, an old man in the cantina addresses him as *compañero*. The word "pelado", the thief, fades slowly out of his consciousness, and Geoffrey feels relieved. "Someone had called him compañero too, which was better, much better. It made him happy" (p. 374). But a hint of salvation remains only a hint, and the novel ends with the Consul falling into the abyss of the barranca.

Chapter 8
Freedom

In the previous chapter we saw the Consul escaping from the possibilities of genuine deliverance into the illusory salvation of the infernal Farolito. We also saw him break through his illusion and turn against the powers of hell. Yet the illusion had never been complete. It may have been decisively broken in the last minutes of the Consul's life but, as has been often pointed out, he had always been vaguely aware that the Farolito represents in fact damnation. And it is precisely this lurking awareness that is the source of conflict within the Consul and that provides him with a freedom of choice. There are more or less always two alternative ways before him, two courses of action between which he may choose. Like Doctor Faustus, he is accompanied by two familiars: two angels representing good and evil, each having a different message for his "protégé".

Because the Consul is almost always confronted with such a fundamental choice, his confusion of heaven and hell cannot be attributed only to the deception created by the mystical faculties of alcohol. In other words, the vision of the Farolito as a paradise is conjured up not only by the pseudo-mystical illusions but also by an overwhelming moral consciousness. Precisely because he is aware of the real power of evil, the Consul, just like Faustus, cannot bear it in its revealing nakedness. "That holy shape becomes a devil best" (*Faustus*, iii, 28), says Faustus who has just ordered Mephostophilis to appear before him as a Franciscan friar. Similarly the Consul, if he is not to recoil from evil, has to see the Farolito in a paradisal shape, and his addiction as a way to salvation. But the paradisal vision cannot always be maintained. Geoffrey occasionally has to acknowledge the downfall into hell and damnation, even though it does not affect his constant decisions in favour of the infernal cantina.

Needless to say, the Consul does not desire damnation for its own sake, but he certainly rejects salvation. "I could not find with all my soul that I did desire deliverance", we read in an epigraph taken from John Bunyan, one of the three mottoes of the novel. While the idea expressed in Bunyan's words applies generally to the whole of the Consul's life, it is also woven into the imagery of the novel. At the beginning of Chapter Twelve (the last chapter) it is represented by the image of the scorpion, which symbolizes death and suicide. It is one of those moments when the thought of deliverance (this time through free association) does cross Geoffrey's mind: "Save me, thought the Consul vaguely [. . .] suélteme, help: but maybe the scorpion, not wanting to be saved, had stung itself to death" (p. 338).

All this indicates the Consul's responsibility for his downfall. It shows that his drunkenness is not merely the fatal sickness of the times whose inevitability crushes the dignity of man with an "existential" despair, simply to be endured with melancholy resignation or defiant abandon. To drink or not to drink is up to the Consul, for the sickness is by and large in him, however much it may have been caused by the *zeitgeist*. It is true that he invariably chooses to drink, but that alone does not necessarily render his freedom of choice illusory, as Stephen Spender suggests in his Introduction to *Under the Volcano*. Each time he is faced with a choice, the Consul—just like Faustus—experiences a conflict of conscience and his vacillations show the conflict to be genuine enough. To diagnose all this merely as symptoms of the addiction by which he has let himself be chosen seems as arbitrary as to maintain that Doctor Faustus has lost all freedom of choice once he has signed the pact with the Devil.[1] Geoffrey's will may be paralysed by alcohol, just as Faustus' by the fear of hell, but in neither case is the paralysis complete. In fact, little in *Under the Volcano* seems to confirm Spender's suggestion that "no real choice exists" for the Consul.[2] On the contrary, Lowry often appears to go out of his way to show his hero's painful confrontations with the alternative of redemption versus damnation, and to emphasize with insistence that Geoffrey Firmin is the author of his own fate. Yet the tragic paradox of the Consul's freedom lies in its wilful inversion, since the choices he makes—whether through decision or indecision—lead him into ever greater spiritual captivity.

Contemplating his downfall shortly before his death, the Consul is perfectly aware of the original freedom enjoyed at a time when, like the noble spirits on the prohibitionist poster *Los Borrachones*, he was still ascending into the light:

Yes, but had he desired it, willed it, the very material world, illusory though that was, might have been a confederate, pointing the wise way. Here would have been no devolving through failing unreal voices and forms of dissolution that became more and more like one voice to a death more dead than death itself, but an infinite widening, an

---

[1] It is clear that "the legalistic deed of gift which Lucifer required Faustus to sign is not really binding—in other words, that his initial sin has not damned him once and for all. The utterances of the Good and Bad Angels on their two appearances would be pointless if it were not still possible for Faustus to repent and by so doing to cancel the bond; and the emergency measures taken by Mephostophilis show that he certainly recognizes the possibility . . . In fact, the deed is validated from minute to minute only by Faustus' persistent refusal to relinquish such power as he has acquired by his presumption." John D. Jump, Introduction to Marlowe's *Doctor Faustus*, p. lii.

[2] S. Spender, Introduction to *Under the Volcano*, p. xxv.

infinite evolving and extension of boundaries, in which the spirit was an entity, perfect and whole: ah, who knows why man, however beset his chance by lies, has been offered love? Yet it had to be faced, down, down he had gone, down till—it was not the bottom even now, he realized. (p. 361)

"Had he desired it, willed it", the pregnant words stand at the beginning of an alternative determining the whole of Geoffrey's life. Quite clearly, he has not been merely pushed down the abyss. The Consul has himself to blame for his downfall and he knows it. He may often supress the knowledge but it inevitably breaks through to his consciousness: "his own fruitless selfish ruin" has already appeared to him as "self-imposed" (p. 345); his marriage as "wilfully slaughtered" (pp. 75—76). He may be profoundly sick, but the sickness is of his own doing. A certain doctor Guzmán, from whom Hugh has got the prescription for the strychnine, refuses to waste his time on the Consul. There has never been anything wrong with him, according to the doctor, "save that he wouldn't make up his mind to stop drinking" (p. 117). Of course we would not have to be bound in our interpretation of the Consul by the verdict of Doctor Guzmán, an entirely marginal character, were it not for his appearance at a crucial moment in the novel, when Geoffrey makes a frantic effort to regain his non-alcoholic sanity.

At Laruelle's house, the Consul has for some time refrained from drinking. "You might as well start now as later, refusing the drinks. You might as well start now; as later. Later"—he has been telling himself (p. 206). Notwithstanding his irresolution, Geoffrey still manages not to touch all the drinks within sight. On a sudden impulse he goes to the telephone and tries to call none other than Dr. Guzmán. Earlier on Laruelle and the Consul have been talking about Doctor Vigil and this might have given him the idea to seek medical help. Laruelle has even suggested that Vigil might be of assistance but Geoffrey apparently does not believe in his healing powers. He has seen Vigil completely drunk, himself in need of assistance. No, he specifically wants Dr. Guzmán. We see, moreover, that to get in touch with Guzmán is for Geoffrey a matter of the highest importance. He trembles and sweats, trying to find the doctor's number; he is so nervous that he cannot talk properly once the reciver is off the hook, as if this fact, magnified by the circumstances and endowed with symbolic meaning, occupied his whole attention, confusing him strangely for a while. "He'd already taken the receiver off the hook, the receiver off the hook, off the hook, he held it the wrong way up, speaking, splashing into the earhole" (p. 208). The insistent repetition of the phrase suggests Geoffrey's attempt to suspend his death sentence, to arrest his sucidal flight into the alcoholic abyss. But despite his earnestness, he is unable to cope with the telephone when he gets through. Asked whom he wants, Geoffrey desperately shouts "God!", and hangs up.

It is possible to regard the Consul's outcry merely as an expression of desperation, but also as an answer to the question put to him on the telephone. Since it is a matter of life and death for him, it is hardly surprising that he should call on God for help. Yet it was Guzmán he wanted. Is there perhaps some affinity between the doctor and the Highest Being which makes them coalesce in Geoffrey's mind? Indeed, it seems that the mysterious Guzmán has this in common with God that he recognizes the Consul's inviolate freedom of choice. "The will of man is unconquerable. Even God cannot conquer it", Geoffrey has once told himself (p. 93). A similar attitude, as we saw a moment ago, has been expressed by the doctor who considers the Consul himself to be responsible for his "sickness". Hence it might be supposed that he identifies Guzmán with God precisely because of their recognition of freedom, turning to them at the moment when he is making desperate efforts to exercise it and refrain from drinking. And if such is indeed the case, it implies that the Consul is able, at least at times, to shake off his illusions and seek—even if un-successfully in the end—a genuine command of his destiny. His short-lived attempt to reach the doctor shows that his power of making choices is not il-lusory, and his preference for Guzmán suggests that he is inclined to accept the responsibility for his liquor-induced sickness.

The sickness, as we have already seen, brings the Consul extraordinary suf-ferings. "Horripilating hangovers", pain, anguish, misery, despair, visitations by demons, "tortures of the damned"—all this he has to endure. But the pain, though genuine enough, is accompanied by a sense of unreality and meaninglessness. "Though my suffering seems senseless I am still in agony", he confesses to Virgin Mary. "Let me truly suffer", he bursts out later in the same prayer, "Let me be truly lonely, that I may honestly pray" (p. 289). It is as if the Consul was all the time aware of the freedom to retrace his steps from the path of damnation; aware that his suffering, self-imposed and often sought for, lacks the tragic inevitability which alone could make it genuine. Revocable any time through a sheer effort of will, suffering constitutes no challenge and its reality evaporates. Geoffrey appears to realize this when the voice of his conscience delivers a somewhat confused but morally forceful verdict: "You've been insulated from the responsibility of genuine suffering ... Even the suffering you do endure is largely unnecessary. Actually, spurious. It lacks the very basis you require of it for its tragic nature. You deceive yourself" (p. 219).

Evidently the Consul is no tragic hero entangled in the irrevocable folly of his passions or caught by the adverse decrees of the gods. His suffering, like the thirst of the plants perishing in his garden, is said to be unnecessary. After all, water flows in abundance and a normal happy life with Yvonne is a possibility. Thus the Consul, unlike Oedipus or Hamlet for example, has deliberately chosen his suffering. Chosen, however, not with any intention of sacrifice but, paradoxically, in order to gain the bliss of alcoholic heaven. Therefore he is in love with his own misery (cf. p. 14). Yet the ecstatic bliss is not the only reason for taking a path to hell. The "tortures of the damned" are also brought about by what Geoffrey calls the "dreadful tyranny of self" (p. 289), that is, an extreme personal isolation, inability to forgive, a morbid preoccupation with his own and others' guilt, and a feeling of being sustained by Yvonne's blame. Indeed, it seems that the Consul both escapes into suffering and seeks there revenge for the injuries received from the world, first of all from Yvonne. Through his own ruin he wants to establish her guilt.

Naturally, the "tyranny of self" and the allurements of alcoholic ecstasies affect the Consul's freedom. His choices are almost invariably negative: freedom is used for acts of rejection, affirmation being left for the delights of hell. The Consul, as we have seen, rejects love, life, salvation, and renounces gradually every support that holds him from ultimate disaster. Therefore Yvonne's attempts to help him are doomed to failure. Her voice does not reach his consciousness, if only because her letters remain unread until it is too late. It is true that her first postcard, written immediately after their separation, has been delayed for over a year. It might have changed everything—so one would think—had it arrived on time. Not only has Yvonne expressed her love for Geoffrey in it but she also questioned their separation: "Darling, why did I leave? Why did you let me?" (p. 193). Yet, implying that in a fundamental sense they are still very much together, the message has deprived Geoffrey of a foundation for his suffering. The postcard, as he now realizes, "proved the lonely torment unnecessary, proved, even, he must have wanted it" (p. 214). And the "lonely torment" has been also unnecessary in another sense. It came about not only through the freak of fate which had not allowed Yvonne's message of love to reach its destination as soon as possible. The suffering came about through the Consul's sins of omission. Actually the postcard could not have changed anything, and Geoffrey has no illusions about that. Had it arrived in time, he would have probably put it away without reading, just as he has been putting away all her subsequent letters. There is no doubt of the Consul's freedom of choice; there is equally no doubt about the direction his choices tend to take: refusal of good and the ensuing evil, rejection of fulfilment and the resultant desolation.

Another example of the unnecessary suffering is Geoffrey's ride on the loop-the-loop machine, aptly called the Máquina Infernal. Unnecessary because he is not in any way forced to do it. Pursued by children, he boards the machine, as we might remember, merely to avoid them. Figuratively taken, the dash for the monster becomes the epitome of his whole life. It displays the same "eternal" pattern: rejection followed by a leap into hell. Also the separation from

Yvonne and all the suffering it brings have their origin in the Consul's act of rejection. As we have seen, his transcendental pursuits are invariably paid for by personal isolation. However much he needs Yvonne, and however genuine his deep sense of deprivation without her, she stands in the way of his alcoholic mysticism. This conflict—so often unresolved in the Consul's mind ("Could one be faithful to Yvonne and the Farolito both?", p. 201)—throws light on her infidelities. She has been led to betray him with Hugh and Laruelle not only through a weakness of character but, as Lowry delicately suggests, because Geoffrey has actually willed it (cf. pp. 79, 210). His loyalty to the Farolito, so to speak, has made Yvonne unfaithful and cast her upon his friend and his half-brother. His choice of alcoholic bliss, in other words, makes the Consul largely responsible for Yvonne's betrayal and all the suffering it has caused him.

The responsibility implies freedom: it implies that the Consul has freely chosen his suffering, an act which bears resemblance to the Christian way of the cross. But the resemblance—which has misled some critics[3]—is superficial. The Consul does not accept suffering in order to save anyone but on the contrary: to escape from people into the loneliness of his alcoholic mysticism. That is why his suffering is unnecessary and spurious. Far from being sacrificial, his death is deprived of tragic inevitability because it is too much like suicide committed through a lack of will. There is no question of the Consul's vicarious suffering; what he endures is, as we have noted many times, "the tortures of the damned". Indeed, he is like a scorpion which does not want to be saved and finally stings itself to death. He is free but he always chooses escape and perdition. Even Señora Gregorio's cantina, in the Consul's mind associated with the Dantean dark forest, provides an opportunity for the exercise of freedom. "The choice is up to you", one of his familiars tells him. " 'You are not invited to use those means of escape; it is left up to your judgement; to obtain them it is necessary only to—"Señora Gregorio,' he repeated, and the echo came back: 'Orio.'" (p. 226). By calling the proprietess of the cantina, who will provide him with more drinks, the Consul makes up his mind. And his decision does not remain without an echo which carries a faint premonition of death: "Orio"—if we assume that it has a significance beyond the mere accoustic effect—suggests Orion, the giant hunter from Greek mythology, who is known to have died from the sting of a scorpion.[4]

So the Consul, by taking advantage of his freedom, succeeds merely in going further down his path towards the infernal abyss. Not only does he increase his sufferings but he also falls, as has been already pointed out, even more deeply

[3] See chapter 4 above, note 70.
[4] See New Larousse Encyclopaedia of Mythology, p. 144.

into spiritual captivity. In order to defend his freedom—freedom to die, to choose his own way to be damned—the Consul, just like Faustus, embraces a doctrine of fatalism.[5] The doctrine, a sort of historical fatalism which he propounds to Hugh and Yvonne, rests on a radical disbelief in all purposeful action, in what he calls "interference" in human affairs. There is no use interfering in the "stupid course" of history which merely winds throughout the ages, like a barranca choked with refuse. All heroic resistance against injustice and oppression is meaningless since it has nothing to do with "the survival of the human spirit". "Countries, civilizations, empires, great hordes, perish for no reason at all, and their soul and meaning with them" (p. 310). Similarly, the Consul implies, there is no use interfering with his own life, no use trying to prevent his fall. Like Faustus, he renounces hope and refuses redemption. The Consul's outburst against interference is, however, more involved than Faustus' rejection of salvation. Both are tempted by the delights promised by the powers of evil and both are disappointed with the world, but for different reasons. While Faustus is mainly disenchanted by knowledge, the Consul is bitterly wounded by the spuriousness of human efforts to bring about salvation.

Aware of the meaninglessness underlying Hugh's political faith, Geoffrey radically questions the motives for interference. They are no more than an evasion of one's responsibility, or a "justification of the common pathological itch". They have "nothing constructive at bottom, only acceptance really, a piddling contemptible acceptance of the state of affairs that flatters one into feeling thus noble and useful" (p. 311). Hence all interference is not only useless but harmful. It would be far better if all those who do the interfering could mind their own business, the Consul insists. Everyone has a right to die if he wants to, and people as well as countries should be left alone. The man dying by the roadside, the American Indians, Spain, the Consul himself are none the better for the help extended to them. On the contrary, they suffer from it, all because charity is not genuine:

"You're all the same, all of you, Yvonne, Jaques, you, Hugh, trying to interfere with other people's lives, interfering, interfering—why should anyone have interfered with young Cervantes here, for example, given him an interest in cock fighting?—and that's precisely what's bringing about disaster in the world, to stretch a point, yes, quite a point, all because you haven't got the wisdom and the simplicity and the courage [...]" (p. 312).

The Consul accuses those who are trying to help him not only of interference but also of bad faith. He is convinced that Yvonne and Hugh, while

[5] See *Doctor Faustus*, i, 39—47. Cf. also Harry Levin, *Christopher Marlowe: The Overreacher*, pp. 135, 156.

pretending to save him, are involved in a flirtation. That is why he cannot accept the salvation suggested by them. Their well-meaning designs, he feels, have been merely deceptive: "I've been beguiled by your offers of a sober non-alcoholic Paradise", he tells them (p. 313). But he is not to be taken in any more. Faced with the painful illusion of a "sober Paradise", he will choose the "paradise of despair" in the Farolito. Here we touch upon one of Geoffrey's most tragic dilemmas. In a sense he chooses not between good and evil, but between two evils. His denial of salvation is dictated not only by the allurements of alcoholic mysticism but by a bitter experience of a world deficient in true charity. He is convinced that the "sober Paradise" is spurious and that what passes for salvation harbours evil. He therefore rejects false promises and proceeds to his inferno which at least offers immediate gratification.

Nevertheless, the world is not as evil as the Consul makes it out to be. He realizes, even if with only a part of his mind, that his despair is not entirely justified. While inveighing against Yvonne and Hugh, he becomes aware of being cruelly unjust to them. He would like to stop his vehement tirade but it turns out somehow impossible. He must go on, he must assemble all the evidence of the world's wickedness in order to be able to make his final irrevocable decision in favour of the Farolito. Let us note that his "double awareness", an awareness of two contradictory impulses in his soul, so often created by the two Faustian familiars, reveals here the paradox of Geoffrey's freedom. In as much as he knows his judgement of the world to be wrong, in other words, in as much as he knows that the world does not force him into the inferno, he is free. He could, it seems, act other than he does. But he uses the freedom to deprive himself of it, to imprison himself in a seemingly predetermined sequence of events, at the end of which stands the Farolito and waits the abyss of the barranca. We have already seen him constrained to follow the prostitute; an act which will finally condemn him to the infernal cantina. In the Salón Ofélia, he feels just as constrained to pile accusations against the whole world, in order to make his path to damnation into a necessity, and himself a prisoner of inevitable destiny.

The inevitable destiny, to which the Consul has committed himself through his abuse of freedom, is in *Under the Volcano* often suggested by the wheel image. The huge Ferris wheel on the plaza in Quauhnahuac, which figures so prominently in the novel, is identified by the Consul with "*the wheel of the law*" (p. 218), that is to say, with the Buddhist image of the everlasting round of births and rebirths, of ever-recurring imprisonment in sorrow, suffering, disease, old age and death. True, the Buddhist wheel also suggests a release from the painful cycle of rebirths into Nirvana, but only in as far as it suggests an es-

147

cape from the rotating rim to the still centre of the wheel, the realm of the Aristotelian "unmoved mover".[6] And there is nothing in *Under the Volcano* to indicate that positive aspect of the image. On the contrary, the Consul is shown imprisoned in a wild rotating movement of a huge loop-the-loop machine on the same plaza on which a moment before he was sunk in contemplating the giant wheel of the law. It is as if his concentration on the Buddhist image elicited a response which indicates his involvement with the infernal, not the paradisal, aspect of the wheel. Not only is the wheel, on which he madly revolves for some time, called "Máquina Infernal" but it also suggests to him "some huge evil spirit, screaming in its lonely hell, its limbs writhing, smiting the air like flails of paddlewheels" (p. 221).

At the same time the image of the Consul riding on the Máquina Infernal contains a lot more that is essential in his life. It betokens escape, denial of life, unnecessary suffering, dramatic ascents and descents, or precarious balancing between life and death. It shows the whole world spinning madly in Geoffrey's mind: an experience which may be taken to epitomize his drinking debauches and, most importantly perhaps, to symbolize his *inverted* position in relation to the world. Clearly the image is pregnant with multiple meanings relevant to the whole of the Consul's fate presented and related in *Under the Volcano*[7]. It may also appear emblematic of the whole novel, especially if we allow the literary allusion contained in it to come into play.

There is no doubt that the sinister name of the loop-the-loop machine refers to Jean Cocteau's play *La Machine Infernale*, where "the infernal machine is the universe itself: an ingeniously contrived clock-like mechanism in which

---

[6] See Cirlot, *Dictionary of Symbols,* pp. 350—52 ("Wheel") and Joseph Campbell, *The Masks of God: Creative Mythology* (London: Souvenir Press, 1974), pp. 415—22.

[7] The image also seems to have a mythical correlative in a tarot card, the so-called twelfth enigma, representing the Hanged Man, a youth who, like the Consul, hangs upside down in the air, suspended by one foot from a gallows-like tree. This is suggested by the Consul's insistence that his upside-down position on the loop-the-loop machine is certainly symbolic of something (p. 222), by Lowry's claim in the letter to Cape that Chapter Seven contains "stray cards from the tarot pack", and by the fact that the negative significance (each tarot card always has a positive and a negative, reversed, significance) of the twelfth enigma remarkably accords with the Consul's search for transcendence and his mystical failure. Without going into a detailed interpretation of the card, it will be sufficient to point out that the Hanged Man represents a man who lives in a dream of mystical idealism (see Cirlot, p. 132). In his negative aspect he is "the vague idealist who lives in his own imaginary dream world, located neither in Heaven nor on earth, but suspended somewhere between the two in a place of his own invention. His eyes are turned inward and he is blind to the beauty that lies all around him, as he hangs by the thread of his wild fantasy." A. Douglas, *The Tarot* (Harmondsworth: Penguin Books, 1972), p. 87. Cf. also Paul Huson, *The Devil's Picturebook* (London: Sphere Books Ltd., 1972), pp. 200—205.

every part, every minute, has its function in the machine's diabolical purpose—'the mathematical destruction of a human life'".[8] According to Douglas Day, Cocteau's infernal machine serves as a central metaphor of *Under the Volcano*. Set in motion by the infernal gods, "the spring of the machine has been unwinding the whole length of the Consul's life, bringing him inexorably to the morning of November 1st, 1938: the Day of the Dead".[9] Moreover, in Cocteau's play Day sees the origins of the dynamic circular movement of Lowry's book. Extrapolating Day's observation from the source to the image, we might regard the Máquina Infernal as symbolic of the whole novel. The extrapolation seems justifiable because the image of the machine is so comprehensive as to link with everything "in the great chain of the infernal machine" of the Consul's life (to borrow Lowry's expression)[10], and because it reflects the wheel-like form of *Under the Volcano* (see *Letters*, pp. 70—71).

"The book should be seen as essentially *trochal* [writes Lowry to Cape], the form of it as a wheel so that, when you get to the end, if you have read carefully, you should want to turn back to the beginning again, where it is not impossible, too, that your eye might alight once more upon Sophocles' *Wonders are many, and none is more wonderful than man*—just to cheer you up" (*Letters*, p. 88). Elsewhere in the same letter Lowry relates the wheel image to eternity (pp. 71, 83). But if we assume, as we did a moment ago, that the circular form of the novel is reflected in the Máquina Infernal, the eternity must be of a particular kind. It is not the eternity the Consul originally seeks but one that he actually finds; it is not paradisal but infernal. In other words, the great wheel of the novel itself, the wheel of the Máquina Infernal, the Ferris wheel identified with the Buddhist wheel of the law and all the minor wheel images (whose significance is naturally coloured by their major counterparts) do not suggest eternity but infinity,[11] or the eternal recurrence (cf. *Letters*, p. 71). Geoffrey and Yvonne may die but their death does not release them from the circle of existence. As Laura E. Casari aptly remarks,

The circularity of structure gives to the novel a sense of timelessness, stating that what has happened may continue to happen, gathering with each revolution even more destructive force. The structure stresses the endless futility which the endless drunkenness of the Consul symbolizes ... the reader must have the sense that the chaos which results from inability to love will not cease just because the victims and creators of that chaos die. Unless man learns to love, the results of his failure will reappear, in another era and another person in the endless revolution of time.[12]

[8] *Biography*, p. 323.

[9] Ibid., p. 323.

[10] Lowry, *Dark as the Grave Wherein My Friend Is Laid*, p. 62.

[11] Cf. M. Eliade, *The Myth of the Eternal Return*.

[12] Laura E. Casari, "Malcolm Lowry's Drunken Divine Comedy: *Under the Volcano* and Shorter Fiction" (Doctoral dissertation: Univ. of Nebraska, 1967), p. 187.

149

And so the Consul, originally endowed with freedom of choice, ends up in the futility of eternal recurrence. Before closing the chapter let us review his predicament and try to indicate its tragic greatness.

As we have seen, the wheel image symbolizes endless imprisonment and reflects the Consul's inevitable destiny which he has brought upon himself through the abuse of freedom. Against his better knowledge and against his conscience, he has adopted an attitude of hopelessness and fatalism in order to be left alone on his way towards the inferno. Paradoxical though it may seem, his inevitable destiny, because it is self-imposed and freely chosen, is bound with suffering which is devoid of any inevitability. Since the Consul is free and since his suffering is a price paid for his alcoholic mysticism, it is never irrevocable. Through a sheer effort of will, he can always put an end to his suffering. Yet his choices are invariably negative: instead of love, life or salvation Geoffrey chooses loneliness, death, perdition. True, he tries to break the magic circle of choices leading deeper and deeper into the abyss, but he never succeeds. At the same time he is always acutely aware of his freedom of choice, so often represented by the two conflicting voices of his familiars. There is no doubt of his freedom; it is inviolable and it does not leave him until the end. If he forfeits it, he forfeits it through his own free decisions. Hence the paradox of his ever greater captivity, an imprisonment—represented by the image of the wheel—which has its source in freedom. Clearly the Consul bears responsibility for his sickness, his sufferings, his death and damnation. In terms of the whole novel he is responsible not only for his own fall but indirectly, for all the evil with which the universe of *Under the Volcano* is permeated. But there precisely lies his greatness:

The responsibility for evil exalts man instead of humiliating him. It implies that he has a tremendous power of freedom capable of rising against God, of separating itself from him, of creating hell and a godless world of its own. The idea of the Fall is at bottom a proud idea, and through it man escapes from the sense of humiliation. If man fell away from God, he must have been an exalted creature, endowed with great freedom and power.[13]

These words of the Russian philosopher Nicolas Berdyaev are not only strikingly appropriate to the Consul's predicament but they also carry a message of "tragic optimism", which bears upon the whole novel. Restating an old truth, they imply that the "hell fire" (cf. *Letters*, p. 80) described by Lowry in *Under the Volcano* is not inevitable; that the horrors and disasters of human existence are neither necessary nor final. The novel, as Lowry says, is also a

---

[13] N. Berdyaev, *The Destiny of Man*, p. 26.

prophecy and a warning *(Letters*, p. 66). It reveals to man a course of action and a sequence of events which result in his destruction and damnation. But it also shows that his will is unconquerable and that to be or not to be is entirely up to him.

Conclusion

Throughout the eight chapters of this study we have analysed and described a number of themes and motifs, trying to weave them into patterns governed by the quality of "infernal paradise". This procedure does not easily lend itself to a neat concluding statement. The aim of this thesis has been to bring out the quality of "infernal paradise" and the reader has either become aware of it or not. But, having gone through the labour of synthesizing a great deal of various apparently disconnected elements of *Under the Volcano,* we seem to have reached a new vantage point from which to consider the novel. While our synthesis has been attempted with regard to the *Gestalt* quality of the novel, we have not yet had the occasion to reconstruct its poetic story. By "poetic story" I mean the significant sequence of events supplied not so much by the rudimentary realistic plot but by the mythical and poetic evocations, that is, by everything Lowry has chosen to suggest rather than state. Let me therefore, by way of conclusion, attempt a very brief reconstruction of the "poetic story" evoked by *Under the Volcano.*

When we meet Consul Geoffrey Firmin for the first time, his already shattered life is almost entirely concentrated on drinking. Why does he do it, we may wonder. Surely the apocalyptic tone of *Under the Volcano* suggests more than a case of over-indulgence. Gradually we discover the tragic dimension of Geoffrey's drunkenness and become aware of its mythical overtones and symbolic value. "It *isn't* drinking, somehow", says Yvonne with conviction (p. 117), and the careful reader is inclined to agree with her. Besides much else, on close examination the alcoholic sickness turns out to represent no less than the fall of man. It symbolizes his unlawful attempt to become god-like as well as destruction and death following the loss of paradise. When we meet the Consul he has been already exiled from the Garden of Eden. His exile consists in his having to remain there, cut off from God and the fountain of life. Ruined and full of weeds, the garden retains only traces of its former Edenic splendour in the midst of which the ever-thirsty Consul suffers the tortures of Tantalus. What has he done to deserve this fate?

The Consul has committed an act of double betrayal. He has betrayed God by abusing divine mysteries, and his fellow men by failing to be compassionate towards his foes. While the profanation of divine mysteries is, as we saw in chapter 4, bound up with the idea of man's fall, Geoffrey's failure in compassion distinctly stands at the onset of the downward course of his life. Therefore, for the purposes of our "poetic story", we shall assume that the act of cruelty perpetrated on the German officers on board the s.s. *Samaritan* is the original sin committed at the beginning of time. If so, the Consul owes the loss of paradise to his betrayal of the brotherhood of man. And, in as much as he fails to be a Samaritan later in his life, he not only for ever seals the gates of paradise but actually falls into damnation. Meanwhile his fallen condition condemns him to loneliness and isolation: cut off from the communion with God, from love, and from genuine relations with his fellow men, he suffers the "tortures of the damned".

At the same time he tries to regain paradise by way of drinking. In alcohol he finds his "eternal sacrament", his "draught of immortality", supposed to bring him mystical enlightenment as well as the joys of heaven. But the mystical fruits of inebriation prove deceptive. Through drinking the Consul abuses both the divine mysteries and the brotherhood of man, and thus constantly repeats his fall. His isolation increases and his mystical strivings—like Adam's reach for a god-like existence—are more and more assisted by the powers of evil. Before the fall the Consul may have been a genuine adept of the occult path, a mystic in search of God and eternity (cf. my discussion of the Consul's mysticism in chapter 4). After the failure in compassion his mysticism fills with demonic content. Geoffrey is still bound for heaven but his path is no longer straight. "Divinity, adieu!", he may have repeated after Doctor Faustus, "these metaphysics of magicians and necromantic books are heavenly" (*Faustus*, i, 47—49).

Having abused divine mysteries the Consul is led into black magic. Not surprisingly, therefore, he follows Faustus in confusing hell with Elysium. Having once allied himself with evil powers, the Consul pursues his course into the infernal abyss, deceiving himself that he is on the way to paradise and heaven. He confuses, as we have seen, fall with ascent, darkness with light, perdition with immortality, and damnation with salvation. Incapable of love and charity, immersed in his black magic of alcoholism, the Consul falls ever deeper into destruction and death through his persistent refusal to exercise the God-given freedom. Willingly he transforms freedom into spiritual captivity, just as more or less willingly he has turned his whole world upside down. Yet his abuse of freedom shows that his fall has not been merely decreed by fate. It reveals his responsibility for much suffering and evil and, by the same token, his tragic greatness.[1]

---

[1] See chapter 8 above, footnote 13.

In the "poetic story" evoked by *Under the Volcano* I have tried to reconstruct its mythical drama expressed through the fall of the protagonist. I feel, however, that I have attempted the impossible. Through giving an outline of the Consul's history as Everyman I have been forced to leave many things unsaid and unexplained. What, for example, is the exact relationship between the betrayal of the brotherhood of man and black magic? Why did the Consul abuse divine mysteries or take to drinking in the first place? Or simply: what kind of God and what kind of devil does he believe in? Such questions, however, cannot be answered without resorting to speculation based on the fragile foundations of Lowry's mythology; a mythology which contains "a fecundity of suggestive detail that tends to over-stimulate the imagination, that is, to set it off in more ways than can be decently encompassed within an overall design."[2] Thus the mythical drama cannot be reconstructed without either ignoring some ambiguities or by-passing essential elements of the novel's imaginative universe. Whether this is a virtue or a fault is, of course, open to debate. There are readers who would always prefer obscurity and suspension of meaning to clarity and distinctness. Personally I am inclined to think that obscurity created by an overabundance of ambiguous detail mars the power of artistic expression. The wealth of meanings *per se* does not imply artistic excellence. Nor is it a virtue when it testifies to a miscarried attempt at universality. In the Introduction I suggested that *Under the Volcano* is an imaginative universe capable of revealing ever new meanings. Having now considered the novel in detail, it seems that the "ever new meanings" bring at times this universe to the point of dissolution. Presumably the burden of controlling his *creatio continua* was too heavy for Lowry, just as it would have been, I think, too heavy for any writer not gifted with superhuman powers.

Perhaps Lowry was trying to play God but perhaps his brilliant semantic polyphony had to hide som essential weakness which condemned him to all the complex "oratio obliqua" of mythical and literary allusions. Writing in an age uncertain of its spiritual whereabouts and no doubt affected by its atmosphere, he may have found suggestion and allusion more congenial than simplicity and directness of expression. To break through the spiritual vacuum of his times his mythopoeic mind must have endlessly searched in the world of myth and symbol. But myths and symbols have no force except through the faith man has in them, and search alone does not imply commitment to the faith which nourishes and stimulates the powers of creative imagination.[3] In so far, there-

[2] Robert B. Heilman, "The Possessed Artist and the Ailing Soul", *Canadian Literature*, 8 (Spring 1960), p. 8.

[3] See Jacques Maritain, *Creative Intuition in Art and Poetry* (New York: Pantheon Books, 1953), pp. 180—81; for a discussion on the relations between art and faith see also Karl Jaspers, *Philosophy*, I, pp. 326—35, III, pp. 168—75.

fore, as Lowry was uncertain of his metaphysical commitments he could not breathe life into the manifold images assembled in a somewhat wayward manner from various mythical and cultural traditions. In effect he created a "loose impressionism, in which a mass of suggestive enterprises sets off so many associations, echoes, and conjectures that the imaginative experience becomes crowded and finally diffuse."[4] Therefore the mythical drama of *Under the Volcano* can never be fully reconstructed. Its elements are too many, their ambiguous meanings perpetually and indecisively open. What seems to hold them together is not so much the "poetic story" as the quality of "infernal paradise" manifested in the demonic inversion of the protagonist's world. As we have seen, this quality permeates the whole of the novel and creates a unique aesthetic phenomenon of *concordia discors*. And if we allow this phenomenon to exert its fascinating influence upon us we might become reconciled to the diffuse contours of the mythical drama behind it. For whatever its riddles and obscurities, the "infernal paradise" reveals enough depth of meaning and enough artistic harmony to mark *Under the Volcano* as one of the greatest novels of the century.

[4] Heilman, p. 16.

Appendix: Ingarden's Metaphysical Qualities.

With the aid of conceptual tools worked out by Husserlian phenomenology Roman Ingarden has made a very thoroughgoing attempt to describe and analyse the literary work in its entirety. Like many adherents of organic formalism, he was largely concerned with problems of structure and coherence, and in his *Das literarische Kunstwerk* (1931)[1] gave "the most coherent account of a theory which sees that the work of art is a totality but a totality composed of different heterogeneous strata."[2] Unlike the formalist critics, however, he made elaborate and phenomenologically substantiated inquiries into aesthetic phenomena, and developed a theory of distinctly aesthetic qualities and values. At the same time, he did not lose sight of a metaphysical significance of the literary work. While categorically denying that art had anything to do with philosophical, moral, or scientific assertions,[3] he put forward the conception of "metaphysical qualities" which made it possible "to reintroduce questions of 'philosophical meaning' of works of art without the risk of the usual intellectualist errors."[4]

What are the metaphysical qualities? According to Ingarden, all of us experience them in certain unique moments of our lives. Such moments come rarely and quite gratuitously. Against everyday ordinariness they bring an experience always charged with significance—either positive or negative—which, as it were, reveals depths of our own life and all existence. Metaphysical qualities, as Ingarden describes them, are

einfache oder auch "abgeleitete" Qualitäten (Wesenheiten), wie z. B. das Erhabene, das Tragische, das Furchtbare, das Erschütternde, das Unbegreifbare, das

---

[1] *Das literarische Kunstwerk. Eine Untersuchung aus dem Grenzgebiet der Ontologie, Logik und Literaturwissenschaft* (Halle: Max Niemeyer, 1931); Polish edition: *O dziele literackim,* trans. M. Turowicz (Warszawa: PWN, 1960). Second German edition—verbesserte und erweiterte Auflage (Tübingen: Max Niemeyer, 1960); third German edition, 1965; fourth German edition, 1972.

[2] René Wellek, *Concepts of Criticism,* pp. 67—68.

[3] See R. Ingarden, "O różnych rozumieniach 'prawdziwości' w dziele sztuki" (On the different meanings of 'truth' in a work of art); "O tzw. 'prawdzie' w literaturze" (Concerning the so-called "truth" in literature) in *Studia z estetyki* (Studies in aesthetics), (Warszawa: PWN, 1966), vol. I.

[4] Wellek and Warren, *Theory of Literature* (Harmondsworth: Penguin Books, 1963), p. 152.

Dämonische, das Heilige, das Sündhafte, das Traurige, die unbeschreibbare Helligkeit des Glückes, aber auch das Groteske, das Reizende, das Leichte, die Ruhe usw. Diese Qualitäten sind keine gegenständlichen "Eigenschaften" im gewöhnlichen Sinne, aber im allgemeinen auch keine "Merkmale" dieser oder jener psychischen Zustände, sondern sie offenbaren sich gewöhnlich in komplexen und oft untereinander sehr verschiedenen Situationen, Ereignissen, als eine spezifische Atmosphäre, die über den in diesen Situationen sich befindenden Menschen und Dingen schwebt und doch alles durchdringt und mit ihrem Lichte verklärt.[5]

Despite the name given to these qualities, Ingarden refrains from ascribing to them any metaphysical status. They are simply experiential data, however unusual and extraordinary, in that they are highly intense and bear the stamp of value and "revelation" of life's meaning. To experience metaphysical qualities even once may profoundly affect our lives, as well as instil in us a peculiar longing to behold them again. This longing, maintains Ingarden, is the *spiritus movens* of philosophy and art. Yet the intensity of the experience of metaphysical qualities in our lives and the rarity of their occurrence make it hardly possible to grasp and contemplate them.

In art, on the other hand, the perceiver experiences a characteristic distance between himself and metaphysical qualities which belong only to an aesthetic concretization[6] of a work of art. Consequently, they are, in Ingarden's technical language, "existentially heteronomous", which means that they have no independent existence of their own, and are, so to speak, removed one stage from reality. This is exactly why they cannot be genuinely actualized and as tangibly felt as in life. They lose intensity and dynamism but instead become accessible, as though in miniature, to calm and prolonged contemplation.[7]

But, it may be asked, how do metaphysical qualities come about in a work of art? Now one of the crucial stages in the process of aesthetic concretization consists in actualizing in the reader's consciousness the stratum of the presented objects[8] (the novelist's world). It is the function of this stratum to reveal metaphysical qualities which become phenomenally given to perception. This function, however, can be fulfilled only if *all* the strata interact and harmonize with one another. Therefore metaphysical qualities are revealed in works of art and not, for example, in press reports where the matter-of-fact tone and lack of artistic harmony do not allow metaphysical qualities to

---

[5] Ingarden, *Das literarische Kunstwerk,* Tübingen: Max Niemeyer, 1960, pp. 310—11.

[6] Aesthetic concretization may be described as an imaginative synthetic reconstruction of a work of art arrived at within the aesthetic attitude and being an end result of the work's aesthetic perception. See R. Ingarden, *O dziele literackim,* §§ 62, 63.

[7] See ibid., § 49.

[8] There are four strata in a literary work of art: sound-stratum, units of meaning, presented objects, and appearances. See also Wellek and Warren, p. 151.

appear as a phenomenon in our perception. Reading in a newspaper about someone's tragic death, we can reflect on the quality of the tragic (which theoretically belongs to the described situation) but not actually see it. Metaphysical qualities are, furthermore, conditioned by what Ingarden calls polyphonic interaction of aesthetically valuable qualities. This polyphonic consonance must not only call forth but also harmonize with a given metaphysical quality which will then be felt as its necessary complement.[9] Therefore, when we at all experience metaphysical qualities in a work of art, they appear in their full aesthetic "brilliance". That is to say, their perception should necessarily entail a perception of various aesthetically valuable elements. And finally, their very presence constitutes an aesthetic value in itself. In metaphysical qualities, says Roman Ingarden, a work of art reaches its peak and cannot be perfect without them.[10]

---

[9] See Ingarden, *O dziele literackim,* p. 376.
[10] Ibid., pp. 376—377.

Selected Bibliography

Principal works by Malcolm Lowry

Dark as the Grave Wherein my Friend Is Laid. Harmondsworth: Penguin Books, 1972.
Hear Us O Lord from Heaven Thy Dwelling Place. Harmondsworth: Penguin Books, 1969.
Lunar Caustic. London: Cape, 1968.
October Ferry to Gabriola. London: Cape, 1971.
"Preface to a Novel", *Canadian Literature*, 9 (Summer 1961), 23—29.
The Selected Letters of Malcolm Lowry. Ed. Harvey Breit & Margerie Bonner Lowry. London: Cape, 1965.
Ultramarine: a Novel. Harmondsworth: Penguin Books, 1974.
Under the Volcano. London: Cape, 1967.
Selected Poems. Ed. Earle Birney with the assistance of Margerie Bonner Lowry. San Francisco: City Lights Books, 1962.

Lowry criticism

(List of works consulted)

Albaum, Elvin. "La Mordida: Myth and Madness in the Novels of Malcolm Lowry". Unpublished doctoral dissertation: State Univ. of New York at Stony Brook, 1971.
Barnes, Jim. "The Myth of Sisyphus in *Under the Volcano*". *Prairie Schooner*, 42 (Winter 1968—69), 341—348.
Bradbrook, M. C. *Malcolm Lowry: His Art and Early Life. A Study in Transformation*. Cambridge: Cambridge Univ. Press, 1975.
Bradbury, Malcolm. *Possibilities: Essays on the State of the Novel*. London, Oxford, New York: OUP, 1973. Ch. X.
Casari, Laura Elizabeth Rhodes. "Malcolm Lowry's Drunken Divine Comedy: *Under the Volcano* and Shorter Fiction". Unpublished doctoral dissertation: Univ. of Nebraska, 1967.
Christella Marie, Sister. "*Under the Volcano*: A Consideration of the Novel by Malcolm Lowry", *Xavier University Studies*, 4 (1965), 13—27.
Corrigan, Matthew. "Malcolm Lowry, New York Publishing, and the 'New Illiteracy'." *Encounter* (July 1970), pp. 82—93.
—"Phenomenology and Literary Criticism: A Definition and an Application". Unpublished doctoral dissertation: State Univ. of New York at Buffalo, 1970.

Costa, Richard Hauer. "Lowry's Overture as Elegy", *A Malcolm Lowry Catalogue*, ed. by J. Howard Woolmer. New York, 1968, pp. 26—44.

—*Malcolm Lowry*. New York: Twayne, 1972.

—"*Pietà, Pelado*, and 'The Ratification of Death': The Ten-Year Evolvement of Malcolm Lowry's *Volcano*". *Journal of Modern Literature*, (Sept. 1971), pp. 3—18.

—"A Quest for Eridanus: The Evolving Art of Malcolm Lowry's *Under the Volcano*". Unpublished doctoral dissertation: Purdue Univ., 1969.

—"*Ulysses*, Lowry's *Volcano* and the Voyage Between: A Study of an Unacknowledged Literary Kinship". *Univ. of Toronto Quarterly*, 36 (July 1967), 335—52.

Day, Douglas. *Malcolm Lowry: A Biography*. London: Oxford Univ. Press, 1974.

—"Of Tragic Joy", *Prairie Schooner*, (Winter 1963—64), pp. 354—62.

—Preface to Malcolm Lowry, *Dark as the Grave Wherein My Friend is Laid*. Harmondsworth: Penguin Books, 1972.

Dodson, Daniel B. *Malcolm Lowry* (Columbia Essays on Modern Writers, 51). New York and London: Columbia Univ. Press, 1970.

Doyen, Victor. "Elements Towards a Spatial Reading of Malcolm Lowry's *Under the Volcano*", *English Studies*, 50, 1 (February 1969), 65—74.

Edmonds, Dale. "Malcolm Lowry: A Study of His Life and Work". Unpublished doctoral dissertation: Univ. of Texas, 1965.

—"*Under the Volcano:* A Reading of the 'Immediate Level'", *Tulane Studies in English,* 16 (1968), 63—105.

Epstein, Perle. "Malcolm Lowry: In Search of Equilibrium", *A Malcolm Lowry Catalogue,* ed. J. Howard Woolmer. New York, 1968, pp. 15—25.

—*The Private Labyrinth of Malcolm Lowry:* Under the Volcano *and the Cabbala*. New York: Rinehart, 1969.

—"Swinging the Maelstrom: Malcolm Lowry and Jazz", *Canadian Literature,* 44 (Spring 1970), 57—66.

Heilman, Robert B. "The Possessed Artist and the Ailing Soul", *Canadian Literature,* 8 (Spring 1960), 7—16.

Kazin, Alfred. *Bright Book of Life: American Novelists and Story Tellers*. Boston-Toronto: Little, Brown & Co., 1971, pp. 18—19.

Kilgallin, Anthony R. "Eliot, Joyce and Lowry", *Canadian Author and Bookman,* 40(1965), 3—4, 6.

—"Faust and *Under the Volcano*", *Canadian Literature*, 26 (Autumn 1965), 43—54.

—*Lowry*. Erin, Ontario: Press Porcepic, 1973.

—"The Use of Literary Sources for Theme and Style in *Under the Volcano*". Unpublished M.A. thesis: Univ. of Toronto, 1965.

"Malcolm Lowry", *The Times Literary Supplement,* Jan. 26, 1967, pp. 57—59.

Markson, David. "Malcolm Lowry: A Study of Theme and Symbol in *Under the Volcano*". Unpublished M.A. thesis: Columbia Univ., 1952.

—"Myth in *Under the Volcano*", *Prairie Schooner,* 37, No. 4, (Winter 1963—64), 339—46.

New, William H. "Lowry's Reading: An Introductory Essay", *Canadian Literature,* 44 (Spring 1970), 5—12.

—*Malcolm Lowry*. Toronto: McClelland and Stewart, 1972.

"A Prose Wasteland", *The Times Literary Supplement,* May 11, 1962, p. 338.

Spender, Stephen. Introduction to *Under the Volcano,* edition used in this dissertation, pp. vii—xxvi.

160

Tiessen, Paul G. "Malcolm Lowry and the Cinema", *Canadian Literature,* 44 (Spring 1970), 38—49.

Wild, Sister Bernadette. "Malcolm Lowry: A Study of the Sea Metaphor", *University of Windsor Review,* 4, No. 1 (1968), 46—60.

Woodcock, George. "Malcolm Lowry's *Under the Volcano", Modern Fiction Studies,* 4, No. 2 (Summer 1958), 151—56.

—"Under Seymour Mountain", *Canadian Literature,* 8 (Spring 1960), 3—6.

Wright, Terence. *"Under the Volcano*: The Static Art of Malcolm Lowry". *Ariel,* 1, No. 4 (October 1970), 67—76.

Other Works

(Only works referred to in the text are included)

Bacon, Francis. *The Essays: The Wisdom of the Ancients; New Atlantis.* London: Cassel, 1907.

Bevan, Edwyn. *Symbolism and Belief.* Boston: Beacon Press, 1957.

Barfield, Owen. *Poetic Diction: A Study in Meaning.* Middletown, Connecticut: Wesleyan Univ. Press, 1973.

Berdyaev, Nicolas. *The Destiny of Man.* New York: Harper, 1960.

Bonhoeffer, Dietrich. *Ethics.* London: SCM Press Ltd., 1955.

Bradbury, Malcolm. "Introduction: The State of Criticism Today", in *Contemporary Criticism* (Stratford-upon-Avon Studies, 12) Ed. M. Bradbury and D. Palmer. London: Edward Arnold, 1970.

Brooks, Cleanth. "Implications of an Organic Theory of Poetry", in M. H. Abrams. *Literature and Belief.* (English Institute Essays, 16). New York: Columbia Univ. Press, 1958.

Brunner, Emil. *The Christian Doctrine of Creation and Redemption.* London: Lutterworth Press, 1952.

Buber, Martin. *Good and Evil: Two Interpretations.* New York: Scribner, 1952.

Butler, E. M. *The Fortunes of Faust.* Cambridge: Cambridge Univ. Press, 1952.

Campbell, Joseph. *The Masks of God: Creative Mythology.* London: Souvenir Press, 1974.

Cassirer, Ernst. *An Essay on Man: An Introduction to a Philosophy of Human Culture.* New York: Doubleday, 1956.

—*Language and Myth.* New York: Dover Publications, 1953.

Cirlot, J. E. *A Dictionary of Symbols.* New York: Philosophical Library, 1962.

Coomaraswamy, Ananda K. Article on "Symbolism" in *Dictionary of World Literary Terms.* Ed. by Joseph T. Shipley. London: Allen & Unwin, 1970.

Daiches, David. *A Study of Literature: For Readers and Critics.* New York: W.W. Norton & Co., 1964.

Dante, Aligheri. *The Divine Comedy: 1. Hell.* Harmondsworth: Penguin Books, 1949.

De Quincey, Thomas. "On the Knocking at the Gate in *Macbeth*", in *A Book of English Essays.* Selected by W. E. Williams. Harmondsworth: Penguin Books, 1951.

Donnelly, Ignatius. *Atlantis: The Antediluvian World.* New York: Rudolf Steiner Publications, 1971.

Dostoevsky, Fyodor Mikhailovich. *Crime and Punishment*. Harmondsworth: Penguin Books, 1966.

Douglas, Alfred. *The Tarot: The Origins, Meaning and Uses of the Cards*. Harmondsworth: Penguin Books, 1973.

Eliade, Mircea. "Methodological Remarks on the Study of Religious Symbolism", in *The History of Religions: Essays in Methodology*. Ed. by M. Eliade and Joseph M. Kitagawa. Chicago and London: The Univ. of Chicago Press, 1959.

—*The Myth of the Eternal Return: or, Cosmos and History*. Princeton: Princeton Univ. Press, 1971.

—*Patterns in Comparative Religion*. London and Sydney: Sheed & Ward, 1958.

—*The Sacred and the Profane: The Nature of Religion*. New York: Harcourt, 1959.

Eliot, T. S. *Selected Essays*. London: Faber, 1934.

Frank, Joseph. "Spatial Form in Modern Literature", in *Sewanee Review*, 53 (1945), 221—40, 433—56.

Frankfort, Henri, et. al. *Before Philosophy: The Intellectual Adventure of Ancient Man*. Harmondsworth: Penguin Books, 1949.

Frankl, Viktor Emil. *The Will to Meaning: Foundations and Applications of Logotherapy*. New York: The New American Library, 1969.

Frieling, Rudolf. *Hidden Treasure in the Psalms*. London: The Christian Community Press, 1967.

Goethe, Johann Wolfgang von. *Goethes Werke in sechs Bänden: Im Auftrage der Goethe-Gesellschaft ausgewählt und herausgegeben von Erich Schmidt*. Leipzig: Insel Verlag, 1910, I.

Graves, Robert. *The Greek Myths*. Harmondsworth: Penguin Books, 1960.

Halevi, Z'ev ben Shimon. *Tree of Life: An Introduction to the Cabala*. London: Rider, 1972.

Huson, Paul. *The Devil's Picturebook*. London: Sphere Books, 1972.

Huxley, Aldous. *The Doors of Perception and Heaven and Hell*. Harmondsworth: Penguin Books, 1959.

—*The Perennial Philosophy*. London: Collins, 1958.

—*Point Counter Point*. Harmondsworth: Penguin Books, 1955.

Ingarden, Roman. *O dziele literackim: Badania z pogranicza ontologii, teorii jezyka i filozofii literatury*. Warszawa: PWN, 1960.

—*Das literarische Kunstwerk* (Second German edition—verbesserte und erweiterte Auflage). Tübingen: Max Niemeyer Verlag, 1960.

—*Studia z estetyki* (Studies in aesthetics). Warszawa: PWN, 1966.

James, William. *The Varieties of Religious Experience: A Study in Human Nature*. London: Collins, 1960.

Jaspers, Karl. *Philosophy*. Chicago and London: Univ. of Chicago Press, 1969.

—*Philosophical Faith and Revelation*. London: Collins, 1967.

Jaspers, Karl, and Bultmann, Rudolf. *Myth and Christianity: An Inquiry into the Possibility of Religion Without Myth*. New York: The Noonday Press, 1958.

Jonas, Hans, *The Gnostic Religion: The Message of the Alien God and the Beginnings of Christianity*. Boston: Beacon Press, 1963.

Jump, J. D. Introduction to Ch. Marlowe, *Doctor Faustus*. London: Methuen, 1968.

Langer, Susanne K. *Feeling and Form: A Theory of Art*. New York: Scribner, 1953.

—*Philosophy in a New Key: A Study in the Symbolism of Reason, Rite, and Art*. New York: The New American Library, 1948.

Lévi, Éliphas. *The History of Magic: Including a Clear and Precise Exposition of Its*

Procedure, Its Rites and Its Mysteries. London: Rider, 1969.

—*Transcendental Magic: Its Doctrine and Ritual.* London: Rider, 1923.

Levin, Harry. *Christopher Marlowe: The Overreacher.* London: Faber, 1961.

—*Contexts of Criticism.* Cambridge, Mass.: Harvard Univ. Press, 1957.

—*James Joyce: A Critical Introduction.* London: Faber, 1968.

Maritain, Jaques. *Creative Intuition in Art and Poetry.* New York: Pantheon Books, 1953.

Marlowe, Christopher. *The Tragical History of the Life and Death of Doctor Faustus.* Ed. by John D. Jump. London: Methuen, 1968.

Marvell, Andrew. "Clorinda and Damon", in *The Poems and Letters of Andrew Marvell.* Oxford: The Clarendon Press, 1927.

Mathers MacGregor,S. L. *The Book of the Sacred Magic of Abra-Melin the Mage* (As delivered by Abraham the Jew unto his son Lamech, A.D. 1458. Translated from the original Hebrew into the French, and now rendered from the latter language into English. From a unique and valuable MS. in the "Bibliothèque de l'Arsenal" at Paris.) 1898; rpt. London: John Watkins, 1956.

Merezhkovsky, Dimitri. *Atlantis/Europe: The Secret of the West.* New York: Rudolf Steiner Publications, 1971.

Milton, John. *Paradise Lost.* New York, London: Collier-Macmillan Ltd., 1962.

New Larousse Encyclopedia of Mythology. London, New York, Sydney, Toronto: Hamlyn, 1968.

Nowottny, Winifred. *The Language Poets Use.* London: The Athlone Press, 1972.

Odenberg, Hugo. *Enoch or the Hebrew Book of Enoch.* Cambridge: Univ. Press, 1928.

Osborne, Harold. *Aesthetics and Criticism.* London: Routledge, 1955.

Paz, Octavio. *The Labyrinth of Solitude: Life and Thought in Mexico.* London: Allen Lane The Penguin Press, 1967.

Plato. *Timaeus.* Harmondsworth: Penguin Books, 1965.

Rayan, Krishna. *Suggestion and Statement in Poetry.* London: The Athlone Press, 1972.

Ricoeur, Paul. *The Symbolism of Evil.* Boston: Beacon Press, 1969.

Rougemont, Denis de. *The Devil's Share.* New York: Pantheon Books, 1944.

—*Love in the Western World.* New York: Harper, 1974.

Sayers, Dorothy. Introduction and Commentary to Dante, *The Divine Comedy.* Harmondsworth: Penguin Books, 1949.

Schaya, Leo. *The Universal Meaning of the Kabbalah.* Baltimore: Penguin Books Inc., 1973.

Scholem, Gershom G. "Kabbalah", article in *Encyclopaedia Judaica.* Jerusalem, 1971.

—*On the Kabbalah and Its Symbolism.* New York: Schocken Books, 1969.

—*Major Trends in Jewish Mysticism.* New York: Schocken Books, 1961.

—"On Sin and Punishment", in *Myths and Symbols: Studies in Honor of Mircea Eliade.* Ed. Joseph M. Kitagawa and Charles H. Long. Chicago: The Univ. of Chicago Press, 1969.

—*Zohar: The Book of Splendor: Basic Readings from the Kabbalah.* New York: Schocken Books, 1963.

Scott, Nathan A., Jr. "The Broken Center: A Definition of the Crisis of Values in Modern Literature", in *Symbolism in Religion and Literature.* Ed. Rollo May. New York: G. Braziller, 1960.

Shaw, Franklin J. *Reconciliation: A Theory of Man Transcending*. Ed. Sydney M. Jourard and Dan C. Overlade, Princeton: D. Van Nostrand Co. Ltd., 1966.

Shelley, Percy Bysshe. "Alastor", in *Poems of Shelley*. London: Thomas Nelson & Sons Ltd. [no date].

Spence, Lewis. *Atlantis in America*. London: E. Benn Ltd., 1925.

—*An Encyclopaedia of Occultism: A Compendium of Information on the Occult Sciences, Occult Personalities, Psychic Science, Magic, Demonology, Spiritism and Mysticism*. London: Routledge, 1920.

—*The Magic and Mysteries of Mexico or the Arcane Secrets and Occult Lore of the Ancient Mexicans and Maya*. London: Rider, 1930.

—*The Myths of Mexico and Peru*. London: George G. Harrap, 1913.

—*The Occult Sciences in Atlantis*. London: Rider, 1943.

—*The Problem of Atlantis*. London: Rider, 1924.

Spengler, Oswald. *Man and Technics: A Contribution to a Philosophy of Life*. New York/London: Alfred A. Knopf/Allen & Unwin, 1963.

Steiner, Rudolf. *Occult Science: An Outline*. London: Rudolf Steiner Press, 1969.

Swedenborg, Emanuel. *Heaven and Its Wonders and Hell: from Things Heard and Seen*. London: The Swedenborg Society, 1966.

Tillich, Paul. *The Boundaries of Our Being: A Collection of His Sermons with His Autobiographical Sketch*. London: Collins, 1973.

—*The Protestant Era*. Chicago: The Univ. of Chicago Press, 1957.

—*Systematic Theology*. Chicago: The Univ. of Chicago Press, 1957.

Waite, Arthur Edward. *The Secret Doctrine in Israel: A Study of the Zohar and its Connections*. London: Rider, 1913.

Watts, Alan W. *Myth and Ritual in Christianity*. Boston: Beacon Press, 1968.

—*The Two Hands of God: The Myths of Polarity*. New York: Collier Books, 1969.

Wellek, René. *Concepts of Criticism*. New Heaven and London: Yale Univ. Press, 1963.

Wellek, René and Warren, Austin. *Theory of Literature*. Harmondsworth: Penguin Books, 1963.

Wheelwright, Philip. *The Burning Fountain: A Study in the Language of Symbolism*. Bloomington: Indiana Univ. Press, 1954.

"Myth", article in *Princeton Encyclopedia of Poetry and Poetics*. Ed. Alex Preminger. Princeton: Princeton Univ. Press, 1972.

Williams, Monier. *Indian Wisdom or Examples of the Religious, Philosophical, and Ethical Doctrines of the Hindus: With a Brief History of the Chief Departments of Sanskrit Literature and Some Account of the Past and Present Condition of India, Moral, and Intellectual*. London: Wm. H. Allen & Co., 1875.

Wilson, Edmund. *Axel's Castle: A Study in the Imaginative Literature of 1870 to 1930*. New York: Scribner, 1959.

Wimsatt, W. K., Jr., and Beardsley, M. C. "The Intentional Fallacy", in W. K. Wimsatt, Jr. *The Verbal Icon*. London: Methuen, 1970.

Zaehner, R. C. *Mysticism Sacred and Profane: An Inquiry into some Varieties of Praeternatural Experience*. London, Oxford, New York: Oxford Univ. Press, 1961.

Zimmer, Heinrich. *The King and the Corpse: Tales of the Soul's Conquest of Evil*. Princeton: Princeton Univ. Press, 1971.

Index of Major Themes